The Charlton Standard Catalogue of ROYAL DOULTON JUGS

First Edition

By
Jean Dale

W.K. Cross
Publisher

The Charlton Press

Birmingham, Michigan • Toronto, Ontario

The Charlton Press

Editorial Office
2010 Yonge Street
Toronto, Ontario. M4S 1Z9

EDITORIAL AND PRODUCTION

Editor   Jean Dale
Editorial Assistant   Mary Cross
Layout   Frank Van Lieshout
Advertising Manager   Janet Cross

ACKNOWLEDGEMENTS

The Publisher would like to thank:

Dick and Alison Nicholson of The British Toby for contributing to the manuscript, reviewing the manuscript, and the photographing of their collection.

Nick Tzimas of Gossland Collectibles for reviewing the manuscript and data.

Barry Weiss for allowing the reproduction of the photographs of the rare and unusual jugs from his book.

Pat O'Brien of RDICC, Canadian Branch, for responding quickly and helpfully to all our questions.

Royal Doulton (U.K.) Ltd. for allowing the reproduction of the photographs of some of the rare jugs.

Also, the publisher would like to thank those dealers who faithfully mailed us their direct mail brochures, helping us keep abreast of the ever changing Doulton market:

Arnie and Judie Berger, Yesterday's South   Charles and Joanne Dombeck

Ed Pascoe, Pascoe & Company   Tom Power, The Collector, Alfies Antique Market

Stan Worrey, Colonial House Antiques & Gifts

CORRECTIONS

We have taken great care in compiling and listing the large volume of data that makes up this price guide. However, errors will surface, errors of omission, accuracy and typographical, whatever category you find them in, it would be greatly appreciated if they were brought to our attention.

CONTENTS

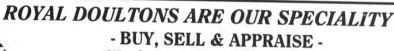

THE COLLECTOR AND THIS BOOK

The purpose of this book is two fold, one to serve as a timely price guide to Royal Doulton Jugs and secondly to provide the collector with the comparative information and illustrations necessary to help them form a meaningful and rewarding collection.

The first purpose, pricing jugs is much more difficult. It is an on going project and as a result an explanation of our thoughts on pricing is needed.

The second purpose is reasonably easy to acheive, with this and the next one or two editions we will be able to present to the collector a comprehensive technical guide on Jugs.

A price guide is just that, "a guide", it is a guide to the most current retail prices possible at the time of publication. It is not a fixed price list, it does not list a price at which dealers must sell their jugs. The guide is an indication of the current market price arrived at by submissions, price lists and auction results.

However, the Charlton Standard Catalogue of Royal Doulton Jugs goes a step farther than any guide has gone before in pricing and that is to show current market prices in three regional areas, United Kingdom, United States and Canada in one catalogue.

When using this guide the collector must carefully assess the three market prices from a number of points:

1. The region of the prices being examined.
2. The duties, taxes and shipping to move the jug to another region.
3. The foriegn exchange calculations required to move between currencies.
   (Remembering that small amounts of funds convert at wide spreads.)

Even with these points taken into account there are major price differences between regional markets. The Royal Doulton Jug market is not perfectly elastic, there is not a uniform demand across all markets. There is also not a uniform supply in all markets. The U.K. market, which is older and supplied first by Doulton must have more depth of product avaliable at any one moment. Prices there, as a result, should be lower. Will dealers and collectors be able to use the guide to buy in the lowest market? Maybe, but again , maybe not. The seller will probably have the guide also and will immediately adjust to the higher market, especially when it is on the side favourable to them. Careful examination of prices is called for, wach market has its own peculiarities and prices can and do vary.

The guide will certainly give the collector an opportunity to explore prices more thoroughly and through that make an intelligent decision when purchasing jugs for their collection.

INTRODUCTION

It is well known that Royal Doulton figurines are immensely popular as collectibles. In recent years, another product of the Doulton company has joined the figurines in capturing the interest of collectors world-wide: that is the character jug.

The earliest Doulton Toby Jug dates back to the 1820's, a representation of Admiral Lord Nelson created by John Doulton. Since that first production, the firm embarked upon a series of Toby Jugs, following the traditional English style of a man standing or seated, sometimes astride a barrel. It is from this form that the jugs acquired their name "Toby", a derivative of the French "tope", to toast.

During the 1930's, Charles J. Noke, then Art Director at Doulton, reintroduced the "face" or character jug. A concept which illustrates characters from history, legend , literature and song.

Today there are over 200 different styles of character jugs.

The purpose of our first edition of the Standard Catalogue of Royal Doulton Jugs is to provide the interested collector with a complete information package. Information needed to create or complete a meaningful collection of Royal Doulton Jugs.

COLOURWAY

Each jug designed by a Royal Doulton designer is hand painted. Skilled artists handpaint and decorate to an original standard laid down by the designer. However, since each jug is handpainted, minor colourway variations are the norm rather than the exception. These minor variations do not affect a jug's value.

However, when the colouring is dramatically changed by the designer and a new colourway is produced, a new variation of the design is launched. Now, depending on the circumstances a price differential will occur between these two colourways of the same jug.

STEPS IN PAINTING

WHITE JUGS

There exist, in limited quantities, white, unpainted, glazed jugs in the same design as their coloured counterparts. The great majority of these white jugs are damaged in some way, leading to the belief that they may be "seconds" that slipped out of the factory or that had been offered to Doulton employees.

In some cases, such as that of Winston Churchill, the value of the white jug exceeds that of the coloured version although in general these oddities are of limited value.

It is important to note that some concern exists among experts that white jugs are being painted and sold as coloured or as coloured variations. These are fakes of no value and a collector interested in purchasing a supposed variation of a standard design should be wary and check its authenticity before purchase.

HANDLE DESIGN VARIATIONS

The handles of the Toby jugs are an integral part of their overall design. They have developed in much the same way as the jugs themselves, growing from the merely functional in early examples of the 1930's and 1940's to the very artistic and sophisticated designs, such as that of the Ugly Duchess in the Alice in Wonderland series.

Again, as with the jugs themselves, slight variations in the handles are the norm and do not affect their values. There are a few cases, however, where one design will sport two handles of sufficient difference to be of the collector's interest. The handle of the Anne of Cleves jug, for example, is a horse with flattened ears. The early version of this same design shows the horse with ears upright and is valued at an higher price.

The variety of handles within a design, such as that of the Beefeater with two, (more including colour variations as well), can be an interesting focus for the collector who wishes to include all the possibilities within their set.

BACKSTAMPS

All general issue Royal Doulton Jugs carry a Doulton backstamp. It is the logo, the maker marks or the signautre that tells you who produced the item. It is located on the bottom, the underneath side of the jug. This backstamp can take many forms depending upon the date or the market for which the jug was issued.

Early jugs (1930's) carried the simple lion and crown stamp. From that time forward the bacstamps became increasingly more complicated, mainly as a result of copyright implications.

Now some backstamps are domiciled to companies for special events, some to clubs and shows for special anniversaries. The backstamp today is being utilized more and more in this manner to personalize the jug for the occasions.

Jugs that were produced for promotional or commemorative purposes have special backstamps. Interest in collecting these jugs has grown in recent years and this demand has affected their value. Almost all of these designs were produced in very limited quantities and command a premium.

The George Washington jug, for example, has a special backstamp in its 1989 production commemorating the bicentennial of the election of the first president of the U.S.A. This jug is priced slightly higher than the "regular issue" without the commemorative stamp.

The Yeoman of the Guard is a good example of a retail commission backstamp. As well as the regular design, a limited edition of this jug was produced to commemorate the anniversary of the opening of a Royal Doulton Room at the retailers, Strawbridge and Clothier. Only seventy five of this limited edition were produced and it is of considerable value.

RESTORATIONS

Due to the great interest in collecting Toby jugs and the high value of rarer pieces, there has developed a market for those that have been professionally restored. Generally, restoration pieces retail at considerably lowe prices than the same unamdged design. It is not recommended to collectors to pursue these repaired jugs if perfect examples can still be found. It is only in the case of very rare jugs that restoration pieces have any market value of interest.

PROTOTYPES

The most rare and valuable of all Royal Doulton Jugs are the prototypes. Indeed, in some cases they may be priceless. They are test or pilot pieces produced to judge market acceptance. Very few examples of these prototypes exist, and even fewer ever come onto the market, making them difficult to price.

ABOUT PRICING

The prices listed in each currency are a reflection of the market in that country. The prices may not be a striaght mathematical calculation of shipping, handling and currency conversion, but reflect the supply and demand within that market.

Jugs in current production are priced at the suggested retail price of the Royal Doulton Company. These will vary between markets and so will the discounts offered by the retailers in the different markets.

Pricing is for jugs in mint condition. Scratched, damaged or repaired jugs are worth less and should be for most instances ignored.

Please be aware that neither this nor any catalogue which reflects market pricing, has prices which are infallible. In all buy and sell markets the final price is still between the buyer and seller.

SPECIAL COMMISSION AND PROMOTIONAL ITEMS

Beyond a couple of early examples, it was not until the late 1970's that Royal Doulton really began to accept commissions for jugs from the outside world. Since that time, the number and type of commissions has grown rapidly. Individuals, organizations and corporations may request a jug design, usually in a limited or special edition.

Commissioned jugs appear with a special backstamp designed for the event.

LIMITED EDITION:
used to describe individually hand numbered jugs.

SPECIAL EDITION:
describes specific commissioned quantities without individual jug numbering.

COLLECTOR SERIES

Over the years, the Royal Doulton Company has produced character ugs that form part of a grouping or series. These have been created around a specific theme, such as "The Circus" or "Great Generals". Collectors who want to assemble a cohesive collection of character jugs have often found it helpful to use these series as a guide.

All of the different character jug series to date are listed below:

Alice in Wonderland: The Cook and the Cheshire Cat; Mad Hatter; The March Hare; The Red Queen; Ugly Duchess; The Walrus and Carpenter.

The Antagonists Collection: Chief Sitting Bull and George Armstrong Custer; Davy Crockett and Santa Anna; George Washington and George III; Ulysses S. Grant and Robert E. Lee.

The Armed Forces: The Airman; The Sailor; The Soldier.

The Beatles: George Harrison; John Lennon; Paul McCartney; Ringo Starr.

The Canadians, On Guard for Thee: The Airman; The Sailor; The Soldier.

Canadian Centennial Series: The Lumerjack; North American Indian; The Trapper.

The Celebrity Collection: Clark Gable; Groucho Marx; Jimmy Durante; Louis Armstrong; Mae West; W.C. Fields.

Characters from Life: The Angler; The Baseball Player (style two); Bowls Player; The Gardener (style two); The Golfer (style two); The Jockey (style two); The Snooker Player (style two).

Characters from Literature: Aramis; Athos; D'Artagnan; Don Quixote; Falstaff; Long John Silver; Merlin; Porthos; Rip Van Winkle; Robin Hood; Scaramouche.

Characters from Williamsburg: Apothecary; Blacksmith; Bootmaker; Goaler; Guardsman; Gunsmith; Night Watchman.

Charles Dickens Commemorative Set / Dickens Tinies: Artful Dodger; Betsy Trotwood; Bill Skyes; Charles Dickens (style one); David Copperfield ;Fagin; Little Nell; Mr. Bumble; Mrs. Bardell; Oliver Twist; Scrooge; Uriah Heep.

The Circus: The Clown (style two); The Elephant Trainer; The Juggler; The Ringmaster.

The Collectors World: The Antique Dealer; The Auctioneer; The Collector.

The Great Generals Collection: Duke of Wellington; General Gordon.

Henry VIII and His Six Wives: Anne Boleyn; Anne of Cleves; Catherine of Aragon; Catherine Howard; Catherine Parr; Henry VIII (style one); Jane Seymour; Sir Thomas More.

The Heroes of the Blitz: A.R.P. Warden; Auxiliary Fireman; Home Guard.

Heroic Leaders: Earl Mountbatten of Burma; Sir Winston Churchill; Viscount Montgomery of Alamein.

Journey Through Britain: The Engine Driver; The Fireman (style two); The Policeman; The Postman

The London Collection: Beefeater; The Busker; Chelsea Pensioner; City Gent; The Guardsman; The London 'Bobby'; Lord Mayor of London; Pearly King; Pearly Queen; Yeoman of the Guard.

Mystical Characters: Genie; Witch; The Wizard.

The Shakespearean Collection: Hamlet; Henry V; MacBeth; Othello; Romeo; William Shakespeare.

The Star-Crossed Lovers Collection: Antony and Cleopatra; King Arthur and Guinevere; Napoleon and Josephine; Samson and Delilah.

The Three Musketeers: Aramis; Athos; Porthos.

The Wild West Collection: Annie Oakley; Buffalo Bill (style two); Doc Holliday; Geronimo; Wild Bill Hickock; Wyatt Earp.

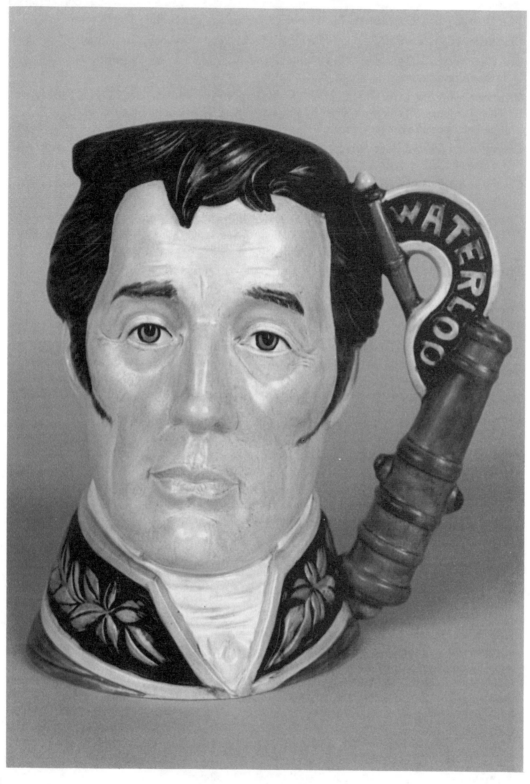

CHARACTER JUGS

AIRMAN

A member of the armed forces, an airman works particularly for the Air Force as either a pilot or a member of the crew. This series pays tribute to those servicemen of the Royal Air Force, Army and Navy who fought in the Second World War.

STYLE ONE: *WHITE SCARF*

SERIES: Armed Forces, one of three.

Royal Doulton®
THE AIRMAN
D 6870
Modelled by

William K. Harper

© **1990 ROYAL DOULTON**

Designer: W. K. Harper **Handle:** German fighter plane shot down in flames **Backstamp:** Doulton

Colourway: Brown cap and flight jacket, white scarf

Doulton Number	Size	Backstamp	Height	Intro.	Discon.	Current Market Value		
						U.K. £	U.S. $	Can. $
D6870	Small	Doulton	4 1/2"	1991	Current	26.50	65.00	90.00

AIRMAN

Commissioned by The British Toby in a limited edition of 250 pieces. Sold originally in a set of three at $465.00 Canadian Funds.

STYLE TWO: RED SCARF WITH R.C.A.F. CYPHER

SERIES: The Canadians, one of three.

Designer: W. K. Harper   **Handle:** German fighter plane shot down in flames   **Backstamp:** Doulton/
British Toby

Colourway: Brown cap and flight jacket, red scarf

Doulton Number	Size	Backstamp	Height	Intro.	Discon.	Current Market Value		
						U.K. £	U.S. $	Can. $
D6903	Small	Doulton/British	4 1/2"	1991	1991	100.00	170.00	200.00

THE ANGLER

Angling, meaning to fish with hook and bait, is the preferred term used by sport fishermen. A pastime well-known for its popularity, angling was a fitting choice of subject for the Characters from Life series.

SERIES: Characters from Life, one of seven.

Designer: Stanley J. Taylor   **Handle:** A fish and lure   **Backstamp:** Doulton

Colourway: Green jacket, brown hat, cream pullover

Doulton Number	Size	Backstamp	Height	Intro.	Discon.	Current Market Value		
						U.K. £	U.S. $	Can. $
D6866	Small	Doulton	4"	1990	Current	26.50	65.00	90.00

ANNE BOLEYN

(1502-1536). Anne became the second wife of Henry VIII in a secret ceremony performed in January, 1533. Their marriage was officially sanctioned in May by the Archbishop of Canterbury, Thomas Cramner, and she was crowned Queen on June 1, 1533 in Westminster Hall. Unable to produce the son he desired, Henry imprisoned her in the tower of London, on false grounds of adultery. She was beheaded, with a sword on May 19, 1536 in a courtyard of the Tower of London. The modeller, in using an axe on the handle, was not quite correct. Anne Boleyn was the mother of Queen Elizabeth the First, born September 7th, 1533.

SERIES: Henry VIII and his Six Wives, one of eight.

Designer: D.V. Tootle   **Handle:** An axe and chopping block   **Backstamp:** Doulton

Colourway: Black and grey

Doulton Number	Size	Backstamp	Height	Intro.	Discon.	Current Market Value U.K. £	U.S. $	Can. $
D6644	Large	Doulton	7 1/4"	1975	1990	50.00	95.00	145.00
D6650	Small	Doulton	3 1/2"	1980	1990	35.00	60.00	80.00
D6651	Miniature	Doulton	2 1/2"	1980	1990	35.00	40.00	60.00

ANNE OF CLEVES

(1515-1557). In a political arrangement by Thomas Cromwell, Anne was chosen to marry Henry VIII. Upon seeing his dull and unattractive betrothed, whom he later referred to as his 'Flanders Mare', Henry attempted unsuccessfully to break the contract. Anne became his forth wife on January 6th, 1540, for only a brief time. Henry had the marriage annulled on July 8th of that year and gave Anne a pension for life.

SERIES: Henry VIII and his Six Wives, one of eight.

Designer: Michael Abberley   **Handle:** Head of a horse   **Backstamp:** Doulton

Colourway: Black and red

VARIATIONS

VARIATION NO. 1: Handle: Horse's ears pointing up.

The original design of the handle had the ears of the horse pointing upwards.

Doulton Number	Size	Variation	Height	Intro.	Discon.	Current Market Value		
						U.K. £	U.S. $	Can. $
D6653	Large	Var. 1	7 1/4"	1980	1981	125.00	275.00	325.00

EARS FLAT   EARS POINTING UP

Royal Doulton
ANNE OF CLEVES
D 6653
Modelled by

© ROYAL DOULTON TABLEWARE
LIMITED 1979

Royal Doulton®
ANNE OF CLEVES
D 6753
Designed by M. Abberley
Modelled by

Peter A Gee

© 1979 ROYAL DOULTON (U.K.)

VARIATION NO. 2: Handle: Horse's ears flat against head.

It was found that during the packaging and shipping of the jug, the horse ears would tend to break off. The design was then changed to have the ears of the horse lying flat against the head.

Doulton Number	Size	Variation	Height	Intro.	Discon.	Current Market Value		
						U.K. £	U.S. $	Can. $
D6653	Large	Var. 2	7 1/4"	1980	1990	50.00	85.00	145.00
D6753	Small	Var. 2	4 1/4"	1987	1990	35.00	60.00	80.00
D6754	Miniature	Var. 2	2 1/2"	1987	1990	35.00	40.00	60.00

ANNIE OAKLEY

(1860-1926). Phoebe Anne Moses learned to shoot at the age of eight and helped support her family by killing game for a hotel in Cincinatti, Ohio. At fifteen, Anne defeated professional marksman Frank Butler in a shooting contest. She married him in 1876 and became a regular performer in shooting exhibitions, using the stage name "Annie Oakley." She was a star of "Buffalo Bill's Wild West Show" from 1885 unitl 1901, when she was injured in a train accident and forced to retire. During W.W. I she worked again, training American soldiers in marksmanship.

SERIES: The Wild West Collection, one of six.

Royal Doulton

THE WILD WEST
Collection

ANNIE OAKLEY
D6732
Modelled by

Stanley James Taylor.

© ROYAL DOULTON TABLEWARE
LIMITED 1984

Designer: Stanley J. Taylor **Handle:** Rifle and belt **Backstamp:** Doulton

Colourway: Yellow hair, cream hat, brown tunic

Doulton Number	Size	Backstamp	Height	Intro.	Discon.	Current Market Value		
						U.K. £	U.S. $	Can. $
D6732	Mid	Doulton	5 1/4"	1985	1989	40.00	75.00	110.00

THE ANTIQUE DEALER

In the world of collecting, the Antique dealer would mostly be involved with old and valuable furniture, paintings, and other decorative items which he would buy and sell to the public.

Commissioned by Kevin Francis Ceramics Ltd. (KFC) in 1988. Issued in a limited edition of 5,000 pieces.

SERIES: The Collecting World, one of three.

Original Concept by Kevin Pearson and Geoff Blower

Royal Doulton®
THE ANTIQUE DEALER
D 6807
Modelled by
G Blower
A Special Edition of 5000
From "The Collecting World" series
Produced by Royal Doulton
for Kevin Francis Ceramics
© 1988 ROYAL DOULTON
AND KEVIN FRANCIS CERAMICS

Designer: Geoff Blower   **Handle:** Flintlock handgun and candlestick   **Backstamp:** Doulton / Kevin Francis

Colourway: Black hat, blue coat

Doulton Number	Size	Backstamp	Height	Intro.	Discon.	Current Market Value		
						U.K. £	U.S. $	Can. $
D6807	Large	Doulton/KFC	7 1/4"	1988	Ltd. Ed.	75.00	150.00	195.00

ANTONY AND CLEOPATRA

Marcus Antonius (83-30 B.C.). Antony, a skilled soldier, was co-ruler of Rome with Caesar's nephew Octavian from 43 to 32 B.C.

Cleopatra (68-30 B.C.). Well known for her charm and beauty, Cleopatra was Queen of Egypt and ally and lover of Julius Caesar. In 41 B.C. Antony and Cleopatra met and fell in love, marrying in 37 B.C. Antony gave to Cleopatra and their children a share of his Roman provinces in 34 B.C., a move which enraged Octavian. He waged war on the couple, pursuing them in their defeat to Alexandria.

Antony, hearing a rumour of Cleopatra's death, stabbed himself in grief. He was carried to her and died in her arms. Cleopatra in turn committed suicide, apparently from fear of Octavian, by placing an asp on her chest.

Issued in 1985 in a limited edition of 9,500 pieces.

SERIES: The Star-Crossed Lovers Collection, (Two Faced Jug), one of four.

Designer: M. Abberley

Handle: Eagle's head, dagger and shield/ Asp and harp

Colourway: Black, grey, brown

Backstamp: Doulton

Doulton Number	Size	Backstamp	Height	Intro.	Discon.	Current Market Value		
						U.K. £	U.S. $	Can. $
D6728	Large	Doulton	7 1/4"	1985	Ltd. Ed.	65.00	95.00	175.00

ANTONY AND CLEOPATRA

PROTOTYPE

A prototype of this Character Jug exists with Antony having a pudgy face, wide eyes and brown hair and Cleopatra with lighter make-up around the eyes, beads around her neck and a dark red head-dress. Only one known to exist.

PROTOTYPE   REGUALR ISSUE

Doulton Number	Size	Variation	Height	Intro.	Discon.	U.K. £	Current Market Value U.S. $	Can. $
D6728	Large	Prototype	7 1/4"	1984	1984		Unique	

APOTHECARY

Along with the other characters in the Williamsburg series, the apothecary was central to colonial life in 18th century U.S.A. The term "apothecary," replaced by modern day "pharmacist," referred to a seller and dispenser of drugs.

SERIES: Characters from Williamsburg, one of seven.

Character Jugs from Williamsburg
Apothecary
D 6567
COPR 1962
DOULTON & CO LIMITED
Rd No 906337
Rd No 43444
Rd No 9223
Rd No 287/62

Designer: Max Henk   **Handle:** Mortar and pestle   **Backstamp:** Doulton

Colourway: Green coat with white cravat, white wig

Doulton Number	Size	Backstamp	Height	Intro.	Discon.	Current Market Value		
						U.K. £	U.S. $	Can. $
D6567	Large	Doulton	7"	1963	1983	50.00	100.00	145.00
D6574	Small	Doulton	4"	1963	1983	40.00	65.00	95.00
D6581	Miniature	Doulton	2 1/2"	1963	1983	35.00	55.00	80.00

ARAMIS

One of the three musketeers, Aramis joined Athos, Porthos and D'Artagnan in a fictional life of adventure in Alexandre Dumas' 18th century novel, led by their code "All for one, and one for all"

SERIES: One of the "Three Musketeers," one of four.
Now part of the Characters from Literature, one of eleven.

Aramis
(One of the Three Musketeers)
D. 6441
COPR. 1955
DOULTON & CO LIMITED
Rd Nº 877527
Rd Nº 34108
Rd Nº 7247
Rd Nº 289/55

Designer: Max Henk

Handle: Handle of a sword

Colourway: See Variations

Backstamp: See Backstamps

VARIATIONS

VARIATION NO. 1: Colourway: Black hat, white feather, brown tunic.

BACKSTAMPS

A: Doulton

B: Doulton / (One of the "Three Musketeers")

The wording "One of the Three Musketeers" was included to enlighten the unknowledgeable that "Aramis" was one of the famous Musketeers.

Doulton Number	Size	Variation	Height	Intro.	Discon.	Current Market Value U.K. £	Current Market Value U.S. $	Current Market Value Can. $
D6441	Large	Var. 1A	7 1/4"	1956	Current	41.00	130.00	145.00
D6441	Large	Var. 1B	7 1/4"	1956	1970	41.00	130.00	145.00
D6454	Small	Var. 1B	3 1/2"	1956	Current	22.50	65.00	80.00
D6508	Miniature	Var. 1A	2 1/2"	1960	Current	15.50	50.00	60.00

Royal Doulton®
ARAMIS
D 6829
Modelled by

© 1955 ROYAL DOULTON
NEW COLOURWAY 1988
SPECIAL COMMISSION 1000
PETER JONES CHINA
LEEDS AND WAKEFIELD

VARIATION NO. 2: Colourway: Yellow hat, maroon tunic.

Commissioned by Peter Jones China Ltd., England. Issued in 1988 in a limited edition of 1,000.

BACKSTAMP: Doulton/Peter Jones China Ltd.

Doulton Number	Size	Backstamp	Height	Intro.	Discon.	Current Market Value U.K. £	Current Market Value U.S. $	Current Market Value Can. $
D6829	Large	Jones	7 1/4"	1988	Ltd. Ed.	75.00	125.00	195.00

'ARD OF 'EARING

With hand held to cup his ear, this cockney gentleman is a comic representation of the popular euphemism for deafness. The jug was discontinued in 1967 and has since become valuable and difficult to find.

'ard of 'earing
D 6586
COPR 1963
DOULTON & CO LIMITED
Rd No 913137
Rd No 45356
Rd No 9681
Rd No 811/63

Designer: David Biggs　　**Handle:** A hand held to the ear　　**Backstamp:** Doulton

Colourway: Dark purple tricorn; green, white and yellow clothing

Doulton Number	Size	Backstamp	Height	Intro.	Discon.	Current Market Value U.K. £	U.S. $	Can. $
D6588	Large	Doulton	7 1/2"	1964	1967	500.00	1,100.00	1,400.00
D6591	Small	Doulton	3 1/2"	1964	1967	400.00	750.00	900.00
D6594	Miniature	Doulton	2 1/2"	1964	1967	475.00	1,000.00	1,250.00

ARP WARDEN

Commissioned by Lawley's By Post in a limited edition of 9,500 sets.

SERIES: Dad's Army, Heroes of the Blitz, one of three.

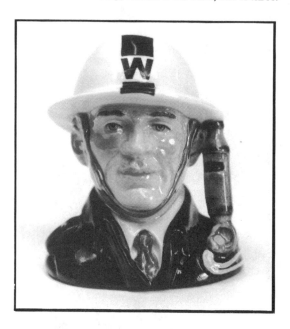

Designer: Stanley J. Taylor   **Handle:** Grey whistle   **Backstamp:** Doulton / Lawley's

Colourway: Dark blue jacket, white helmet with black stripe and the initial "W"

Doulton Number	Size	Backstamp	Height	Intro.	Discon.	Current Market Value U.K. £	U.S. $	Can. $
D6872	Small	Doulton/Lawley's	4"	1991	1991	40.00	70.00	80.00

'ARRIET

'Arriet is a coster or costermonger. A cockney woman who sold fruits and vegetables from a barrow in the streets of London.

'Arriet is a derivative of Pearly Girl. Please see page 215 for the Pearly Girl character jug.

'arriet.

COPR.1946.
DOULTON & CO LIMITED
RdN⁰ 647682
RdN⁰ 23909
RdN⁰ 132/46
RdN⁰ 5195

Designer: Harry Fenton   **Handle:** Hat feather   **Backstamp:** Doulton

Colourway: Green hat, brown coat, yellow scarf

Doulton Number	Size	Backstamp	Height	Intro.	Discon.	Current Market Value		
						U.K. £	U.S. $	Can. $
D6208	Large	Doulton	6 1/2"	1947	1960	120.00	225.00	285.00
D6236	Small	Doulton	3 1/4"	1947	1960	60.00	110.00	140.00
D6250	Miniature	Doulton	2 1/4"	1947	1960	45.00	85.00	110.00
D6256	Tiny	Doulton	1 1/4"	1947	1960	75.00	200.00	265.00

'ARRY

'Arriet's husband 'Arry is also a costermonger, plying his trade in London.

'Arry is a derivative of Pearly Boy. Please see page 213 for the Pearly Boy character jug. The original design of 'Arry featured the word "Blimey" across the back, it was never produced.

Designer: Harry Fenton   **Handle:** Plain   **Backstamp:** Doulton

Colourway: Brown hat and coat, red and yellow scarf

Doulton Number	Size	Backstamp	Height	Intro.	Discon.	Current Market Value U.K. £	U.S. $	Can. $
D6207	Large	Doulton	6 1/2"	1947	1960	120.00	225.00	285.00
D6235	Small	Doulton	3 1/2"	1947	1960	60.00	110.00	140.00
D6249	Miniature	Doulton	2 1/2"	1947	1960	45.00	75.00	95.00
D6255	Tiny	Doulton	1 1/2"	1947	1960	75.00	200.00	265.00

ARTFUL DODGER

The Artful Dodger is a member of a gang of thieves who meets and enlists Oliver in Dickens' novel of Victoria London, "Oliver Twist."

Issued to commemorate the 170th Anniversary of the birth of Charles Dickens. There are twelve jugs in this set, which were issued with a certificate of authenticity. A mahogany display shelf completes the set. The set was first sold by Lawley's By Post in the U.K. during 1982 to 1988, and in 1985 forward in North America and Austrialia.

SERIES: Charles Dickens Commemorative Set / Dickens Tinies, one of twelve.

*Photograph
Not Available
At Press Time*

Designer: Peter Gee   **Handle:** Plain   **Backstamp:** Doulton

Colourway: Yellow and black

Doulton Number	Size	Backstamp	Height	Intro.	Discon.	Current Market Value U.K. £	U.S. $	Can. $
D6678	Tiny	Doulton	1 1/2"	1982	1989	30.00	50.00	60.00

ATHOS

Under the banner of "All for one and one for all," Athos joined his three cohorts in a life of adventure in Alexandre Dumas' 18th century novel.

SERIES: One of the "Three Musketeers", one of four.
Now part of the Characters from Literature, one of eleven.

Athos
(One of the "Three Musketeers")
D 6452
COPR 1955
DOULTON & CO LIMITED
Rd No 677528
Rd No 34106
Rd No 7245
Rd No 290/55

Athos
D 6439
©DOULTON & CO LIMITED 1955

Designer: Max Henk   **Handle:** Upper half of a sword   **Backstamp:** See Backstamps

Colourway: See Variations

VARIATIONS

VARIATION NO. 1: Colourway: Black hat, white feather, green tunic with gold trim.
Mould: Feathers above rim of hat.

BACKSTAMP: Doulton

Doulton Number	Size	Variation	Height	Intro.	Discon.	Current Market Value U.K. £	U.S. $	Can. $
D6439	Large	Var. 1	7 1/2"	1956	Unknown	45.00	135.00	145.00

VARIATION NO. 2: Colourway: Black hat, white feather, green tunic with gold trim.
Mould: Feathers run along rim of hat.

BACKSTAMPS

A: Doulton

B: Doulton / (One of the "Three Musketeers")

The wording "One of the Three Musketeers" was included in the early backstamp to enlighten the unknowledgeable that "Athos" was one of the famous Musketeers.

Doulton Number	Size	Backstamp	Height	Intro.	Discon.	Current Market Value U.K. £	U.S. $	Can. $
D6439	Large	Doulton	7 1/4"	Unknown	Current	41.00	130.00	145.00
D6439	Large	Doulton/One	7 1/4"	Unknown	Current	41.00	130.00	145.00
D6452	Small	Doulton/One	3 3/4"	Unknown	Current	22.50	65.00	80.00
D6509	Miniature	Doulton/One	2 1/2"	Unknown	Current	15.50	50.00	60.00

Royal Doulton®
ATHOS
D 6827
Modelled by

© 1955 ROYAL DOULTON
NEW COLOURWAY 1988
SPECIAL COMMISSION 1000
PETER JONES CHINA
LEEDS AND WAKEFIELD

VARIATION NO. 3: Colourway: Black hat, white feather, yellow tunic with blue trim.

BACKSTAMP: Doulton / Peter Jones China Ltd.

Commissioned by Peter Jones China Ltd., England. Issued in 1988 in a limited edition of 1,000.

Doulton Number	Size	Variation	Height	Intro.	Discon.	Current Market Value U.K. £	U.S. $	Can. $
D6827	Large	Var. 3	7 1/4"	1988	Ltd. Ed.	75.00	150.00	195.00

THE AUCTIONEER

Unlike a store or market, an auction requires a prospective buyer to bid a price on an item, the object being sold to the individual offering the highest bid. The auctioneer presents the merchandise, controls the bidding, and declares the buyer of each item.

Commissioned by Kevin Francis Ceramics Ltd. (KFC). Issued in 1988 in a limited edition of 5,000.

SERIES: The Collecting World, one of three.

Designer: Geoff Blower

Handle: Auctioneer's gavel
HN687 The Bather

Backstamp: Doulton /
Kevin Francis

Colourway: Green coat and bow tie, light brown cap

Doulton Number	Size	Backstamp	Height	Intro.	Discon.	Current Market Value		
						U.K. £	U.S. $	Can. $
D6838	Large	Doulton/KFC	6 1/4"	1988	Ltd. Ed.	85.00	160.00	195.00

AULD MAC

Sir Harry Lauder, a 20th century singer/comedian, sang a song which inspired this piece. His Scotsman Mac found the prices too high in London because every time he made a move, "Bang Went Saxpence." The phrase is incised on back of his hat below "Auld Mac."

Auld Mac
D.5823

Designer: Harry Fenton	**Handle:** Plain	**Backstamp:** See Backstamps

Colourway: Green tam, brown coat

BACKSTAMPS

A: Doulton - "OWD MAC"

"Owd Mac" incised in the tam and printed in the backstamp c. 1937.

B: Doulton - "AULD MAC"

"Auld Mac" incised in the tam in 1938, but "Owd Mac" continued in the backstamp until approximately 1940.

C: Doulton - "AULD MAC"

"Auld Mac" incised in tam and printed in backstamp.

"OWD MAC"   "AULD MAC"

Doulton Number	Size	Backstamp	Height	Intro.	Discon.	Current Market Value U.K. £	U.S. $	Can. $
D5823	Large	A "Owd"/"Owd"	6 1/4"	1937	c. 1937	65.00	125.00	250.00
D5823	Large	B "Auld/Owd"	6 1/4"	1938	1940	45.00	100.00	150.00
D5823	Large	C "Auld/Auld"	6 1/4"	1940	1986	45.00	100.00	150.00
D5824	Small	A "Owd"/"Owd"	3 1/4"	1937	1937	65.00	40.00	125.00
D5824	Small	B "Auld/Owd"	3 1/4"	1938	1940	30.00	35.00	95.00
D5824	Small	C "Auld/Auld"	3 1/4"	1940	1985	30.00	30.00	95.00
D6253	Miniature	C "Auld/Auld"	2 1/4"	1946	1985	25.00	35.00	70.00
D6257	Tiny	C "Auld/Auld"	1 1/4"	1946	1960	90.00	225.00	275.00

Miscellaneous "Auld Mac" Items

Doulton Number	Item	Height	Intro.	Discon.	Current Market Value U.K. £	U.S. $	Can. $
D5889	Musical Jug	6 1/4"	1938	c. 1939	350.00	800.00	925.00
D6006	Ash Bowl	3"	1938	1960	65.00	125.00	140.00

Note: Tune to the Musical Jug: "The Campbells are Coming".

AUXILIARY FIREMAN

Commissioned by Lawley's By Post in a limited edition of 9,500 sets.

SERIES: Dad's Army, Heroes of the Blitz, one of three.

Designer: Stanley J. Taylor   **Handle:** Hose and nozzle   **Backstamp:** Doulton / Lawley's

Colourway: Black jacket, grey helmet with white initials "A.F.S."

Doulton Number	Size	Backstamp	Height	Intro.	Discon.	Current Market Value U.K. £	U.S. $	Can. $
D6887	Small	Doulton/Lawley's	4"	1991	1991	40.00	70.00	80.00

BACCHUS

In Roman mythology, Bacchus, son of Zeus, was the god of wine and nature. He traditionally inspired men and women to music and poetry. The harvest celebrations to honour him, "Bacchanalia" were reputed to be such orgies of excess that the Roman government had them banned.

Some of the earlier versions of the miniature jug had the leaves on the vine handle painted green. There is no current premium value for this variety.

Designer: Max Henk   **Handle:** Grapevine   **Backstamp:** See Backstamps

Colourway: Purple robes, green leaves and purple grapes adorn the head

Bacchus
D 6505
COPR 1958
DOULTON & CO LIMITED
Rd No 889570
Rd No 38226
Rd No 8036
Rd No 423/58

Bacchus
D 6499
COPR 1958
DOULTON & CO LIMITED
Rd No 889570
Rd No 38226
Rd No 8036
Rd No 423/58

CITY OF
STOKE-ON-TRENT
JUBILEE YEAR
1959-1960
WITH THE COMPLIMENTS OF
LORD MAYOR AND LADY MAYORESS
ALDERMAN HAROLD CLOWES O.B.E. J.P.
AND
MISS CHRISTINE CLOWES

BACKSTAMPS

A: Doulton

B: Doulton / City of Stoke-on-Trent "With the compliments of Lord Mayor and Lady Mayoress Alderman Harold Clowes, O.B.E., J.P. and Miss Christine Clowes"

Overprinted for the jubilee year, 1959-1960, of the city.

Doulton Number	Size	Backstamp	Height	Intro.	Discon.	Current Market Value		
						U.K. £	U.S. $	Can. $
D6499	Large	Doulton	7"	1959	Current	41.00	130.00	145.00
D6499	Large	Doulton/City	7"	1959	1960	475.00	800.00	950.00
D6505	Small	Doulton	4"	1959	Current	22.50	65.00	80.00
D6521	Miniature	Doulton	2 1/2"	1960	Current	15.50	50.00	60.00

Miscellaneous "Bacchus" Items

Doulton Number	Item	Height	Intro.	Discon.	Current Market Value		
					U.K. £	U.S. $	Can. $
D6505	Table Lighter	3 1/2"	1964	1974	60.00	100.00	225.00

BASEBALL PLAYER

Only two jugs known to exist. These jugs are test pieces and were never put into production. Each jug is different.

STYLE ONE: HANDLE: BAT AND BALL

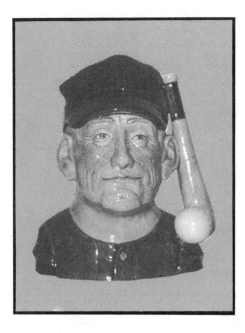

Designer: David Biggs   **Handle:** Bat and ball   **Backstamp:** Doulton

Colourway: See Variations

VARIATIONS

VARIATION NO. 1: Colourway: Blue / green jersey, red sleeves and cap.

Doulton Number	Size	Variation	Height	Intro.	Discon.	U.K. £	Current Market Value U.S. $	Can. $
Unknown	Large	Var. 1	7 1/2"		Unknown		Extremely Rare	

VARIATION NO. 2: Colourway: Striped blue and black jersey and cap.

Doulton Number	Size	Variation	Height	Intro.	Discon.	U.K. £	Current Market Value U.S. $	Can. $
Unknown	Large	Var. 2	7 1/2"		Unknown		Extremely Rare	

THE BASEBALL PLAYER

The "great American pastime" of baseball is an obvious choice in a series inspired by favourite hobbies.

SERIES: Characters from Life, one of seven.

STYLE TWO: HANDLE: BALL, BAT AND GLOVE.

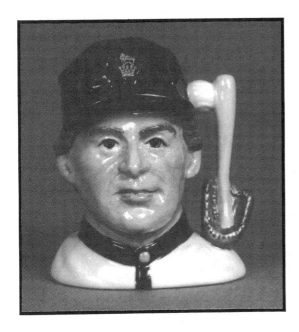

Designer: Stanley J. Taylor   **Handle:** Ball, bat and glove   **Backstamp:** See Backstamps

Colourway: Dark blue cap and white jersey

BACKSTAMPS

A: Doulton

For General Issue: 1991.

B: Doulton / Britannia Limited

Commissioned by Britannia Limited to celebrate the 5th anniversary of their Doulton Convention and Sale, January 1991. Issued in 1991 in a limited edition of 500 pieces.

Doulton Number	Size	Backstamp	Height	Intro.	Discon.	Current Market Value U.K. £	U.S. $	Can. $
D6878	Small	Doulton	4 1/4"	1991	Current	28.50	70.00	90.00
D6878	Small	Doulton/Britannia	4 1/4"	1991	Ltd. Ed.	45.00	85.00	85.00

BEEFEATER

The Yeomen of the Guard and warders of the Tower of London are colloquially referred to as Beefeaters. The name "Beefeater" came from a visiting Grand Duke who was astonished by the large amounts of beef the Yeoman Guards ate. He nicknamed them "Beefeaters." The monarch's cypher at the base of the handle, G.R., is an abbreviation of George Regina, for King George VI. In 1953, after his death, the cypher was changed to E.R., (Elizabeth Regina), for Queen Elizabeth II and continues today.

SERIES: The London Collection, one of ten.
The current Beefeater is included in this series.

Designer: Harry Fenton
Robert Tabbenor

Handle: See Variations

Backstamp: See Backstamps

Colourway: See Variations

VARIATIONS

VARIATION NO. 1: Colourway: Black hat, white ruff, pink tunic.
Handle: Pink with a "GR" cypher.

BACKSTAMP: Doulton/"Beefeaters"

The plural name was used on all three size jugs from 1947 through 1953.

`` Beefeaters''

COPR 1946
DOULTON & CO LIMITED
Rd Nº 847680
Rd Nº 23907
Rd Nº 119/46
Rd Nº 5193

Doulton Number	Size	Variation	Height	Intro.	Discon.	Current Market Value		
						U.K. £	U.S. $	Can. $
D6206	Large	1, "Beefeaters"	6 1/2"	1947	1953	65.00	150.00	195.00
D6233	Small	1, "Beefeaters"	3 1/4"	1947	1953	45.00	75.00	85.00
D6251	Miniature	1, "Beefeaters"	2 1/2"	1947	1953	40.00	70.00	75.00

VARIATION NO. 2: Colourway: Black hat, white ruff, pink tunic.
Handle: Yellow with a "GR" cypher.

BACKSTAMP: Doulton/"Beefeaters"

Doulton Number	Size	Variation	Height	Intro.	Discon.	Current Market Value U.K. £	U.S. $	Can. $
D6206	Large	Var. 2	6 1/2"	1947	1947	900.00	1,500.00	1,750.00
D6233	Small	Var. 2	3 1/4"	1947	1947	800.00	1,300.00	1,500.00

VARIATION NO. 3: Colourway: Black hat, white ruff, pink tunic.
Handle: Pink with an "ER" cypher.

BACKSTAMPS

A: Doulton/"Beefeaters"

The plural name was found only on early versions of the "ER" jugs.

B: Doulton/"Beefeater"

In late 1953 the backstamp was adjusted and the singular "Beefeater" name was incorporated.

C: Doulton/"Beefeater" "Fired in the last firing of a traditional Bottle Oven 1978 Longton Stoke-on-Trent, England"

Doulton Number	Size	Variation	Height	Intro.	Discon.	Current Market Value U.K. £	U.S. $	Can. $
D6206	Large	3A, "Beefeaters"	6 1/2"	1953	1953	70.00	140.00	160.00
D6206	Large	3B, "Beefeater"	6 1/2"	1953	1987	65.00	130.00	145.00
D6206	Large	3C, Bottle Oven	6 1/2"	1978	1978	750.00	1,250.00	1,500.00
D6233	Small	3A, "Beefeaters"	3 1/4"	1953	1953	45.00	70.00	80.00
D6233	Small	3B, "Beefeater"	3 1/4"	1953	1987	35.00	65.00	80.00
D6251	Miniature	3A, "Beefeaters	2 1/2"	1953	1953	40.00	60.00	70.00
D6251	Miniature	3B, "Beefeater"	2 1/2"	1953	1987	35.00	50.00	60.00

VAR. 3   VAR. 1   VAR. 4

VARIATION NO. 4: Colourway: Black hat, white ruff, scarlet tunic.
Handle: Scarlet with an "ER" cypher.

BACKSTAMPS

Royal Doulton
BEEFEATER
D 6233
Modelled by

H. Fenton

© ROYAL DOULTON TABLEWARE
LIMITED 1946

A: Doulton

B: Doulton / Royal Doulton International Collectors Club

The "Tiny" Beefeater was issued in 1988 for the RDICC members.
Robert Tabbenor miniaturized Fenton's design of 1947.

Doulton Number	Size	Backstamp	Height	Intro.	Discon.	Current Market Value U.K. £	Current Market Value U.S. $	Current Market Value Can. $
D6206	Large	Doulton	6 1/2"	1987	Current	47.00	130.00	145.00
D6233	Small	Doulton	3 1/4"	1987	Current	24.50	65.00	80.00
D6251	Miniature	Doulton	2 1/2"	1987	Current	16.50	50.00	60.00
D6806	Tiny	Doulton/RDICC	1 1/2"	1988	1988	35.00	60.00	125.00

Miscellaneous "Beefeater" Items

Doulton Number	Item	Height	Intro.	Discon.	Current Market Value U.K. £	Current Market Value U.S. $	Current Market Value Can. $
D6233	Table Lighter	3 1/2"	1958	1973	65.00	145.00	225.00

BENJAMIN FRANKLIN

(1706-1790). An American publicist, scientist and statesman, Franklin was a signatory to the peace between Britain and the U.S.A. after the war of Independence. In 1748 he left his printing business to his foreman and devoted his life to science. His most famous discovery, that lightning is electricity, was accomplished with the simple objects of a knife and a metal key. It lead to the invention of the lightning rod, still used today to divert lightning harmlessly into the ground.

This jug was modelled for "The Queen's Table," Royal Doulton's Exhibit at the United Kingdom Showcase at Walt Disney's Epcot Centre in Orlando, Florida. The jug was sold exclusively to Epcot tourists visiting the exhibition during 1982. It was released for general sale in 1983.

Royal Doulton
Benjamin Franklin
D.6695
Hand made and Hand decorated
© ROYAL DOULTON
TABLEWARE LTD. 1982

Designer: Eric Griffiths   **Handle:** A kite and key   **Backstamp:** Doulton

Colourway: Black coat, white shirt, blue scarf

Doulton Number	Size	Backstamp	Height	Intro.	Discon.	Current Market Value		
						U.K. £	U.S. $	Can. $
D6695	Small	Doulton	4"	1982	1989	45.00	65.00	85.00

BETSY TROTWOOD

In Dickens' novel "David Copperfield," Betsy is David's curt yet loving aunt.

Issued to commemorate the 170th Anniversary of the birth of Charles Dickens. There are twelve jugs in this set, which were issued with a certificate of authenticity. A mahogany display shelf completes the set. The set was first sold by Lawley's By Post in the U.K. during 1982 to 1988, and in 1985 forward in North America and Austrialia.

SERIES: Charles Dickens Commemorative Set / Dickens Tinies, one of twelve.

*Photograph
Not Available
At Press Time*

Designer: Michael Abberley   **Handle:** Plain   **Backstamp:** Doulton

Colourway: Yellow, white and black

Doulton Number	Size	Backstamp	Height	Intro.	Discon.	Current Market Value U.K. £	U.S. $	Can. $
D6685	Tiny	Doulton	1 1/2"	1982	1989	30.00	50.00	60.00

BILL SYKES

In Dickens' "Oliver Twist," Sykes is a cruel cohort of Fagin and his band of child thieves.

Issued to commemorate the 170th Anniversary of the birth of Charles Dickens. There are twelve jugs in this set, which were issued with a certificate of authenticity. A mahogany display shelf completes the set. The set was first sold by Lawley's By Post in the U.K. during 1982 to 1988, and in 1985 forward in North America and Austrialia.

SERIES: Charles Dickens Commemorative Set / Dickens Tinies, one of twelve.

*Photograph
Not Available
At Press Time*

Designer: Michael Abberley   **Handle:** Plain   **Backstamp:** Doulton

Colourway: Green and dark blue

Doulton Number	Size	Backstamp	Height	Intro.	Discon.	Current Market Value U.K. £	U.S. $	Can. $
D6684	Tiny	Doulton	1 1/2"	1982	1989	30.00	50.00	60.00

BLACKSMITH

In 18th Century Williamsburg, Virginia, the blacksmith was an essential part of colonial life. Working a forge, he made horseshoes and other iron tools needed to cultivate the land.

SERIES: Characters from Williamsburg, one of seven.

Designer: David Biggs   **Handle:** Hammer and anvil   **Backstamp:** Doulton

Colourway: Salmon hat, white shirt, light brown apron

Doulton Number	Size	Backstamp	Height	Intro.	Discon.	Current Market Value		
						U.K. £	U.S. $	Can. $
D6571	Large	Doulton	7 1/4"	1963	1983	50.00	100.00	145.00
D6578	Small	Doulton	4"	1963	1983	40.00	70.00	95.00
D6585	Miniature	Doulton	2 1/2"	1963	1983	35.00	55.00	80.00

BLACKSMITH

PROTOTYPE

A large prototype of the Blacksmith with older features, different hat and hair style. Only one copy known to exist.

Designer: David Biggs **Handle:** Hammer, anvil and horseshoe **Backstamp:** Doulton

Colourway: Beige, white and black

Doulton Number	Size	Backstamp	Height	Intro.	Discon.	Current Market Value U.K. £	U.S. $	Can. $
Not Issued	Large	Doulton	7 1/4"		c. 1963		Unique	

BONNIE PRINCE CHARLIE

(1720-1788). Grandson of James II, the "Young Pretender" was born Charles Edward Stuart in Rome. He became the hopeful leader of the Jacobites, adherents to the Stuart line, and led them in an unsuccessful uprising in 1745. Being defeated at Culloden Moor in 1746, he escaped to France with the help of Flora McDonald, Charles roamed Europe, a drunkard, until settling in Rome where he passed the remainder of his life.

Royal Doulton®
BONNIE PRINCE CHARLIE
D 6858
Modelled by
Stanley James Taylor.
© 1989 ROYAL DOULTON

Designer: Stanley J. Taylor   **Handle:** Crown atop thistles   **Backstamp:** Doulton

Colourway: Blue plaid tam, red coat trimmed with yellow collar, white ruffles at the neck

Doulton Number	Size	Backstamp	Height	Intro.	Discon.	Current Market Value		
						U.K. £	U.S. $	Can. $
D6858	Large	Doulton	6 1/2"	1990	Current	57.00	175.00	225.00

BOOTMAKER

This 18th Century American craftsman differed from a cobbler by his product. Although he may have made shoes as well as boots, it is doubtful he would have done so often - Virginia winters were much too harsh for more delicate footwear.

SERIES: Characters from Williamsburg, one of seven.

Designer: David Biggs **Handle:** A boot, hammer and a pair of shoes at the base

Colourway: Salmon cap, white shirt

Backstamp: Doulton

Character Jugs from Williamsburg

Bootmaker
D 6572
COPR 1962
DOULTON & CO LIMITED
Rd No 906342
Rd No 43449
Rd No 9228
Rd No 282 .62

Doulton Number	Size	Backstamp	Height	Intro.	Discon.	Current Market Value U.K. £	U.S. $	Can. $
D6572	Large	Doulton	7 1/2"	1963	1983	50.00	100.00	145.00
D6579	Small	Doulton	4"	1963	1983	40.00	75.00	95.00
D6586	Miniature	Doulton	2 1/2"	1963	1983	35.00	55.00	80.00

BOOTMAKER

PROTOTYPE

A large size prototype of the Bootmaker with younger features, different hair, handle and hat designs. Only one copy known to exist.

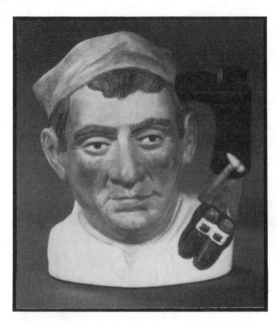

Designer: David Biggs   **Handle:** Shoes, boot and hammer   **Backstamp:** Doulton

Colourway: Beige, white and black

Doulton Number	Size	Backstamp	Height	Intro.	Discon.	Current Market Value U.K. £	Current Market Value U.S. $	Current Market Value Can. $
Not Issued	Large	Doulton	7 1/2"	c. 1963			Unique	

BOWLS PLAYER

SERIES: Characters from Life, one of seven.

Designer: Stanley J. Taylor   **Handle:** Bowl, jack and measure   **Backstamp:** Doulton

Colourway: White and yellow

Doulton Number	Size	Backstamp	Height	Intro.	Discon.	Current Market Value U.K. £	U.S. $	Can. $
D6896	Small	Doulton	4"	1991	Current	27.50	70.00	90.00

BUFFALO BILL

(1846-1917) William Frederick Cody was a scout, plainsman, soldier in the Civil War, hotelier, rancher and finally showman. His expert marksmanship while working as a buffalo hunter earned him his nickname Buffalo Bill. In 1883, Cody and others formed "Buffalo Bill's Wild West Show," a theatrical shooting exhibition which became very successful and travelled through the U.S. and Europe.

This jug was piloted but never put into production. Only three jugs are known to exist. "W.F. Cody Buffalo Bill" is incised on the right shoulder in raised letters.

STYLE ONE: PROFILE OF BUFFALO BILL

Designer: Unknown   **Handle:** A rifle and buffalo head.   **Backstamp:** Doulton

Colourway: Brown hat, grey moustache and goatee

Doulton Number	Size	Backstamp	Height	Intro.	Discon.	U.K. £	Current Market Value U.S. $	Can. $
D —	Large	Doulton	7 1/2"	Unknown			Extremely Rare	

BUFFALO BILL

SERIES: The Wild West Collection, one of six.

STYLE TWO: BUFFALO HEAD WITH HORNS

Designer: Robert Tabbenor   **Handle:** Buffalo head   **Backstamp:** Doulton

Colourway: Light brown hat and buckskin jacket

Doulton Number	Size	Backstamp	Height	Intro.	Discon.	Current Market Value U.K. £	U.S. $	Can. $
D6735	Mid	Doulton	5 1/2"	1985	1989	45.00	75.00	110.00

THE BUSKER

Finding its roots with the early wandering minstrels, busking is still widely practiced today. Entertaining for money in public places has long been an honourable way for artists to support themselves while gaining public exposure for their work.

SERIES: The London Collection, one of ten.

Royal Doulton®

THE BUSKER
D 6775
Modelled by
Stanley James Taylor
© 1987 ROYAL DOULTON

Designer: Stanley J. Taylor   **Handle:** An open concertina   **Backstamp:** Doulton

Colourway: Grey cap, green coat, yellow scarf

Doulton Number	Size	Backstamp	Height	Intro.	Discon.	Current Market Value		
						U.K. £	U.S. $	Can. $
D6775	Large	Doulton	6 1/2"	1988	Current	47.00	130.00	145.00

BUZFUZ

This is an excellent example of the literary character designs of early Character Jugs. In Dickens' "Pickwick Papers," Sergeant Buzfuz was the counsel of Mrs. Bardell in the breach of promise suit she brought against Mr. Pickwick.

Designer: Leslie Harradine Harry Fenton

Handle: Plain

Backstamp: Doulton

Colourway: White collar, brown waistcoat, dark green coat, black robe.

Doulton Number	Size	Backstamp	Height	Intro.	Discon.	Current Market Value U.K. £	U.S. $	Can. $
D5838	Mid	Doulton	5 1/2"	1938	1948	95.00	200.00	230.00
D5838	Small	Doulton	4"	1948	1960	45.00	95.00	125.00

Miscellaneous "Buzfuz" Items

Doulton Number	Item	Height	Intro.	Discon.	Current Market Value U.K. £	U.S. $	Can. $
D5838	Table Lighter	3 1/2"	1958	1959	100.00	200.00	250.00
D6048	Bust	3"	1939	1960	60.00	100.00	135.00

CABINET MAKER

PROTOTYPE

In 1980 plans to continue the Williamsburg series were still in force. A new jug, the Cabinet Maker was announced in 1981 based on the prototype. With the Williamsburg series being cancelled in 1983 the new jug was never put into production.

SERIES: Characters from Williamsburg

Designer: Micheal Abberley   **Handle:** Brace   **Backstamp:** Doulton

Colourway: Red, white and brown

Doulton Number	Size	Backstamp	Height	Intro.	Discon.	Current Market Value U.K. £	U.S. $	Can. $
Not Issued	Large	Doulton	7 1/2"	1980	1980		Unique	

CAP'N CUTTLE

The wonderful characters of Dickens' novels were the inspiration of many early jug designs. Captain Edward Cuttle was an eccentric English gentleman in "Dombey and Son," (1846), who is best known for saying "When found, make a note of it."

Designer: Leslie Harradine
Harry Fenton

Handle: Plain

Backstamp: Doulton

Colourway: Blue-black coat and hat, white collar

Doulton Number	Size	Backstamp	Height	Intro.	Discon.	Current Market Value U.K. £	U.S. $	Can. $
D5842	Mid	Doulton	5 1/2"	1938	1948	95.00	200.00	235.00
D5842	Small	Doulton	4"	1948	1960	45.00	110.00	125.00

Miscellaneous "Cap'n Cuttle" Items

Doulton Number	Item	Height	Intro.	Discon.	Current Market Value U.K. £	U.S. $	Can. $
D5842	Table Lighter	3 1/2"	1958	1959	100.00	220.00	250.00

CAPT AHAB

Captain Ahab sailed the whaler, "Pequod" in Herman Melville's great 19th century American classic "Moby Dick." He lost a leg and then his life in pursuit of the great white whale who triumphed in the chase and sunk his ship.

Capt Ahab
D 6522
COPR 1958
DOULTON & CO LIMITED
Rd No 889571
Rd No 38227
Rd No 8037
Rd No 422/58

Designer: Garry Sharpe　　　**Handle:** A grey whale　　　**Backstamp:** Doulton

Colourway: Blue cap and coat, white sweater

Doulton Number	Size	Backstamp	Height	Intro.	Discon.	U.K. £	U.S. $	Can. $
						Current Market Value		
D6500	Large	Doulton	7"	1959	1984	50.00	100.00	160.00
D6506	Small	Doulton	4"	1959	1984	35.00	55.00	95.00
D6522	Miniature	Doulton	2 1/2"	1960	1984	25.00	45.00	80.00

Miscellaneous "Capt Ahab" Items

Doulton Number	Item	Height	Intro.	Discon.	U.K. £	U.S. $	Can. $
					Current Market Value		
D6506	Table Lighter	3 1/2"	1964	1973	125.00	200.00	250.00

CAPT HENRY MORGAN

(1635-1688). A privateer and head of bucaneer pirates in the West Indies, Morgan carried out commissions from the British Authorities. His attack on Panama in 1671 violated a peace treaty between England and Spain. Sent to England to stand trial, he was instead knighted and became Lieutenant Governor of Jamaica where he remained until his death.

Capt Henry Morgan
D 6467
COPR 1957
DOULTON & CO LIMITED
Rd No 886231
Rd No 37211
Rd No 7853
Rd No 388/57

Designer: Garry Sharpe   **Handle:** Sails of a ship   **Backstamp:** Doulton

Colourway: Black tricorn, blue collar trimmed with gold

Doulton Number	Size	Backstamp	Height	Intro.	Discon.	Current Market Value		
						U.K. £	U.S. $	Can. $
D6467	Large	Doulton	6 3/4"	1958	1982	50.00	110.00	160.00
D6469	Small	Doulton	3 1/2"	1958	1982	35.00	55.00	95.00
D6510	Miniature	Doulton	2 1/2"	1960	1982	25.00	40.00	70.00

CAPT HOOK

Captain Hook is the villian and nemesis of Peter Pan in J.M. Barries' famous story. Peter Pan cut off Hook's hand and fed it to a crocodile, who liked it so much he followed the captain around in hopes of eating the rest of him. Hook managed to keep eluding his predator because the crocodile had accidentally swallowed a clock that ticked inside him and ruined the element of suprise in his attacks.

Capt Hook
D 6597
COPR 1964
DOULTON & CO LIMITED
Rd No 917230
Rd No 46676
Rd No 9999
Rd No 594/64

Designer: Max Henk
David Biggs

Handle: An alligator and clock

Backstamp: Doulton

Colourway: Blue tricorn trimmed with gold, green coat trimmed with gold, white ruffles at the neck

Doulton Number	Size	Backstamp	Height	Intro.	Discon.	Current Market Value U.K. £	U.S. $	Can. $
D6597	Large	Doulton	7 1/4"	1965	1971	250.00	500.00	695.00
D6601	Small	Doulton	4"	1965	1971	180.00	375.00	450.00
D6605	Miniature	Doulton	2 1/2"	1965	1971	180.00	400.00	495.00

THE CARDINAL

Easily recognized by his red robes, the cardinal is a leading dignitary of the Roman Catholic Church. The Cardinals as a group form the Sacred College of Cardinals. Since 1059, The Sacred College has elected the Pope.

The Cardinal character jug was produced with and without the pink highlighting on the raised character name. The hair colour ranges from brown to grey.

Designer: Charles Noke

Handle: Plain

Colourway: Scarlet robes

Backstamp: Doulton

The Cardinal

Doulton Number	Size	Backstamp	Height	Intro.	Discon.	Current Market Value U.K. £	U.S. $	Can. $
D5614	Large	Doulton	6 1/2"	1936	1960	75.00	150.00	225.00
D6033	Small	Doulton	3 1/2"	1939	1960	45.00	75.00	110.00
D6129	Miniature	Doulton	2 1/4"	1940	1960	40.00	50.00	95.00
D6258	Tiny	Doulton	1 1/2"	1947	1960	90.00	150.00	275.00

CATHERINE OF ARAGON

(1485-1536). Daughter of Ferdinand and Isabella of Spain, the princess was married to Arthur, Prince of Wales, in a political arrangement between the two countries. When Arthur died shortly after their wedding, she was married to Henry VIII to continue the arrangement. This first marriage for Henry lasted 24 years until he became restless at the lack of male heir and met Anne Boleyn. In 1527 Henry attempted to have his marriage annulled, a move that led to his excommunication by the Pope and, eventually, to the English Reformation. Catherine was banished from the Royal Court and lived until the age of 50, unhappy and lonely.

SERIES: Henry VIII and his Six Wives, one of eight.

Designer: Alan Maslankowski   **Handle:** A tower   **Backstamp:** Doulton

Colourway: Red, gold, black and white

Doulton Number	Size	Backstamp	Height	Intro.	Discon.	Current Market Value U.K. £	U.S. $	Can. $
D6643	Large	Doulton	7"	1975	1989	55.00	85.00	145.00
D6657	Small	Doulton	4"	1981	1989	45.00	65.00	80.00
D6658	Miniature	Doulton	2 3/4"	1981	1989	35.00	50.00	60.00

CATHERINE HOWARD

(1521-1542). Niece to the Duke of Norfolk, Catherine became Henry VIII's fifth wife on July 28, 1540 in a marriage arranged by her family. In 1541 Henry accused her of adultery and had her beheaded in the Tower of London.

SERIES: Henry VIII and his Six Wives, one of eight.

Royal Doulton
**CATHERINE
HOWARD**
D 6645
Modelled by

Peter A Gee .

© ROYAL DOULTON TABLEWARE
LIMITED 1977

Designer: Peter Gee   **Handle:** An axe   **Backstamp:** Doulton

Colourway: Green, brown and white

Doulton Number	Size	Backstamp	Height	Intro.	Discon.	Current Market Value U.K. £	U.S. $	Can. $
D6645	Large	Doulton	7"	1978	1989	50.00	85.00	145.00
D6692	Small	Doulton	4"	1984	1989	35.00	65.00	80.00
D6693	Miniature	Doulton	2 1/2"	1984	1989	35.00	50.00	60.00

CATHERINE PARR

(1512-1548). Catherine became Henry VIII's last wife on July 12, 1543 after being twice widowed herself. She came to wield considerable power in the Royal Court, serving for a time as Queen regent in 1544 and overseeing the start of Edward VI's reign. After Henry's death in 1547, she married Baron Seymour of Sudeley but died during childbirth the following year.

SERIES: Henry VIII and his Six Wives, one of eight.

Royal Doulton®

CATHERINE PARR

D 6752

©1980 ROYAL DOULTON (UK)

Royal Doulton

CATHERINE PARR

D 6664

Modelled by

© ROYAL DOULTON TABLEWARE
LIMITED 1980

Designer: Michael Abberley	**Handle:** Bible and pulpit	**Backstamp:** Doulton

Colourway: Black, orange and brown

Doulton Number	Size	Backstamp	Height	Intro.	Discon.	Current Market Value U.K. £	U.S. $	Can. $
D6664	Large	Doulton	6 3/4"	1981	1989	50.00	100.00	145.00
D6751	Small	Doulton	4"	1987	1989	35.00	65.00	80.00
D6752	Miniature	Doulton	2 1/2"	1987	1989	35.00	55.00	60.00

THE CAVALIER

During the English Civil War, the cavaliers were Royalist soldiers who fought for Charles I. They became known for their off-hand gallantry and haughtiness, an attitude today still described as "cavalier."

STYLE ONE: CAVALIER WITH GOATEE

Designer: Harry Fenton   **Handle:** Handle of a sword   **Backstamp:** Doulton

Colourway: Green hat, white ruff

Doulton Number	Size	Backstamp	Height	Intro.	Discon.	Current Market Value U.K. £	U.S. $	Can. $
D6114	Large	Doulton	7"	1940	1950	1,475.00	3,000.00	3,500.00

THE CAVALIER

Originally listed in Royal Doulton's product guide as "The Laughing Cavalier" presumably after the famous Frans Hals' painting.

Slight colour changes along with alterations to the ruff (collar) and removal of the goatee occurred in 1950.

STYLE TWO: CAVALIER WITHOUT GOATEE

Designer: Harry Fenton   **Handle:** Handle of a sword   **Backstamp:** Doulton

Colourway: Green hat, white ruff

Doulton Number	Size	Backstamp	Height	Intro.	Discon.	Current Market Value U.K. £	Current Market Value U.S. $	Current Market Value Can. $
D6114	Large	Doulton	7"	1950	1960	75.00	135.00	200.00
D6173	Small	Doulton	3 1/4"	1941	1960	45.00	80.00	110.00

CHARLES DICKENS

Issued to commemorate the 170th Anniversary of the birth of Charles Dickens. There are twelve jugs in this set, which were issued with a certificate of authenticity. A mahogany display shelf completes the set. The set was first sold by Lawley's By Post in the U.K. during 1982 to 1988, and in 1985 forward in North America and Austrialia.

SERIES: Charles Dickens Commemorative Set / Dickens Tinies, one of twelve.

STYLE ONE: HANDLE: PLAIN

Designer: Eric Griffiths   **Handle:** Plain   **Backstamp:** Doulton

Colourway: Grey and black

Doulton Number	Size	Backstamp	Height	Intro.	Discon.	Current Market Value U.K. £	U.S. $	Can. $
D6676	Tiny	Doulton	1 1/2"	1982	1989	40.00	60.00	70.00

CHARLES DICKENS

Commissioned by the Royal Doulton International Collectors Club in a limited edition of 7,500 pieces.

SERIES: Royal Doulton International Collectors Club

STYLE TWO: *HANDLE: QUILL PEN AND INK POT*

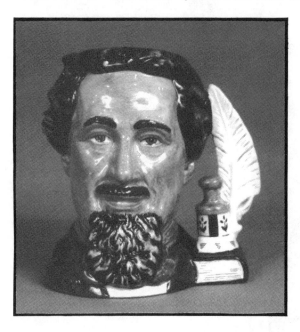

Designer: W.K. Harper

Handle: Quill pen and ink pot, book "The Old Curiosity Shop"

Backstamp: Doulton / RDICC

Colourway: Black and olive green

Doulton Number	Size	Backstamp	Height	Intro.	Discon.	Current Market Value		
						U.K. £	U.S. $	Can. $
D6901	Small	Doulton/RDICC	4"	1991	1991	60.00	100.00	125.00

CHELSEA PENSIONER

Charles II founded the Royal Hospital in Chelsea for "worthy old soldiers broken in the wars." It was built by Christopher Wren and completed in 1692. Each year on Founders Day, the hospital's opening is celebrated by the soldiers in full dress uniform, as worn by the gentlleman depicted on the jug.

SERIES: The London Collection, one of ten.

Royal Doulton®

CHELSEA PENSIONER
D 6817
Modelled by
Stanley James Taylor.
© 1988 ROYAL DOULTON

Designer: Stanley J. Taylor   **Handle:** Medals of honour   **Backstamp:** See Backstamps

Colourway: Black tricorn trimmed with gold, scarlet tunic with black collar

BACKSTAMPS

A: **Doulton**

For General Issue: 1989

Pre-released in the U.S.A. in 1988 at the following four stores in a limited edition of 1,000 pieces, with 250 jugs per store.

B: Doulton/Joseph Horne's "To commemorate the First Anniversary of the opening of the Royal Doulton Room Joseph Horne's, Pittsburgh, Pennsylvania, U.S.A."

C: Doulton/D. H. Holme's "To commemorate the First Anniversary of the opening of the Royal Doulton Room D. H. Holme's, New Orleans, Louisiana, U.S.A."

D: Doulton/Higbee Company "To commemorate the Third Anniversary of the opening of the Royal Doulton Room The Higbee Company, Cleveland, Ohio, U.S.A."

E: Doulton/Strawbridge and Clothier "To commemorate the Second Anniversary of the opening of the Royal Doulton Room Strawbridge and Clothier, Philadelphia, Pennsylvania, U.S.A."

Doulton Number	Size	Backstamp	Height	Intro.	Discon.	Current Market Value U.K. £	U.S. $	Can. $
D6817	Large	Doulton	6 1/2"	1989	Current	49.00	155.00	180.00
D6830	Large	Doulton/Horne's	6 1/2"	1988	Ltd. Ed.	165.00	300.00	350.00
D6831	Large	Doulton/Holme's	6 1/2"	1988	Ltd. Ed.	165.00	300.00	350.00
D6832	Large	Doulton/Higbee	6 1/2"	1988	Ltd. Ed.	165.00	300.00	350.00
D6833	Large	Strawbridge	6 1/2"	1988	Ltd. Ed.	165.00	300.00	350.00

CHIEF SITTING BULL
GEORGE ARMSTRONG CUSTER

Chief Sitting Bull (1831-1890). As chief of the Sioux Indians, Sitting Bull spent his life working for the rights of his people to own and control their land. He was shot by Indian Police on a questionable charge of resisting arrest.

George Armstrong Custer (1839-1876). The youngest general in the U.S. Army, Custer first saw action in the Civil War. He was later stationed in the Dakota Territory during the gold rush on Sioux Land. In 1876, in the interests of the whites, he led an attack against an Indian encampment at Little Big Horn. Sitting Bull and his men outnumbered Custer's regiment and easily defeated them, leaving no survivors.

This jug was issued in a limited edition of 9,500 pieces.

SERIES: The Antagonists (Two faced jug), one of four.

Designer: Michael Abberley   **Handle:** A pistol and tomahawk   **Backstamp:** Doulton

Colourway: See Variations

BROWN EYES   GREY EYES

VARIATIONS

VARIATION NO. 1: Colourway: Multi-coloured, Sitting Bull has grey eyes.

Doulton Number	Size	Variation	Height	Intro.	Discon.	Current Market Value U.K. £	U.S. $	Can. $
D6712	Large	Var. 1	7"	1984	1989	95.00	125.00	225.00

VARIATION NO. 2: Colourway: Multi-coloured, Sitting Bull has brown eyes.

Doulton Number	Size	Variation	Height	Intro.	Discon.	Current Market Value U.K. £	U.S. $	Can. $
D6712	Large	Var. 2	7"	1984	1989	95.00	125.00	225.00

CHRISTOPHER COLUMBUS

(c.1451-1506). A trader and explorer, Italian-born Columbus was financed by the Spanish royalty, Queen Isabella, to find a quicker route to the gold and spices of India. Believing the world was round, he set sail due west, landing in the Americas in 1492. He is popularly credited with "discovering" the New World.

Designer: Stanley J. Taylor   **Handle:** Map of New World   **Backstamp:** Doulton

Colourway: Dark blue and green

Doulton Number	Size	Backstamp	Height	Intro.	Discon.	Current Market Value U.K. £	U.S. $	Can. $
D6891	Large	Doulton	7"	1991	Current	55.00	140.00	180.00

CHURCHILL

(1874-1965). Sir Winston Leonard Spencer Churchill was first lord of the Admiralty, home secretary, and Prime Minister on three occasions. As Wartime Prime Minister he led Britain to victory and captured the spirit of the Allied World with his famous radio broadcasts. He was awarded the Nobel Prize for Literature in 1953.

WINSTON SPENCER CHURCHILL
PRIME MINISTER
OF BRITAIN
— 1940 —
THIS LOVING CUP WAS MADE
DURING THE "BATTLE OF BRITAIN"
AS A TRIBUTE TO A GREAT LEADER

modelled by NOKE

Designer: Charles Noke   **Handle:** See Variations   **Backstamp:** Doulton

Colourway: See Variations

VARIATIONS

VARIATION NO. 1: Colourway: **Cream with two black handles.**
Inscription on base.

Doulton Number	Size	Variation	Height	Intro.	Discon.	Current Market Value U.K. £	Current Market Value U.S. $	Current Market Value Can. $
D6170	Large	Doulton	6 1/2"	1940	1941	2,500.00	10,000.00	10,000.00

VARIATION NO. 2   VARIATION NO. 3

VARIATION NO. 2: Different modelling portraying a younger Churchill.
Colourway: Very lightly coloured overall with two grey handles.
No inscription on base, has green Doulton backstamp.

Doulton Number	Size	Variation	Height	Intro.	Discon.	U.K. £	Current Market Value U.S. $	Can. $
D6170	Large	Var.2	6 1/2"		Unknown		Extremely Rare	

VARIATION NO. 3: Modelling portrays a young Churchill.
Colourway: Fully decorated in natural colours
with two dark brown handles.
No inscription on base.

Doulton Number	Size	Variation	Height	Intro.	Discon.	U.K. £	Current Market Value U.S. $	Can. $
D6170	Large	Var. 3	6 1/2"		Unknown		Extremely Rare	

CITY GENT

This archetypal British aristocrat represents the finery and style of London. Strolling along the street, perhaps on his way to the House of Lords, he's sure to tip his hat at the ladies he passes on the way.

SERIES: The London Collection, one of ten.

Royal Doulton®
CITY GENT
D 6815
Modelled by
Stanley James Taylor
© 1988 ROYAL DOULTON

Designer: Stanley J. Taylor   **Handle:** Umbrella   **Backstamp:** Doulton

Colourway: Black and grey hat, black coat, white shirt, grey tie

Doulton Number	Size	Backstamp	Height	Intro.	Discon.	Current Market Value U.K. £	U.S. $	Can. $
D6815	Large	Doulton	7"	1988	Current	47.00	130.00	180.00

CLARK GABLE

(1901-1960). An Ohio native, Gable worked in a tire factory and as a lumberjack before he took up acting. He began his career in 1930 and appeared in over seventy films. He won an Academy Award in 1934 for his performance in "It Happened One Night" but is perhaps best remembered as Rhett Butler in "Gone With the Wind."

This jug was issued in the U.S.A. prior to approval of the Estate, and had to be withdrawn when permission was not forthcoming. A small number of jugs are known to exist.

SERIES: The Celebrity Collection

Designer: Stanley J. Taylor   **Handle:** Movie camera entwined in film.   **Backstamp:** Doulton

Colourway: Brown, light brown suit and tan tie.

Doulton Number	Size	Backstamp	Height	Intro.	Discon.	Current Market Value U.K. £	U.S. $	Can. $
D6709	Large	Doulton	7"	1984	1984	2,000.00	3,000.00	3,500.00

THE CLOWN

From the early jesters of the Royal Courts to the present day, clowns have entertained audiences of all ages with their acrobatics, tricks, and humourous satires of human life.

STYLE ONE: CLOWN WITHOUT HAT

The Clown.
COPR. 1950.
DOULTON & CO. LIMITED.
RᵈNᵒ 28163.
RᵈNᵒ 6207.
RᵈNᵒ 92/30.

Designer: Harry Fenton

Handle: See Variations

Colourway: See Variations

Backstamp: Doulton

VARIATIONS

VARIATION NO. 1: Colourway: Red hair.
Handle: Multi-coloured.

Doulton Number	Size	Colour	Height	Intro.	Discon.	Current Market Value U.K. £	U.S. $	Can. $
D5610	Large	Red hair	7 1/2"	1937	1942	1,400.00	2,400.00	2,750.00

VARIATION NO. 2: Colourway: Brown hair.
Handle: Plain brown.

Doulton Number	Size	Colour	Height	Intro.	Discon.	Current Market Value U.K. £	U.S. $	Can. $
D5610	Large	Brown hair	7 1/2"	c. 1937	1942	1,400.00	2,400.00	2,750.00

VARIATION NO. 3: Colourway: White hair.
Handle: Multi-coloured.

Doulton Number	Size	Colour	Height	Intro.	Discon.	Current Market Value U.K. £	U.S. $	Can. $
D6322	Large	White hair	7 1/2"	1951	1955	500.00	950.00	1,600.00

A black haired example has appeared on the market, however its authencity has never been determined.

THE CLOWN

SERIES: The Circus, one of four.

STYLE TWO: *CLOWN WITH HAT*

Royal Doulton®
THE CLOWN
D 6834
Modelled by
Stanley James Taylor
© 1988 ROYAL DOULTON

Designer: Stanley J. Taylor   **Handle:** Hand touches cap   **Backstamp:** Doulton

Colourway: Green cap, yellow bow-tie with black spots, red nose and mouth

Doulton Number	Size	Backstamp	Height	Intro.	Discon.	Current Market Value U.K. £	U.S. $	Can. $
D6834	Large	Doulton	6 1/2"	1989	Current	57.00	175.00	225.00

THE COLLECTOR

The large size, commissioned by Kevin Francis Ceramics Ltd. (KFC) was issued in 1988 in a special edition of 5,000 pieces. The small size was issued in 1991, is a special edition of 1,500 pieces.

SERIES: The Collecting World, one of three.

Original Concept by Kevin Pearson and Geoff Blower

Royal Doulton®
THE COLLECTOR
D 6796
Modelled by
Stanley James Taylor
A Special Edition of 5000
From "The Collecting World" series
Produced by Royal Doulton
for Kevin Francis Ceramics
© 1987 ROYAL DOULTON
AND KEVIN FRANCIS CERAMICS

Designer: Stanley J. Taylor

Handle: A hand holding a Mephistopheles jug

Backstamp: Doulton / Kevin Francis

Colourway: Black hat and coat with tan shirt

Doulton Number	Size	Backstamp	Height	Intro.	Discon.	Current Market Value U.K. £	U.S. $	Can. $
D6796	Large	Doulton/KFC	7"	1988	Sp. Ed.	90.00	200.00	225.00
D —	Small	Doulton/KFC	4"	1991	Sp. Ed.	50.00	90.00	110.00

THE COOK AND THE CHESHIRE CAT

These are two characters from Lewis Carroll's charming story of Alice's adventures in Wonderland. The Cat's fixed, broad smile has become recognized world wide.

SERIES: Alice in Wonderland, one of six.

THE COOK AND THE CHESHIRE CAT

D. 6842

Modelled by

© 1989 ROYAL DOULTON

Designer: William K. Harper   **Handle:** A cat   **Backstamp:** Doulton

Colourway: White mop-cap trimmed with a blue bow

Doulton Number	Size	Backstamp	Height	Intro.	Discon.	Current Market Value		
						U.K. £	U.S. $	Can. $
D6842	Large	Doulton	7"	1990	Current	57.00	175.00	195.00

D'ARTAGNAN

A character in Alexandre Dumas' lively 18th century fiction, D'Artagnan comes to Paris to join the celebrated band of the Three Musketeers and share their adventures.

SERIES: One of the "Three Musketeers", one of four.
Now part of the Characters from Literature, one of eleven.

Designer: Stanley J. Taylor   **Handle:** An extension of the feathers with a Fleur-de-lis at the base   **Backstamp:** Doulton

Colourway: Black hat trimmed with white feathers, white lace collar

Doulton Number	Size	Backstamp	Height	Intro.	Discon.	Current Market Value U.K. £	U.S. $	Can. $
D6691	Large	Doulton	7 1/2"	1982	Current	41.00	130.00	145.00
D6764	Small	Doulton	4"	1987	Current	22.50	65.00	80.00
D6765	Miniature	Doulton	2 1/2"	1987	Current	15.50	50.00	60.00

DAVID COPPERFIELD

David Copperfield is the orphan protagonist in Dickins' novel "David Copperfield."
Issued to commemorate the 170th Anniversary of the birth of Charles Dickens. There are twelve jugs in this set, which were issued with a certificate of authenticity. A mahogany display shelf completes the set. The set was first sold by Lawley's By Post in the U.K. during 1982 to 1988, and in 1985 forward in North America and Austrialia.

SERIES: Charles Dickens Commemorative Set / Dickens Tinies, one of twelve.

*Photograph
Not Available
At Press Time*

Designer: Michael Abberley   **Handle:** Plain   **Backstamp:** Doulton

Colourway: Dark blue and black

Doulton Number	Size	Backstamp	Height	Intro.	Discon.	Current Market Value		
						U.K. £	U.S. $	Can. $
D6680	Tiny	Doulton	1 1/2"	1982	1989	30.00	50.00	60.00

DAVY CROCKETT AND SANTA ANNA

Davy Crockett (1786-1836). Born "on a mountaintop in Tennessee," as the popular song goes, Crockett was a hunter and expert marksman, as well as a gregarious drinker.

Antonio Lopez de Santa Anna (1795-1876). A Mexican General, he led troops on many missions into the U.S. He was finally defeated in Texas in 1837 and jailed for a year.

This jug was issued in 1985 in a limited edition of 9,500 pieces.

SERIES: The Antagonists' Collection (Two-faced Jug), one of four.

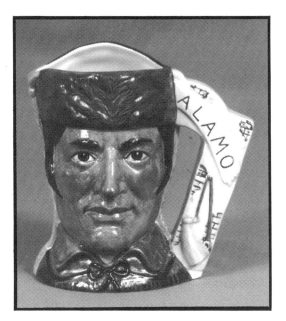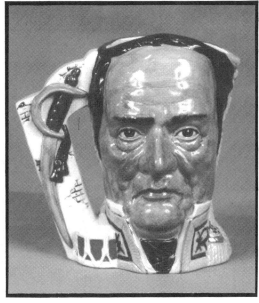

Designer: Michael Abberley **Handle:** The word "Alamo" and a horn/ Part of the mission wall with a sword

Colourway: Yellow and brown

Backstamp: Doulton

Royal Doulton
'The Antagonists'
Collection
D.6729
The Battle of the Alamo 1836
Davy Crockett/Antonio Lopez de Santa Anna
Hand made and Hand decorated
Designed by Michael Abberley

© ROYAL DOULTON (U.K.) 1984
Worldwide Limited Edition of 9,500
This is Number 393.

Doulton Number	Size	Backstamp	Height	Intro.	Discon.	Current Market Value		
						U.K. £	U.S. $	Can. $
D6729	Large	Doulton	7"	1985	1985	65.00	100.00	125.00

DICK TURPIN

(1706-1739). The son of an innkeeper, Turpin worked with a band of petty thieves in his youth until joining Tom King as a highwayman. They worked the road between London and Oxford, robbing unsuspecting travellers. Turpin was finally arrested in York for stealing horses and hanged. He has become a romantic figure, immortalized in literature atop his faithful horse, "Black Bess."

The first style of Dick Turpin has the mask up on the brim of the tri-corn, and the handle is a pistol. All of the style ones have "R.T." inscribed on the pistol grip. Depending on the casting detail, it may or may not be obvious. There is no premium value with or without the "R.T." inscription.

STYLE ONE: HANDLE: A PISTOL

Designer: Charles Noke   **Handle:** Pistol   **Backstamp:** See Backstamps
     Harry Fenton

Colourway: Brown hat with black mask up at the front, green coat, white cravat

BACKSTAMPS

A: Doulton

B: Doulton/Bentalls, "Souvenir From Bentalls 1936"

Doulton Number	Size	Backstamps	Height	Intro.	Discon.	Current Market Value U.K. £	U.S. $	Can. $
D5485	Large	Doulton	6 1/2"	1935	1960	75.00	150.00	200.00
D5618	Small	Doulton	3 1/2"	1936	1960	45.00	70.00	110.00
D5618	Small	Doulton/Bentalls	3 1/2"	1936	1936	350.00	750.00	850.00
D6128	Miniature	Doulton	2 1/4"	1940	1960	35.00	50.00	95.00

Miscellaneous "Dick Turpin" Items

Doulton Number	Item	Height	Intro.	Discon.	Current Market Value U.K. £	Current Market Value U.S. $	Current Market Value Can. $
D5601	Matchstand/Ashtray	3"	1936	1960	85.00	125.00	160.00

DICK TURPIN

This second style of Dick Turpin has the mask covering the eyes, and the handle depicts a horse's head and neck.

STYLE TWO: *HANDLE: NECK AND HEAD OF HORSE*

Dick Turpin
D 6528
COPR 1959
DOULTON & CO LIMITED
Rd No 893841
Rd No 39649
Rd No 8313
Rd No 420/59

Designer: David Biggs   **Handle:** Head and neck of a horse   **Backstamp:** Doulton

Colourway: Green tricorn, black mask over the eyes, red jacket

Doulton Number	Size	Backstamp	Height	Intro.	Discon.	Current Market Value U.K. £	U.S. $	Can. $
D6528	Large	Doulton	7"	1960	1981	45.00	90.00	135.00
D6535	Small	Doulton	3 3/4"	1960	1981	30.00	50.00	95.00
D6542	Miniature	Doulton	2 1/4"	1960	1981	30.00	45.00	70.00

DICK WHITTINGTON

The first Dick Whittington Jug was styled on the character of a poor orphan boy who is employed in a London kitchen, as described in a play dated 1605. He gave his cat to his employer to sell to earn money, but then ran away to escape his evil employer's cook who mistreats him. The Bow Bells rang as he fled and seemed to say "Turn back Whittington, Lord Mayor of London." He obeyed and found that his cat had fetched a huge sum, making him a wealthy man. The Pantomine Dick Whittington and His Cat can be seen at Christmas time at theatres in Great Britain.

STYLE ONE: DRESSED AS A POOR BOY

Dick Whittington
D 6375
COPR 1952
DOULTON & CO LIMITED
Rd No 868419
Rd No 30500
Rd No 193/52
Rd No 6649

Designer: Geoff Blower   **Handle:** A stick and handkerchief   **Backstamp:** Doulton

Colourway: Dark green cap and robes

Doulton Number	Size	Backstamp	Height	Intro.	Discon.	Current Market Value		
						U.K. £	U.S. $	Can. $
D6375	Large	Doulton	6 1/2"	1953	1960	200.00	400.00	450.00

DICK WHITTINGTON
LORD MAYOR OF LONDON

(1358-1423). Richard Whittington, in actual fact, made his fortune as a textile dealer. He entered London politics as a councilman and rose to Lord Mayor of London in 1397, an office he held three times.

Commissioned by "The Guild of Specialist China and Glass Retailers" Peter Jones China, Wakefield, England. Issued in 1989 in a limited edition of 5,000 pieces.

STYLE TWO: DRESSED AS LORD MAYOR OF LONDON

Designer: William K. Harper **Handle:** Handle is of a sign-post to London; the "Bow Bells" are above the sign-post, and a sack of gold is at the base.

Backstamp: Doulton / Guild

Colourway: Blue tricorn hat trimmed with white feathers, blue coat trimmed with white fur, yellow chain of office.

Doulton Number	Size	Backstamp	Height	Intro.	Discon.	Current Market Value		
						U.K. £	U.S. $	Can. $
D6846	Large	Doulton/Guild	7 1/2"	1989	Ltd. Ed.	50.00	100.00	150.00

DOC HOLLIDAY

(1852-1887). The son of a lawyer, John Henry Holliday worked as a dentist in Baltimore, Maryland. At the age of twenty he learned he had tuberculosis and must move to a warmer climate to prolong his life. He moved west, became adept at both firearms and the Bowie knife, and became known for his wild gambling, brawls and shootouts. He survived the famous gunfight at the O.K. Corral, but died in a sanatorium at age thirty-five.

SERIES: The Wild West Collection, one of six.

Designer: Stanley J. Taylor   **Handle:** Pistol in a holster and dice   **Backstamp:** Doulton

Colourway: Black and grey hat, black coat

Doulton Number	Size	Backstamp	Height	Intro.	Discon.	Current Market Value		
						U.K. £	U.S. $	Can. $
D6731	Mid	Doulton	5 1/2"	1985	1989	40.00	70.00	110.00

DON QUIXOTE

Hero of the novel by Cervantes, Don Quixote is a satirical parody of the chivalrous knight. He is inspired to lead a life of adventure, capturing many hearts along the way. "Quixotic", meaning impractical, enthusiastic or honourable finds its origins in this character.

Helmet colour varies from dark grey to light grey with no difference in value.

SERIES: Characters from Literature, one of eleven.

"Don Quixote".
D 6455
COPR 1956
DOULTON & CO LIMITED
Rd Nº 881509
Rd Nº 35705
Rd Nº 7560
Rd Nº 332/56

Designer: Geoff Blower   **Handle:** A feather; a shield at the base   **Backstamp:** Doulton

Colourway: Blue-grey helmet, purple robes

Doulton Number	Size	Backstamp	Height	Intro.	Discon.	Current Market Value U.K. £	U.S. $	Can. $
D6455	Large	Doulton	7 1/4"	1957	1991	41.00	130.00	145.00
D6460	Small	Doulton	3 1/4"	1957	1991	22.50	65.00	80.00
D6511	Miniature	Doulton	2 1/2"	1960	1991	15.50	50.00	60.00

DRAKE

(1540-1596). Sir Francis Drake was an English navigator and admiral. He was Queen Elizabeth I's right hand against the Spanish, going on many plundering expeditions in the Spanish West Indies. On one of these voyages, Drake became the first Englishman to sail around the world, between 1577 and 1580. As Admiral of the British Navy, he repelled the Spanish Armada sent to invade England.

STYLE ONE: *WITHOUT HAT (HATLESS)*

Designer: Harry Fenton **Handle:** Plain **Backstamp:** Doulton

Colourway: See Variations

VARIATIONS

VARIATION NO. 1: Colourway: White ruff, red coat.

Doulton Number	Size	Backstamp	Height	Intro.	Discon.	U.K. £	Current Market Value U.S. $	Can. $
D6115	Large	Doulton	5 3/4"	1940	1941	1,500.00	3,000.00	3,500.00

VARIATION NO. 2: Colourway: White ruff, green coat.

Doulton Number	Size	Backstamp	Height	Intro.	Discon.	U.K. £	Current Market Value U.S. $	Can. $
D6115	Large	Doulton	5 3/4"	1940	1941		Extremely Rare Only Two Known	

DRAKE

STYLE TWO: *WITH HAT*

Designer: Harry Fenton   **Handle:** Plain   **Backstamp:** Doulton

Colourway: Brown hat, green robes, white ruff

Doulton Number	Size	Backstamp	Height	Intro.	Discon.	Current Market Value U.K. £	U.S. $	Can. $
D6115	Large	Doulton	5 3/4"	1940	1960	75.00	150.00	200.00
D6174	Small	Doulton	3 1/4"	1941	1960	45.00	75.00	110.00

DUKE OF WELLINGTON

(1769-1852). Arthur Wellesley, First Duke of Wellington, was a British General and Statesman. He led the British forces in the defeat of Napoleon at Waterloo in 1815 and served as Prime Minister from 1828-1830.

Commissioned by UK International Ceramics Ltd in a special edition. The number of jugs to be produced is in question, the backstamp/Doulton indicate 5,000 while U.K. International states 3,500 pieces.

SERIES: The Great Generals Collection, one of ten.

Designer: William K. Harper   **Handle:** Cannon above a banner "Waterloo"   **Backstamp:** Doulton/UK Int'l

Colourway: Blue and gold

Doulton Number	Size	Backstamp	Height	Intro.	Discon.	Current Market Value U.K. £	U.S. $	Can. $
D6848	Large	Doulton/UK Int'l	7 1/4"	1989	Sp. Ed.	90.00	200.00	250.00

EARL MOUNTBATTEN OF BURMA

(1900-1979). A British naval and military leader, Louis Francis Albert Victor Nicholas Mountbatten was the last viceroy of India. Mountbatten was Governor General of the Dominion of India from 1947 to 1948, relinquishing power to native rule in 1948.

Upon his retirement form the Navy in 1959 he became the principal military adviser to the Ministry of Defence. He was killed when a bomb exploded his fishing boat off the coast of Ireland.

Commissioned by Lawley's By Post. Issued as a set of three in 1989 in a limited edition of 9,500 pieces.

SERIES: Heroic Leaders, one of three.

EARL MOUNTBATTEN OF BURMA
1900-1979
D 6851
Modelled by
Stanley James Taylor
© 1989 ROYAL DOULTON
A LIMITED EDITION OF 9500
THIS IS NO. 1609

Designer: Stanley J. Taylor   **Handle:** White ensign   **Backstamp:** Doulton / Lawley's

Colourway: White naval uniform trimmed with gold

Doulton Number	Size	Backstamp	Height	Intro.	Discon.	Current Market Value		
						U.K. £	U.S. $	Can. $
D6851	Small	Doulton/Lawley's	3 1/4"	1989	Ltd. Ed.	45.00	135.00	155.00

THE ELEPHANT TRAINER

No circus is complete without the marvellous trained elephants doing their acrobatics. With their trainer (and a few peanuts) they've continued to captured hearts of all ages.

SERIES: The Circus, one of four.

Royal Doulton®
THE ELEPHANT TRAINER
D 6841
Modelled by
Stanley James Taylor
© 1989 ROYAL DOULTON

Designer: Stanley J. Taylor   **Handle:** Head of an elephant   **Backstamp:** See Backstamps

Colourway: Orange turban, black coat trimmed with green and yellow

BACKSTAMPS

A: Doulton

General Issue: 1990.

B: Doulton/The Higbee Company   "To commemorate the Fourth Anniversary of the opening of The Royal Doulton Room The Higbee Company, Cleveland, Ohio, U.S.A."

Commissioned by The Higbee Company, Cleveland, Ohio. Issued in 1989 in a limited editon of 250 pieces.

Doulton Number	Size	Backstamp	Height	Intro.	Discon.	Current Market Value U.K. £	U.S. $	Can. $
D6841	Large	Doulton	7"	1990	Current	57.00	175.00	225.00
D6856	Large	Doulton/Higbee	7"	1989	Ltd. Ed.	150.00	175.00	300.00

ELVIS PRESLEY

PROTOTYPE

(1935-1977) Elvis Aaron Presley, the "King of Rock 'n Roll" was the most popular artist in the history of American rock music. After his debut in 1955, he appeared in thirty-three films, as well as issuing numerous albums. His home in Graceland is visited by thousands of fans every year. The only example of this jug is in the Henry Doulton Museum. Not issued due to copyright problems. While at least two prototypes are known to exist, none are known to be in private collections.

SERIES: The Celebrity Collection

Designer: Unknown   **Handle:** Guitar and strap   **Backstamp:** Doulton

Colourway: Black hair, white shirt with gold trim

Doulton Number	Size	Backstamp	Height	Intro.	Discon.	U.K. £	Current Market Value U.S. $	Can. $
D —	Large	Doulton	7 1/4"	1987	1987		Unique	

THE ENGINE DRIVER

Rail travel in Britain has played a large part in the development of the country and remains the most-used method of transportation of many. In a skilled and important job, the engine driver is responsible for the safe arrival of his freight and passengers.

Each jug in the Journey Through Britain series was given a specially designed backstamp relating to the subject of the jug. The "Engine Driver" backstamp has the wording within the outline of a locomotive engine. Issued through Lawley's By Post in a limited edition of 5,000 pieces.

SERIES: Journey Through Britain, one of four.

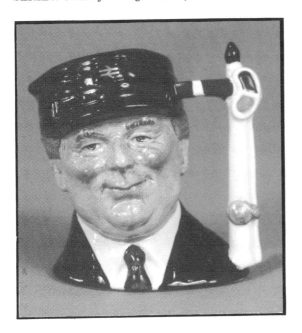

Designer: Stanley J. Taylor   **Handle:** A railway signal   **Backstamp:** Doulton / Lawley's

Colourway: Black cap and coat, white shirt

Doulton Number	Size	Backstamp	Height	Intro.	Discon.	Current Market Value U.K. £	U.S. $	Can. $
D6823	Small	Doulton/Lawley's	4"	1988	Ltd. Ed.	40.00	85.00	135.00

FAGIN

Fagin runs the bank of child thieves with a hard hand in Dickens' novel "Oliver Twist."

Issued to commemorate the 170th Anniversary of the birth of Charles Dickens. There are twelve jugs in this set, which were issued with a certificate of authenticity. A mahogany display shelf completes the set. The set was first sold by Lawley's By Post in the U.K. during 1982 to 1988, and in 1985 forward in North America and Austrialia.

SERIES: Charles Dickens Commemorative Set / Dickens Tinies, one **of twelve**

*Photograph
Not Available
At Press Time*

Designer: Robert Tabbenor   **Handle:** Plain   **Backstamp:** Doulton

Colourway: Orange and brown

Doulton Number	Size	Backstamp	Height	Intro.	Discon.	Current Market Value U.K. £	U.S. $	Can. $
D6679	Tiny	Doulton	1 1/2"	1982	1989	30.00	50.00	60.00

THE FALCONER

Once called "The Sport of Kings," falconry is the art of training birds of prey for the hunt. The sport began in China more than 3,000 years ago and still enjoys popularity in Europe and North America, even though the addition of firearms to hunting almost brought it to an end in the 18th century.

Designer: Max Henk   **Handle:** A falcon   **Backstamp:** See Backstamps

Colourway: See Variations

The Falconer
D 6540
COPR 1959
DOULTON & CO LIMITED
Rd No 893846
Rd No 39654
Rd No 8318
Rd No 415/59

VARIATIONS

VARIATION NO. 1: Colourway: Green with black and white striped fur hat, green coat, grey and white falcon.

BACKSTAMP: Doulton

Doulton Number	Size	Backstamp	Height	Intro.	Discon.	Current Market Value U.K. £	U.S. $	Can. $
D6533	Large	Doulton	7 1/2"	1960	Current	41.00	130.00	145.00
D6540	Small	Doulton	3 3/4"	1960	Current	22.50	65.00	80.00
D6547	Miniature	Doulton	2 3/4"	1960	Current	15.50	50.00	60.00

VARIATION NO. 2 VARIATION NO. 3

VARIATION NO. 2: Colourway: Dark green and brown striped fur hat, dark brown coat, ginger beard, brown falcon.

Specially commissioned from Royal Doulton by the Joseph Horne Company, Pittsburgh, Pennsylvania, U.S.A. Issued in 1987 in a limited edition of 250 pieces.

BACKSTAMP: Doulton/Joseph Horne Company "Celebrating the opening of The RoyalDoulton Room, Hornes, Pittsburgh, Pennsylvania, U.S.A.

Doulton Number	Size	Backstamp	Height	Intro.	Discon.	Current Market Value U.K. £	U.S. $	Can. $
D6798	Large	Doulton/Horne	7 1/2"	1987	Ltd. Ed.	225.00	400.00	450.00

VARIATION NO. 3: Colourway: Black with maroon and white striped fur hat, red-brown coat, brown falcon.

BACKSTAMP: Doulton/Peter Jones China Ltd "New Colourway 1987 Special Commission 1000 Peter Jones Collection Leeds and Wakefield"

Commissioned by Peter Jones China Ltd, Leeds and Wakefield, England. Issued in 1987 in a special edition of 1,000 pieces.

Royal Doulton®

THE FALCONER
D 6800
Modelled by

© 1959 ROYAL DOULTON
NEW COLOURWAY 1987
SPECIAL COMMISSION 1000
PETER JONES COLLECTION
LEEDS AND WAKEFIELD

Doulton Number	Size	Backstamp	Height	Intro.	Discon.	Current Market Value U.K. £	U.S. $	Can. $
D6800	Large	Doulton/Jones	7 1/2"	1987	Sp. Ed.	50.00	95.00	175.00

FALSTAFF

Sir John Falstaff, is a fat convivial, good-humoured braggart who figures in Shakespeare's "Henry IV" and "The Merry Wives of Windsor."

A trial piece exists in a red and dark green colourway.

SERIES: Characters from Literature, one of eleven.

Falstaff
D 6287
COPR 1949
DOULTON & CO LIMITED

Designer: Harry Fenton   **Handle:** Plain   **Backstamp:** See Backstamps

Colourway: See Variations

VARIATIONS

VARIATION NO. 1: Colourway: Rose-pink tunic, black hat trimmed with rose-pink plumes, grey beard.

BACKSTAMP: Doulton

Doulton Number	Size	Backstamp	Height	Intro.	Discon.	Current Market Value U.K. £	U.S. $	Can. $
D6287	Large	Doulton	6"	1950	Current	41.00	130.00	145.00
D6385	Small	Doulton	3 1/2"	1950	Current	22.50	65.00	80.00
D6519	Miniature	Doulton	2 1/2"	1960	Current	15.50	50.00	60.00

Produced Exclusively for U.K. Fairs Ltd. in a Special Edition of 1500

Royal Doulton®
FALSTAFF
D 6795
Modelled by
H. FENTON
© 1949 ROYAL DOULTON
NEW COLOURWAY 1987

VARIATION NO. 2: Colourway: Yellow tunic, black hat trimmed with yellow plumes, brown beard

Commissioned by UK Fairs Ltd. Issued in 1988 in a special edition of 1,500 pieces.

BACKSTAMP: Doulton / UK Fairs Ltd.

Doulton Number	Size	Backstamp	Height	Intro.	Discon.	Current Market Value U.K. £	U.S. $	Can. $
D6797	Large	Doulton/ UK Fairs	6"	1987	Sp. Ed.	60.00	120.00	175.00

Miscellaneous "Falstaff" Items

Doulton Number	Item	Height	Intro.	Discon.	Current Market Value U.K. £	U.S. $	Can. $
D6385	Table lighter	4 1/2"	1958	1973	95.00	125.00	175.00
D6854	Teapot		1989	Current	60.00	125.00	250.00

FARMER JOHN

The archetypal English farmer, "John" is cheerful and hard-working from his early morning chores until dusk finds him at the local pub with his daily draught of ale.

STYLE ONE: HANDLE "INSIDE" JUG

Designer: Charles Noke

Handle: Brown handle which is set within the neck of the jug

Colourway: Brown

Backstamp: See Backstamps

BACKSTAMPS

A: **Doulton**

B: **Doulton/Coleman's "Coleman's Compliments"**

Doulton Number	Size	Backstamp	Height	Intro.	Discon.	U.K. £	U.S. $	Can. $
							Current Market Value	
D5788	Large	Doulton	6 1/2"	1938	1960	75.00	150.00	225.00
D5788	Large	Doulton/Coleman's	6 1/2"	1938	1938	1,000.00	1,700.00	2,000.00
D5789	Small	Doulton	3 1/4"	1938	1960	45.00	85.00	130.00

FARMER JOHN

STYLE TWO: HANDLE "OUTSIDE" JUG

Designer: Charles Noke   **Handle:** Brown handle which sits at   **Backstamp:** Doulton
the top of the neck.

Colourway: Brown

Doulton Number	Size	Backstamp	Height	Intro.	Discon.	Current Market Value U.K. £	U.S. $	Can. $
D5788	Large	Doulton	6 1/2"	1938	1960	75.00	150.00	225.00
D5789	Small	Doulton	3 1/4"	1938	1960	45.00	85.00	120.00

Miscellaneous "Farmer John" Items

Doulton Number	Item	Height	Intro.	Discon.	Current Market Value U.K. £	U.S. $	Can. $
D6007	Ash bowl	3"	1939	1960	65.00	120.00	140.00

FAT BOY

Another wonderful Dickens' character, Joe, the Fat Boy was the lazy, glutton who worked as servant to Mr. Wardle in "The Pickwick Papers."

Designer: Leslie Harradine
Harry Fenton

Handle: Plain

Backstamp: Doulton

Colourway: Blue shirt, white scarf

Doulton Number	Size	Backstamp	Height	Intro.	Discon.	Current Market Value U.K. £	U.S. $	Can. $
D5840	Mid	Doulton	5"	1938	1948	95.00	200.00	240.00
D5840	Small	Doulton	4"	1948	1960	50.00	125.00	125.00
D6139	Miniature	Doulton	2 1/2"	1940	1960	40.00	65.00	95.00
D6142	Tiny	Doulton	1 1/2"	1940	1960	50.00	95.00	150.00

Miscellaneous "Fat Boy" Items

Doulton Number	Item	Height	Intro.	Discon.	Current Market Value U.K. £	U.S. $	Can. $
M59	Napkin Ring	3 1/2"	1935	1939	350.00	600.00	625.00

THE FIREMAN

Admired as courageous and gallant, the profession of fireman has often been the envy of all the aspiring heroes.

Launched exclusively by Griffith Pottery House in 1983 and then released into the general range in 1984. Varieties exist with the nozzle handle ranging from dark orange to light yellow. There is no premium value for these colourway variations

A Fireman character jug exists which is an error jug. The red background of the helmet badge was not applied during painting, resulting in a white badge. This is a curiosity piece with very little premium value.

STYLE ONE: *HANDLE: NOZZLE OF FIRE HOSE*

Royal Doulton
The Fireman
D.6697
Hand made and Hand decorated
Designed by Jerry D.Griffith
Modelled by Robert Tabbenor
© ROYAL DOULTON
TABLEWARE LTD. 1982

Designer: Robert Tabbenor   **Handle:** Nozzle of fire hose   **Backstamp:** See Backstamps

Colourway: Black, brown and red helmet badge

BACKSTAMPS

A: Doulton/"Hand made and Hand decorated", no credits

B: Doulton/"Hand made and Hand decorated, Modelled by Robert Tabbenor"

C: Doulton/"Hand made and Hand decorated, Designed by Jerry D. Griffith"
Modelled by Robert Tabbenor,

Doulton Number	Size	Backstamp	Height	Intro.	Discon.	Current Market Value U.K. £	U.S. $	Can. $
D6697	Large	A Doulton	7 1/4"	1984	Current	49.00	130.00	145.00
D6697	Large	B Doulton	7 1/4"	1984	Current	49.00	130.00	145.00
D6697	Large	C Doulton	7 1/4"	1983	Current	49.00	130.00	145.00

THE FIREMAN

As with the other pieces in this series, the wording of the backstamp is contained within a design connected with the subject. This design is a coiled hosepipe. Issued through Lawley's By Post in 1988 in a limited edition of 5,000 pieces.

SERIES: Journey Through Britain, one of four.

STYLE TWO: *HANDLE: AXE AND FIRE HOSE*

This is no 3631

Designer: Stanley J. Taylor   **Handle:** An axe and fire hose   **Backstamp:** Doulton / Lawley's

Colourway: Yellow helmet, dark blue jacket

Doulton Number	Size	Backstamp	Height	Intro.	Discon.	Current Market Value U.K. £	Current Market Value U.S. $	Current Market Value Can. $
D6839	Small	Doulton/Lawley's	4 1/4"	1989	Ltd. Ed.	40.00	85.00	120.00

THE FORTUNE TELLER

Fortune telling and other methods of predicting the future have been a part of many cultures throughout history. Astrology uses the position of the stars to provide information on people or events while the Tarot tells fortunes from a deck of seventy-eight cards, each with a different symbolic meaning.

STYLE ONE: HANDLE: SIGNS OF THE ZODIAC

The Fortune Teller
D.6497
COPR 1958
DOULTON & CO LIMITED
Rd No 889568
Rd No 38224
Rd No 8034
Rd No 425,58

Designer: Garry Sharpe   **Handle:** Zodiac design   **Backstamp:** Doulton

Colourway: Green scarf and coat

Doulton Number	Size	Backstamp	Height	Intro.	Discon.	Current Market Value U.K. £	U.S. $	Can. $
D6497	Large	Doulton	6 3/4"	1959	1967	250.00	500.00	600.00
D6503	Small	Doulton	3 3/4"	1959	1967	180.00	350.00	400.00
D6523	Miniature	Doulton	2 1/2"	1960	1967	180.00	325.00	375.00

THE FORTUNE TELLER

Beginning in 1991 one special jug will be selected as "Character Jug of the Year" and will be produced for one year only. The "Character Jug of the Year" will be issued with a certificate of authenticity.

STYLE TWO: HANDLE: TAROT CARDS

Royal Doulton®
CHARACTER JUG OF THE YEAR
THE FORTUNE TELLER
D 6874
Modelled by

Stanley James Taylor

This special edition will only
be available during the year
1991
© 1990 ROYAL DOULTON

Designer: Stanley J. Taylor   **Handle:** Bandana and cards   **Backstamp:** Doulton / "Character Jug of the Year"

Colourway: Red polka-dot bandana, light blue shirt

Doulton Number	Size	Backstamp	Height	Intro.	Discon.	Current Market Value U.K. £	Current Market Value U.S. $	Current Market Value Can. $
D6874	Large	Jug of the Year	7"	1991	1991	57.00	130.00	180.00

FRIAR TUCK

Fat and jolly and fond of drink, Friar Tuck joined the legendary Robin Hood and his band of rogues as they robbed the rich to feed the poor in rural England. Living in Sherwood Forest, the merry group shared many hair-raising adventures.

Designer: Harry Fenton   **Handle:** Plain   **Backstamp:** Doulton

Colourway: Brown robes

Doulton Number	Size	Backstamp	Height	Intro.	Discon.	Current Market Value U.K. £	U.S. $	Can. $
D6321	Large	Doulton	7"	1951	1960	180.00	400.00	450.00

GAOLER

During the morally Puritan times experienced in 18th century Virginia it was not uncommon to land in jail for improprietous language or behaviour, among many other things. This gentleman held the unpopular yet necessary job of "keeper of the keys" to one's freedom.

SERIES: Characters from Williamsburg, one of seven.

Character Jugs from Williamsburg
Gaoler
D 6 5 7 0
COPR 1962
DOULTON & CO LIMITED
Rd No 906340
Rd No 43447
Rd No 9226
Rd No 284/62

Designer: David Biggs   **Handle:** Two keys   **Backstamp:** Doulton

Colourway: Black tricorn, white shirt and red vest

Doulton Number	Size	Backstamp	Height	Intro.	Discon.	U.K. £	U.S. $	Can. $
						Current Market Value		
D6570	Large	Doulton	7"	1963	1983	50.00	90.00	145.00
D6577	Small	Doulton	3 3/4"	1963	1983	40.00	70.00	95.00
D6584	Miniature	Doulton	2 3/4"	1963	1983	35.00	55.00	80.00

THE GARDENER

Engaged in a pastime enjoyed world-wide, this cheerful gent is shown with his spade, a friendly robin, and some of the fruits of his labour. From carrots to roses, the cultivation of a garden is an immensely rewarding pursuit.

STYLE ONE: HANDLE: A SPADE AND VEGETABLES

Designer: David Biggs **Handle:** A spade with carrots and a marrow at the base

Colourway: See Variations

Backstamp: Doulton

The Gardener
D.6630
© DOULTON & CO. LIMITED 1972
REGISTRATION APPLIED FOR

VARIATIONS

VARIATION NO. 1: Colourway: Red scarf, red striped shirt, brown hat.

Doulton Number	Size	Backstamp	Height	Intro.	Discon.	Current Market Value U.K. £	U.S. $	Can. $
D6630	Large	Doulton	7 3/4"	1971	1971		Extremely Rare	

VARIATION NO. 2: Colourway: Yellow scarf, white shirt, light brown hat.

Doulton Number	Size	Backstamp	Height	Intro.	Discon.	Current Market Value U.K. £	U.S. $	Can. $
D6630	Large	Doulton	7 3/4"	1973	1981	120.00	180.00	195.00
D6634	Small	Doulton	4"	1973	1981	75.00	90.00	110.00
D6638	Miniature	Doulton	2 3/4"	1973	1981	60.00	65.00	95.00

THE GARDENER

SERIES: Characters from Life, one of seven.

STYLE TWO: HANDLE: A RED FLOWERING POTTED PLANT

Designer: Stanley J. Taylor   **Handle:** A potted plant

Colourway: Yellow hat, green sweater and white shirt

Backstamp: Doulton

Royal Doulton®

THE GARDENER

D 6867

Modelled by

Stanley James Taylor

© 1990 ROYAL DOULTON

VARIATIONS

VARIATION NO. 1: Mould: Younger face with hair in front.

Doulton Number	Size	Variation	Height	Intro.	Discon.	Current Market Value U.K. £	U.S. $	Can. $
D6867	Large	Var. 1	7 1/4"	1990	Current	49.00	130.00	195.00

VARIATION NO. 2: Mould: Older face without hair in front.

Doulton Number	Size	Variation	Height	Intro.	Discon.	Current Market Value U.K. £	U.S. $	Can. $
D6868	Small	Var. 2	4"	1990	Current	26.50	65.00	90.00

GENERAL GORDON

(1833-1885).   Charles George Gordon was known as "Chinese Gordon" after he commanded the Chinese forces against Taiping rebels in 1863. As Governor-General of the Sudan, he was instrumental in closing down the slave trade. In 1884 he was ordered to return to rescue Egypt garrisons there, was beseiged at Khartoum and killed. Commissioned by UK International Ceramics and issued in 1991 in a special edition of 1,500 pieces.

SERIES: The Great Generals Collection, one of ten.

Designer: William K. Harper   **Handle:** Camel's head and neck with Khartoum ensign   **Backstamp:** Doulton / U K Int'l.

Colourway: Red, blue and gold

Doulton Number	Size	Backstamp	Height	Intro.	Discon.	Current Market Value		
						U.K. £	U.S. $	Can. $
D6869	Large	Doulton/UK Int'l	7 1/4"	1990	Sp. Ed.	120.00	275.00	295.00

GENIE

Finding its origins in the Arabic "jinnee," the genie is a sprite with supernatural powers who can change from animal to human form. Popularized through fable and legend, the modern genie is thought to reside in a magic lantern and become the servant of whoever frees it.

SERIES: Mystical Characters, one of three.

Designer: Stanley J. Taylor   **Handle:** Lamp and flame   **Backstamp:** Doulton

Colourway: Grey, black, red and yellow

Doulton Number	Size	Backstamp	Height	Intro.	Discon.	Current Market Value U.K. £	U.S. $	Can. $
D6892	Large	Doulton	7"	1991	Current	59.00	150.00	180.00

GEORGE HARRISON

(b. 1943). One of the original members of the world-famous and legendary rock band, the Beatles, Harrison was born in Liverpool, England. He played guitar in the band, writing songs occasionally, from 1961 to 1970. Since the break-up of the Beatles, Harrison has pursued a solo career in music and film.

SERIES: The Beatles, one of four.

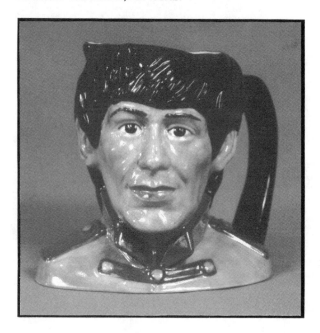

Designer: Stanley J. Taylor   **Handle:** Plain   **Backstamp:** Doulton

Colourway: Green tunic trimmed with orange collar and epaulettes

Doulton Number	Size	Backstamp	Height	Intro.	Discon.	Current Market Value U.K. £	U.S. $	Can. $
D6727	Mid	Doulton	5 1/2"	1984	1991	45.00	65.00	95.00

GEORGE WASHINGTON

(1732-1799). As commander-in-chief of the American States, Washington led them to victory in the War of Independence. In 1789 he became the first president of the United States, governing for two terms, until 1797.

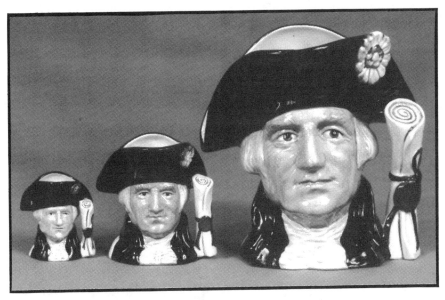

Designer: Stanley J. Taylor   **Handle:** Declaration of Independence

Colourway: Black hat and coat, white shirt

Backstamp: Doulton

© ROYAL DOULTON
TABLEWARE LTD. 1982
D6669

George Washington
1732-1799

First Issued in 1982 to Celebrate
the 250th Anniversary of his Birth

BACKSTAMPS

A: Doulton / George Washington 1732-1799 "FIRST ISSUED IN 1982 TO CELEBRATE
   THE 250TH ANNIVERSARY OF HIS BIRTH"

B: Doulton / George Washington   "TO COMMEMORATE THE 200th ANNIVERSARY
   OF THE ELECTION OF THE FIRST PRESIDENT OF
   THE UNITED STATES OF AMERICA"

Doulton Number	Size	Backstamp	Height	Intro.	Discon.	U.K. £	U.S. $	Can. $
D6669	Large	A	7 1/2"	1982	1991	41.00	130.00	145.00
D6669	Large	B	7 1/2"	1989	1989	70.00	130.00	145.00
D6824	Small	A	4"	1989	1991	24.50	60.00	80.00
D6824	Small	B	4"	1989	1989	40.00	65.00	80.00
D6825	Miniature	A	2 1/2"	1989	1991	16.50	50.00	60.00

GEORGE WASHINGTON AND GEORGE III

George Washington (1732-1799). As commander-in-chief of the American States, Washington led them to victory in the War of Independence. In 1789 he became the first president of the United States, governing for two terms, until 1797.

George III (1738-1820). George William Frederick ruled as King George III from 1760 until his death. He led Great Britain in the war against the American States, which he lost in 1776. England did not recognize the American Independence until 1781.

Issued in a limited edition of 9,500 in 1986.

SERIES: The Antagonists' Collection (Two Faced Jug), one of four.

Designer: Michael Abberley

Handle: Declaration of Independence/ A cannon

Colourway: Red crown and black hat

Backstamp: Doulton

Royal Doulton®
'The Antagonists'
Collection
D.6749
The Siege of Yorktown 1781
George III/George Washington
Hand made and Hand decorated •
Designed by Michael Abberley
© 1985 ROYAL DOULTON (UK)
Worldwide Limited Edition of 9.500
This is Number 3895

Doulton Number	Size	Backstamp	Height	Intro.	Discon.	Current Market Value		
						U.K. £	U.S. $	Can. $
D6749	Large	Doulton	7 1/4"	1986	Ltd.Ed.	60.00	120.00	175.00

GERONIMO

(1829-1909). Geronimo was the last leader of the Apache Indians while they were still independent of Colonial rule by the white American colonists, and he fought many battles to protect their freedom. In 1886 he surrendered to General Nelson Miles, and the Apache territory became the state of Arizona. After a prison term in Florida, Geronimo moved west and settled down to become a prosperous farmer, while his exploits became the stuff of legends.

SERIES: The Wild West Collection, one of six.

Designer: Stanley J. Taylor   **Handle:** Indian game pieces   **Backstamp:** Doulton

Colourway: Black, red and white

Doulton Number	Size	Backstamp	Height	Intro.	Discon.	Current Market Value U.K. £	U.S. $	Can. $
D6733	Mid	Doulton	5 1/2"	1985	1989	45.00	75.00	110.00

GLADIATOR

From about 246 B.C. the gladiator games were a popular form of entertainment for Roman audiences. The gladiators were most often slaves or prisoners condemned to fight, which they did to the death using sword, spear or trident. The most famous gladiator of the period was Spartacus, a slave, who led an unsuccessful rebellion against Rome. Emperor Honorius banned the brutal games in 404 A.D.

Gladiator
D 6550
COPR 1960
DOULTON & CO LIMITED
Rd No 897939
Rd No 40889
Rd No 8598
Rd No 548A/60

Designer: Max Henk   **Handle:** A dagger and shield   **Backstamp:** Doulton

Colourway: Brown helmet, grey armour

Doulton Number	Size	Backstamp	Height	Intro.	Discon.	Current Market Value U.K. £	U.S. $	Can. $
D6650	Large	Doulton	7 3/4"	1961	1967	350.00	600.00	750.00
D6553	Small	Doulton	4 1/4"	1961	1967	200.00	375.00	450.00
D6556	Miniature	Doulton	2 3/4"	1961	1967	200.00	350.00	475.00

GOLFER

An outdoor sport enjoying great popularity in Europe and North America, golf requires the player to shoot a small ball into a hole using the least number of strokes of a wooden or metal club. Usually played to eighteen holes, a typical game of golf can last up to six hours and require a great deal of walking.

The Golfer character jug was modelled in the likeness of W. J. Carey, the former chairman of Doulton U.S.A.

STYLE ONE: HANDLE: GOLD BAG AND CLUBS

Royal Doulton®
GOLFER
D 6757
© 1970 ROYAL DOULTON

Designer: David Biggs **Handle:** A golf bag and clubs **Backstamp:** See Backstamps

Colourway: See Variations

VARIATIONS

VARIATION NO. 1: Colourway: Blue cap, brown sweater, brown golf bag

BACKSTAMP: Doulton

Doulton Number	Size	Backstamp	Height	Intro.	Discon.	Current Market Value U.K. £	U.S. $	Can. $
D6623	Large	Doulton	7"	1971	Current	41.00	130.00	145.00
D6756	Small	Doulton	4 1/2"	1987	Current	22.50	60.00	80.00
D6757	Miniature	Doulton	2 1/2"	1987	Current	15.50	50.00	60.00

VARIATION NO. 2: Colourway: Dark blue cap, blue striped sweater, light brown golf bag

BACKSTAMP: Doulton / John Sinclair

Commissioned by John Sinclair, Sheffield, England. Issued in 1987 in a limited edition of 1,000 pieces.

Doulton Number	Size	Backstamp	Height	Intro.	Discon.	Current Market Value U.K. £	U.S. $	Can. $
D6787	Large	Doulton/Sinclair	7"	1987	Ltd. Ed.	35.00	75.00	100.00

THE GOLFER

In the United States, the Royal Doulton product list carry this jug listed as "The Modern Golfer."

SERIES: Characters from Life, one of seven.

STYLE TWO: HANDLE: 18TH HOLE FLAG, BALL, TEE AND GOLF CLUB

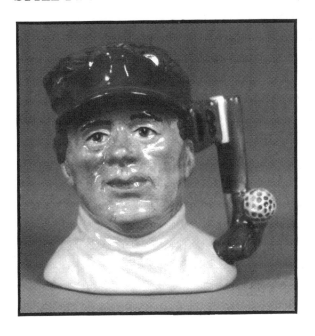

Royal Doulton®
THE GOLFER
D 6865
Modelled by
Stanley James Taylor
© 1990 ROYAL DOULTON

Designer: Stanley J. Taylor   **Handle:** Golf club, eighteenth hole flag, ball and tee   **Backstamp:** Doulton

Colourway: Yellow sweater, green sun visor

Doulton Number	Size	Backstamp	Height	Intro.	Discon.	Current Market Value		
						U.K. £	U.S. $	Can. $
D6865	Small	Doulton	4"	1990	Current	26.50	65.00	90.00

GONDOLIER

The shallow long craft the gondolier pilots through Venetian canals must be painted all black, according to ancient law. When not ferrying or serenading lovers on moonlight rides, the gondolier moors his gondola to a brightly striped pole by the waterside.

Gondolier
D 6589
COPR 1963
DOULTON & CO LIMITED
Rd No 913139
Rd No 45357
Rd No 9682
Rd No 812/63

Designer: David Biggs　　　　**Handle:** Gondola　　　　**Backstamp:** Doulton

Colourway: Yellow hat, blue and white t-shirt, maroon and white pole.

Doulton Number	Size	Backstamp	Height	Intro.	Discon.	Current Market Value U.K. £	U.S. $	Can. $
D6589	Large	Doulton	8"	1964	1969	275.00	600.00	700.00
D6592	Small	Doulton	4"	1964	1969	180.00	425.00	450.00
D6595	Miniature	Doulton	2 1/2"	1964	1969	180.00	400.00	475.00

GONE AWAY

The very British huntsman looks about ready to give this traditional call signalling the loss of the quarry. His prey, the fox, has won this round!

Gone Away
D 6531
COPR 1959
DOULTON & CO LIMITED
Rd No 893844
Rd No 39652
Rd No 8316
Rd No 417/59

Designer: Garry Sharpe   **Handle:** A fox   **Backstamp:** Doulton

Colourway: Red jacket, black cap

Doulton Number	Size	Backstamp	Height	Intro.	Discon.	Current Market Value U.K. £	U.S. $	Can. $
D6531	Large	Doulton	7 1/4"	1960	1982	50.00	90.00	155.00
D6538	Small	Doulton	3 3/4	1960	1982	35.00	60.00	90.00
D6545	Miniature	Doulton	2 1/2"	1960	1982	30.00	45.00	80.00

GRANNY

A delight for children, and often the favourite relative, Granny can always be counted on for a little treat or a big hug.

STYLE ONE: *"TOOTHLESS" GRANNY*

The wimple on this style does not show between the hat and the hair at the front of the head. There is no tooth showing between the lips.

Granny
D 5521

Designer: Harry Fenton   **Handle:** Plain   **Backstamp:** Doulton

Colourway: Dark grey and white

Doulton Number	Size	Backstamp	Height	Intro.	Discon.	Current Market Value		
						U.K. £	U.S. $	Can. $
D5521	Large	Doulton	6 1/4"	1935	Unknown	250.00	1,000.00	1,200.00

GRANNY

PROTOTYPE

This early coloured prototype proved to expensive to produce. Only one copy is known to exist.

STYLE ONE: *"TOOTHLESS" GRANNY*

Designer: Harry Fenton   **Handle:** Plain   **Backstamp:** Doulton

Colourway: Yellows

Doulton Number	Size	Backstamp	Height	Intro.	Discon.	Current Market Value		
						U.K. £	U.S. $	Can. $
D5521	Large	Doulton	6 1/4"	1935	Unknown		Unique	

GRANNY

STYLE TWO: *GRANNY HAS ONE TOOTH SHOWING*

The wimple on this style shows in waves under most of the hat.

Granny
D 6384

Designer: Harry Fenton, Large
Max Henk, Small
and Miniature

Handle: Plain

Backstamp: Doulton

Colourway: Dark grey and white

Doulton Number	Size	Backstamp	Height	Intro.	Discon.	Current Market Value U.K. £	U.S. $	Can. $
D5521	Large	Doulton	6 1/4"	1935	1983	45.00	85.00	145.00
D6384	Small	Doulton	3 1/4"	1953	1983	30.00	50.00	90.00
D6520	Miniature	Doulton	2 1/4"	1960	1983	25.00	40.00	70.00

Miscellaneous "Granny" Items

Doulton Number	Item	Height	Intro.	Discon.	Current Market Value U.K. £	U.S. $	Can. $
D —	Lighter	3 1/2"	Unknown		.00	.00	.00

GROUCHO MARX

(1895-1977). Julius Marx was one of four brothers who became hits of American comedy film. The "Marx Brothers" were known for their crazy slapstick antics and hilarious puns. Groucho led the gang, always smoking his trademark cigar.

SERIES: The Celebrity Collection, one of five.

THE
CELEBRITY
COLLECTION
by Royal Doulton
A hand-made, hand-decorated series
GROUCHO MARX ®
"I've worked myself up
from nothing to a state
of extreme poverty."

Groucho Marx ®

Designer: Stanley J. Taylor

Handle: Cigar

Backstamp: Doulton

Colourway: See Variations

VARIATIONS

VARIATION NO. 1: Colourway: Plain jacket, spotted bow tie.

Doulton Number	Size	Variation	Height	Intro.	Discon.	Current Market Value U.K. £	U.S. $	Can. $
D6710	Large	Var. 1	7"	1984	1988	60.00	100.00	155.00

VARIATION NO. 2: Colourway: Plaid jacket

Doulton Number	Size	Variation	Height	Intro.	Discon.	Current Market Value U.K. £	U.S. $	Can. $
D6710	Large	Var. 2	7"	Unknown			Extremely Rare	

GROUCHO MARX

PROTOTYPE

The design having two of the Marx Brothers peering from behind the cigar was never put into produciton due to htis complicated handle. Only one is known to exist.

Designer: Stanley J. Taylor **Handle:** Cigar with two other Marx brothers   **Backstamp:** Doulton

Colourway: Plain jacket, spotted bow-tie

Doulton Number	Size	Variation	Height	Intro.	Discon.	Current Market Value U.K. £	U.S. $	Can. $
D6710	Large	Prototype	7"		Unknown			Unique

GUARDSMAN

In a new and foreign land, any colony must also be a well protected fortress. Williamsburg, Virginia was no exception and this guardsman was always at the ready to protect the American pioneers against attack.

SERIES: Characters from Williamsburg, one of seven.

STYLE ONE: *TRICORN HAT WITH SPIKE*

Character Jugs from Williamsburg®

Guardsman
D 6575
COPR 1962
DOULTON & CO LIMITED
Rd No 906338
Rd No 43445
Rd No 9224
Rd No 286/62

Designer: Max Henk   **Handle:** Spike   **Backstamp:** Doulton

Colourway: Dark blue and yellow hat and jacket

Doulton Number	Size	Backstamp	Height	Intro.	Discon.	Current Market Value		
						U.K. £	U.S. $	Can. $
D6568	Large	Doulton	6 3/4"	1963	1983	50.00	100.00	145.00
D6575	Small	Doulton	4 1/4"	1963	1983	40.00	65.00	95.00
D6582	Miniature	Doulton	2 1/2"	1963	1983	35.00	50.00	80.00

THE GUARDSMAN

Long a fixture in London, the guardsman is easily identified by his tall bearskin hat and scarlet uniform. Today they still stand outside Buckingham Palace, to protect the Queen.

SERIES: The London Collection, one of ten.

STYLE TWO: *BEARSKIN HAT WITH SWORD*

Designer: Stanley J. Taylor   **Handle:** Sword with draped brown flag

Colourway: Red tunic, black bearskin hat

Backstamp: Doulton

Royal Doulton®

THE GUARDSMAN

D 6755

Modelled by

Stanley James Taylor

© 1986 ROYAL DOULTON

Doulton Number	Size	Backstamp	Height	Intro.	Discon.	Current Market Value U.K. £	U.S. $	Can. $
D6755	Large	Doulton	8"	1986	Current	47.00	130.00	145.00
D6771	Small	Doulton	4"	1987	Current	24.50	65.00	80.00
D6772	Miniature	Doulton	2 1/2"	1987	Current	16.50	50.00	60.00

THE GUARDSMAN

PROTOTYPE

This was the original design of The Guardsman Jug. A prototype, with the Union Jack as the flag.

Designer: Stanley J. Taylor **Handle:** A sword draped with the Union Jack   **Backstamp:** Doulton

Colourway: Red tunic, black bearskin hat

Doulton Number	Size	Variation	Height	Intro.	Discon.	U.K. £	Current Market Value U.S. $	Can. $
D —	Large	Prototype	8"		Unknown		Extremely Rare	

GULLIVER

Jonathon Swift, when he published "Gulliver's Travels" under a pseudonym in 1726, intended to satirize society's leading men and institutions. The book was so fascinating however, that even the intended victims didn't realize they were the butt of a joke.

Gulliver the traveller sails to foreign lands, surviving shipwrecks, giants and many odd adventures. Perhaps his most well-known experience was waking up in the land of Lilliput to find he had been tied up by the miniature people who lived there.

Gulliver
D 6560
COPR 1961
DOULTON & CO LIMITED
Rd No 902091
Rd No 42143
Rd No 8926
Rd No R 85/61

Designer: David Biggs **Handle:** Castle tower with two Lilliputians in the turret **Backstamp:** Doulton

Colourway: Dark blue and grey hat, blue jacket, grey handle

Doulton Number	Size	Backstamp	Height	Intro.	Discon.	Current Market Value		
						U.K. £	U.S. $	Can. $
D6560	Large	Doulton	7 1/2"	1962	1967	300.00	675.00	750.00
D6563	Small	Doulton	4"	1962	1967	200.00	350.00	525.00
D6566	Miniature	Doulton	2 1/2"	1962	1967	200.00	375.00	600.00

GUNSMITH

The produciton of guns in 18th century America was an exacting science, part metalwork and part chemistry. To have a resident expert within the colony meant that arms could be quickly manufactured or repaired in case of danger.

SERIES: Characters from Williamsburg, one of seven

Character Jugs from Williamsburg
Gunsmith
D 6573
COPR·1962
DOULTON & CO LIMITED
Rd No 908698
Rd No 43563
Rd No 9264
Rd No 322/62

Designer: David Biggs   **Handle:** Stock of a musket   **Backstamp:** Doulton

Colourway: Black hat, cream shirt, light brown apron

Doulton Number	Size	Backstamp	Height	Intro.	Discon.	Current Market Value		
						U.K. £	U.S. $	Can. $
D6573	Large	Doulton	7 1/4"	1963	1983	50.00	85.00	145.00
D6580	Small	Doulton	3 1/2"	1963	1983	40.00	65.00	80.00
D6587	Miniature	Doulton	2 1/2"	1963	1983	35.00	50.00	70.00

GUNSMITH

PROTOTYPE

The prototype has a different hat, hair style and handle than the issued design. Only one jug known to exist.

Designer: David Biggs   **Handle:** Stock of a musket and flintlock   **Backstamp:** Doulton

Colourway: Black hat, cream shirt, light brown apron

Doulton Number	Size	Backstamp	Height	Intro.	Discon.	Current Market Value U.K. £	U.S. $	Can. $
D —	Large	Doulton	7 1/4"		c. 1963		Unique	

GUY FAWKES

(1570-1606). Guy Fawkes, a Yorkshire Catholic, was part of the infamous "Gunpowder Plot," a plan by Catholic rebels to blow up the British Houses of Parliament and King James I on November 5, 1605.

The conspiracy was leaked by a mysterious letter to Lord Monteagle and Guy Fawkes was arrested and hanged. Every year on November 5th Guy Fawkes day is celebrated with fireworks and the burning of Fawkes in effigy.

Royal Doulton®
GUY FAWKES
D 6861
Modelled by
William K. Harper
© 1990 ROYAL DOULTON

Designer: W.K. Harper   **Handle:** A lantern above a barrel of gunpowder   **Backstamp:** See Backstamps

Colourway: See Variations

VARIATIONS

VARIATION NO. 1: Colourway: Black hat, red band, white collar on black coat

BACKSTAMP: Doulton

For General Issue: 1990

Doulton Number	Size	Backstamp	Height	Intro.	Discon.	Current Market Value U.K. £	U.S. $	Can. $
D6861	Large	Doulton	7"	1990	Current	49.00	130.00	195.00

VARIATION NO. 2: Colourway: Black hat, orange band, white collar on black coat

BACKSTAMP: Doulton / Canadian Art and Collectables Show

Pre-release limited to 750 for the 3rd Annual Canadian Doulton Show and Sale in conjuction with the 1990 Canadian Collectables Showcase May 5 & 6, 1990, Durham, Ontario

Doulton Number	Size	Backstamp	Height	Intro.	Discon.	Current Market Value U.K. £	U.S. $	Can. $
D6861	Large	Doulton/Can.	7"	1990	Ltd. Ed.	95.00	145.00	195.00

HAMLET

Probably Shakespeare's most famous play, "Hamlet, Prince of Denmark" was first performed between 1599 and 1602. Hamlet became the quintessential tragic hero, driven by conscience and familial obligation to revenge his father's murder.

SERIES: The Shakespearean Collection, one of six.

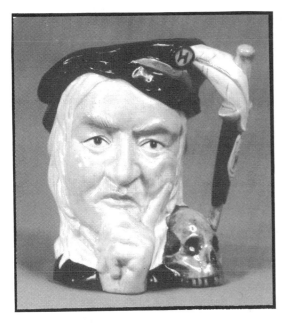

Designer: Michael Abberley **Handle:** A dagger and skull join the feather of the cap **Backstamp:** Doulton

Colourway: Black cap and robes, white hair and feather

Doulton Number	Size	Backstamp	Height	Intro.	Discon.	Current Market Value U.K. £	U.S. $	Can. $
D6672	Large	Doulton	7 1/4"	1982	1989	60.00	100.00	145.00

THE HAMPSHIRE CRICKETER

An honourable and gentlemanly game, cricket enjoys great popularity in the United Kingdom. Two teams of eleven compete on an outdoor field with balls, wickets and bats.

Developed and sold by the Hampshire Cricket Club to celebrate the centenary of the Hampshire cricket grounds. Issued in 1985 in a limited edition of 5,000 pieces.

Designer: Harry Sales   **Handle:** Cricket bat   **Backstamp:** Doulton / Hampshire Cricet Club

Colourway: Black cap, white sweater with two black stripes

Doulton Number	Size	Backstamp	Height	Intro.	Discon.	Current Market Value U.K. £	U.S. $	Can. $
D6739	Small	Doulton/ Hampshire	5"	1985	Ltd. Ed.	45.00	75.00	125.00

HENRY V

(1387-1422). King Henry V during his reign from 1413-1422 renewed the Hundred Years' War against France. At the Battle of Agincourt in 1415, he won one of the most famous victories in English history. Henry married the daughter of King Charles VI of France and by the Treaty of Troyes became heir to the French throne.

The story of his reign and battles was dramatized in a play by William Shakespeare.

SERIES: The Shakespearean Collection, one of six.

© ROYAL DOULTON TABLEWARE LIMITED 1982
D 6671

The Shakespearean Collection

HENRY V̱

A series of hand-made, hand-decorated Character Jugs by Royal Doulton

Designer: Robert Tabbenor   **Handle:** Royal Ensign   **Backstamp:** Doutlon

Colourway: See Variations

VARIATIONS

VARIATION NO. 1: Colourway: Yellow crown with gold, blue and red design.
Handle: Embossed

Doulton Number	Size	Variation	Height	Intro.	Discon.	Current Market Value U.K. £	Current Market Value U.S. $	Current Market Value Can. $
D6671	Large	Var. 1	7 1/4"	1982	c. 1984	135.00	200.00	195.00

VARIATION NO. 2: Colourway: Yellow crown with gold, blue and red design.
Handle: Decorated with a decal.

Doulton Number	Size	Variation	Height	Intro.	Discon.	Current Market Value		
						U.K. £	U.S. $	Can. $
D6671	Large	Var. 2	7 1/4"	c. 1984	1989	60.00	100.00	145.00

VARIATION NO. 3: Colourway: Yellow crown, some blue colouring, no red or gold.
Handle: Embossed.

This jug is actually a factory second, marked and sold as such. One of the steps used when firing and painting the jugs was missed. Hundreds are known to exist.

Doulton Number	Size	Variation	Height	Intro.	Discon.	Current Market Value		
						U.K. £	U.S. $	Can. $
D6671	Large	Var. 3	7 1/4"	Unknown		100.00	250.00	250.00

HENRY VIII

(1491-1547). Henry VIII was king of Great Britain from 1509-1547 during which time he established the English Navy as one of the most powerful in the world. Henry's infamous private life changed the course of history. Attempting to produce a male heir to the throne, he married six times, was excommunicated by the Pope for divorcing, and ultimately founded the Church of England.

STYLE ONE: ONE HANDLED JUG

SERIES: Henry VIII and his Six Wives, one of eight.

HENRY VIII
D 6642
© ROYAL DOULTON
TABLEWARE LTD 1975

Designer: Eric Griffiths   **Handle:** A tower joins the feather in the hat   **Backstamp:** Doulton

Colourway: Black and gold hat, white plume, brown and maroon tunic

Doulton Number	Size	Backstamp	Height	Intro.	Discon.	Current Market Value U.K. £	U.S. $	Can. $
D6642	Large	Doulton	6 1/2"	1975	Current	41.00	130.00	145.00
D6647	Small	Doulton	3 3/4"	1979	Current	22.50	65.00	80.00
D6648	Miniature	Doulton	2 3/4"	1979	Current	15.50	50.00	60.00

HENRY VIII

This is a two handled jug and strictly speaking should be classified as a loving cup. Issued in 1991 in a limited edition of 1991 to commemorate the 500th anniversary of the birth of Henry VIII.

STYLE TWO: *TWO HANDLED JUG*

Designer: William K. Harper   **Handle:** Double handle, three wives on either side   **Backstamp:** Doulton

Colourway: White and black with gold trim

Doulton Number	Size	Backstamp	Height	Intro.	Discon.	Current Market Value		
						U.K. £	U.S. $	Can. $
D6888	Large	Doulton	7"	1991	Ltd. Ed.	250.00	400.00	550.00

HOME GUARD

Commissioned by Lawley's By Post in a limited edtion of 9,500 in a set.

SERIES: Dad's Army, Heroes of the Blitz, one of three.

Designer: Stanley J. Taylor   **Handle:** Sten gun with hand grenade   **Backstamp:** Doulton

Colourway: Khaki uniform and cap

Doulton Number	Size	Variation	Height	Intro.	Discon.	Current Market Value U.K. £	U.S. $	Can. $
D6886	Small	Doulton	4"	1991	1991	40.00	70.00	80.00

HUMPHREY BOGART

Born in New York city, Humphrey DeForest Bogart began his acting career in 1920 on the stage. Turning to film, he had a prolific career, winning an Academy Award in 1952 for his performance in "The African Queen." His most well-known role, however, must be that of Rick in "Casablanca." Not issued due to copyright problems. Not known to be in private collections.

SERIES: The Celebrity Collection

PROTOTYPE

Designer: Eric Griffith   **Handle:** Movie camera pointing right   **Backstamp:** Doulton

Colourway: Black hat and brown coat, black bow-tie

Doulton Number	Size	Variation	Height	Intro.	Discon.	U.K. £	Current Market Value U.S. $	Can. $
D —	Large	Prototype	7"		Unknown		Extremely Rare	

IZAAK WALTON

(1593-1683). An English writer, Walton is best known for his book "The Compleat Angler, or Contemplative Man's Recreation." First published in 1653, this work later became the most famous book written on the sport of fishing in the English language. Styled as a conversation between a fisherman and a hunter, the book breathes serenity and contentment.

TO COMMEMORATE THI
300ᵗʰ ANNIVERSARY
OF THE
COMPLEAT ANGLER
1653 - 1953

IZAAK WALTON.
D. 6404.
COPR.1953.
DOULTON & CO LIMITED
Rᵈ Nº 871560
Rᵈ Nº 31804
Rᵈ Nº 6825
Rᵈ Nº 237/53

CITY OF
STOKE-ON-TRENT
JUBILEE YEAR
1959-1960
WITH THE COMPLIMENTS OF
LORD MAYOR AND LADY MAYORESS
ALDERMAN HAROLD CLOWES O.B.E. J.P
AND
MISS CHRISTINE CLOWES

Designer: Geoff Blower

Handle: A fishing rod resting on a tree trunk

Backstamp: See Backstamps

Colourway: Brown hat, brown coat, white collar

BACKSTAMPS

A: **Doulton**

B: **Doulton / City of Stoke-on-Trent** "With the compliments of Lord Mayor and Lady Mayoress Alderman Harold Clowes, O.B.E., J.P. and Miss Christine Clowes"

Overprinted for the jubilee year, 1959-1960, of the city.

Doulton Number	Size	Backstamp	Height	Intro.	Discon.	Current Market Value		
						U.K. £	U.S. $	Can. $
D6404	Large	Doulton	7"	1953	1982	50.00	100.00	145.00
D6404	Large	Doulton/City	7"	1959	1960	475.00	800.00	950.00

JANE SEYMOUR

(1509-1537). While serving as lady-in-waiting to both Catherine of Aragon and Anne Boleyn, Jane attracted the attention of Henry VIII. She refused any proposal from the King except marriage, a factor leading to the trial of Anne. Two weeks after Anne Boleyn was beheaded, Jane Seymour became the third wife of Henry VIII, and the only one to bear him a male heir. She died shortly after Edward was born, and is the only wife to be buried at Henry's side.

SERIES: Henry VIII and his Six Wives, one of eight.

Designer: Michael Abberley

Handle: A mandolin

Colourway: Turquoise and white

Backstamp: Doulton

Royal Doulton®
JANE SEYMOUR
D 6746
Designed by M Abberley
Modelled by
Peter A Gee
© 1978 ROYAL DOULTON (UK)

Doulton Number	Size	Backstamp	Height	Intro.	Discon.	Current Market Value U.K. £	U.S. $	Can. $
D6646	Large	Doulton	7 1/4"	1979	1990	50.00	80.00	145.00
D6746	Small	Doulton	4 1/4"	1986	1990	35.00	55.00	80.00
D6747	Miniature	Doulton	2 3/4"	1986	1990	35.00	40.00	60.00

JARGE

The dialect form of "George" to name this fellow indicates he's a countryman, probably a farmer, with his polka-dot scarf and the piece of straw in his teeth.

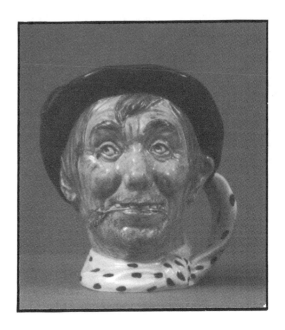

Designer: Harry Fenton   **Handle:** The scarf extends upwards to the cap   **Backstamp:** Doulton

Colourway: Green cap, white scarf with red polka-dots

Doulton Number	Size	Backstamp	Height	Intro.	Discon.	Current Market Value U.K. £	U.S. $	Can. $
D6288	Large	Doulton	6 1/2"	1950	1960	200.00	300.00	400.00
D6295	Small	Doulton	3 1/2"	1950	1960	100.00	200.00	265.00

JESTER

Taking his name form the Latin "gesta" for "exploits," this charcter's comic antics entertained the courts of kings and noblemen. In the modern-day clown one can see the evolution of this funny role which maintains its popularity today.

Note: The green and yellow colouring on either side of the hat may be reversed as a preference of the painter.

Designer: Charles Noke   **Handle:** Plain   **Backstamp:** See Backstamps

Colourway: Brown, green and yellow

BACKSTAMPS

A: Doulton

B: Bentalls "Souvenir From Bentalls 1936"

Commmissioned by Bentalls as an advertising piece.

Doulton Number	Size	Backstamp	Height	Intro.	Discon.	Current Market Value U.K. £	U.S. $	Can. $
D5556	Small	Doulton	3 1/8"	1936	1960	65.00	110.00	125.00
D5556	Small	Bentalls	3 1/8"	1936	1936	350.00	575.00	850.00

Miscellaneous "Jester" Items

Doulton Number	Item	Height	Intro.	Discon.	Current Market Value U.K. £	U.S. $	Can. $
D6111	Wall Pocket	7 1/4"	1940	1941	750.00	1,700.00	2,000.00

JIMMY DURANTE

(1893-1980). James Francis Durante began his entertaining career playing the piano. His comic singing and clowning won him fame in Vaudeville theatre, night clubs, films, radio and television. Using his own large nose as the object of jokes, Durante earned the long-standing nickname "Schnozzle."

SERIES: The Celebrity Collection, one of five.

Designer: David Biggs   **Handle:** A piano keyboard   **Backstamp:** Doulton

Colourway: Grey and black cap, yellow jacket and cream shirt

Doulton Number	Size	Backstamp	Height	Intro.	Discon.	Current Market Value		
						U.K. £	U.S. $	Can. $
D6708	Large	Doulton	7 1/2"	1985	1988	60.00	100.00	145.00

JOCKEY

Winning or losing a horse race can ultimately depend on the skill of the jockey. Master horsemen, these riders are chosen for their small size and weight as well as talent. The brightly coloured clothes they wear are the signature shades of the horse's owner.

Small and miniature sized jugs were test piloted but not produced. A small pilot jug is known to exist.

STYLE ONE: *GOGGLES RESTING ON HIS CHEST; WINNING POLE*

Jockey
D 6625
COPR 1970
DOULTON & CO LIMITED
Rd No 949548
Rd No 57981
Rd No 12388
Rd No 917/70

Designer: David Biggs   **Handle:** The winning pole   **Backstamp:** Doulton

Colourway: Red and yellow striped cap and racing jersey

Doulton Number	Size	Backstamp	Height	Intro.	Discon.	Current Market Value U.K. £	U.S. $	Can. $
D6625	Large	Doulton	7 3/4"	1971	1975	250.00	350.00	495.00

THE JOCKEY

SERIES: Character Jugs from Life, one of seven.

STYLE TWO: GOGGLES RESTING ON CAP; WINNING POLE AND HORSE HEAD

Royal Doulton®
THE JOCKEY
D 6877
Modelled by

Stanley James Taylor

© 1990 ROYAL DOULTON

Designer: Stanley J. Taylor **Handle:** Head of a horse and the winning pole   **Backstamp:** Doulton

Colourway: Grey and black cap, yellow and black racing jersey

Doulton Number	Size	Backstamp	Height	Intro.	Discon.	Current Market Value U.K. £	U.S. $	Can. $
D6877	Small	Doulton	4"	1991	Current	26.50	65.00	90.00

JOHN BARLEYCORN

John is the personification of barley, the grain source of malt liquor. This Character jug is the first design, created by Charles Noke in 1934.

STYLE ONE: HANDLE "INSIDE" JUG - 1934 TO 1939

JOHN BARLEYCORN.

Designer: Charles Noke   **Handle:** Plain brown   **Backstamp:** See Backstamps

Colourway: Brown rim with light brown body

BACKSTAMPS

A: Doulton

B: Doulton/Colemans's "Coleman's Compliments"

> Commissioned by Coleman's as an advertising piece, large size

C: Doulton/Salt River Cement Works "With Compliments From Salt River Cement Works"

> Commissioned by Salt River Cement Works as an advertising piece, large size

Doulton Number	Size	Backstamp	Height	Intro.	Discon.	Current Market Value U.K. £	U.S. $	Can. $
D5327	Large	Doulton	6 1/2"	1934	1939	100.00	160.00	225.00
D5327	Large	Doulton/Coleman's	6 1/2"	Unknown		500.00	850.00	850.00
D5327	Large	Doulton/Salt River	6 1/2"	Unknown		500.00	850.00	850.00
D5735	Small	Doulton	3 1/2"	1937	1939	70.00	110.00	120.00

JOHN BARLEYCORN

STYLE TWO: *HANDLE "OUTSIDE" JUG - 1939 TO 1960*

Designer: Charles Noke   **Handle:** See Variations   **Backstamp:** See Backstamps

Colourway: Brown rim with light brown face

VARIATIONS

VARIATION NO. 1: Handle: Brown shading.

Doulton Number	Size	Backstamp	Height	Intro.	Discon.	Current Market Value U.K. £	U.S. $	Can. $
D5327	Large	Doulton	6 1/2"	1934	1960	75.00	140.00	195.00
D5735	Small	Doulton	3 1/2"	1937	1960	45.00	80.00	110.00
D6041	Miniature	Doulton	2 1/2"	1939	1960	40.00	65.00	85.00

JOHN BARLEYCORN
D.5327
SPECIAL EXHIBITION REPRODUCTION
LIMITED TO 7,500 PIECES
THIS IS NUMBER 249

VARIATION NO. 2: Handle: Black shading.

Issued 1978 to 1982. Similar design, but a new mold as the original John Barleycorn mold was not available. This special exhibition jug, limited to 7,500, was sold at Royal Doulton special events. Modelled by Micheal Abberley.

BACKSTAMP: Doulton/"SPECIAL EXHIBITION REPRODUCTION LIMITED TO 7,500 PIECES"

Doulton Number	Size	Backstamp	Height	Intro.	Discon.	Current Market Value U.K. £	U.S. $	Can. $
D5327	Large	Doulton/Special	6"	1978	Ltd. Ed.	65.00	130.00	195.00

Miscellaneous "John Barleycorn" Items

Doulton Number	Item	Height	Intro.	Discon.	Current Market Value U.K. £	U.S. $	Can. $
D5602	Ashtray	4"	1936	1960	65.00	125.00	140.00

JOHN BARLEYCORN

Commissioned by American Express to form part of a twelve tankard set from various manufactures. The set was test marketed to their card members.

It is estimated that between 500 and 600 were sold.

STYLE THREE: BLUE HAT WITH BARLEY EARS

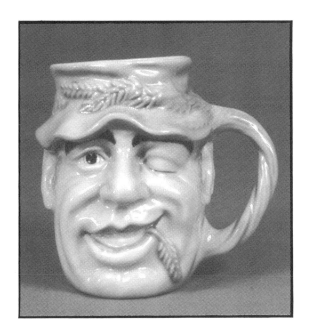

Royal Doulton®
JOHN BARLEYCORN
TANKARD
D 6780
Specially Commissioned
by
AMERICAN EXPRESS
Modelled by
Stanley James Taylor
© 1987 ROYAL DOULTON

Designer: Stanley J. Taylor   **Handle:** Twisted barley stock   **Backstamp:** Doulton /
American Express

Colourway: Pale blue cap and light brown barley ears

Doulton Number	Size	Backstamp	Height	Intro.	Discon.	Current Market Value U.K. £	U.S. $	Can. $
D6780	Mid	Doulton/Amex	5 1/2"	1988	Sp. Ed.	125.00	300.00	375.00

JOHN DOULTON

(1793-1873). John Doulton served a seven year apprenticeship in the pottery industry, as a thrower, before fortune smiled on him and he was able to buy into a pottery partnership. He bought a one-third share of a stoneware pot-house in Vauxhall Walk, Lambeth. Doulton and Watts began its life around 1815 in that small town on the banks of the Thames in South London.

To honour John Doulton, The Royal Doulton International Collectors Club, in 1980, made this jug available to all their orginal charter members.

This first style has the time shown on "Big Ben" as 8 o'clock.

STYLE ONE: *TIME SHOWN ON BIG BEN IS 8 O'CLOCK*

SERIES: Royal Doulton International Collectors Club

D 6656

JOHN DOULTON
1793 · 1873
EXCLUSIVELY FOR
COLLECTORS CLUB
© ROYAL DOULTON
TABLEWARE LTD 1980

Designer: Eric Griffith   **Handle:** The tower of "Big Ben"   **Backstamp:** Doulton / RDICC

Colourway: White cravat, "Big Ben" is grey

Doulton Number	Size	Backstamp	Height	Intro.	Discon.	Current Market Value U.K. £	U.S. $	Can. $
D6656	Small	Doulton/RDICC	4 1/4"	1980	c. 1982	60.00	100.00	185.00

JOHN DOULTON

Starting in 1981 each new member joining the Royal Doulton International Collectors Club had the opporunity of purchasing the John Doulton jug, however, the time shown on 'Big Ben' is 2 o'clock.

SERIES: Royal Doulton International Collectors Club

STYLE TWO: *TIME SHOWN ON "BIG BEN" IS 2 O'CLOCK*

JOHN DOULTON
1793 - 1873
EXCLUSIVELY FOR
COLLECTORS CLUB
© ROYAL DOULTON
TABLEWARE LTD 1980

Designer: Eric Griffiths **Handle:** The tower of "Big Ben" **Backstamp:** Doulton / RDICC

Colourway: Yellow cravat, "Big Ben" is light brown

Doulton Number	Size	Backstamp	Height	Intro.	Discon.	Current Market Value U.K. £	U.S. $	Can. $
D6656	Small	Doulton/RDICC	4 1/4"	1981	Current	25.00	50.00	60.00

JOHN GILPIN

"The Diverting History of John Gilpin" is an 18th century poem by Cowper. Gilpin, a "linen draper bold" and his wife go to Edmonton to celebrate their 20th wedding anniversary. His horse runs out of control on the way, and John careens ten miles beyond Edmonton and back again.

PROTOTYPE

Designer: David Biggs   **Handle:** Brown wood sign post "Edmonton"   **Backstamp:** Doulton

Colourway: Dark green hat, maroon coat

Doulton Number	Size	Backstamp	Height	Intro.	Discon.	U.K. £	Current Market Value U.S. $	Can. $
D —	Large	Doulton	7"	1960's	1960's		Extremely Rare Only Two Known	

JOHN LENNON

(1940-1980). One of the original members of the famous English rock band, the Beatles, John Winston Lennon played guitar and wrote songs until they disbanded in 1970. With his wife Yoko Ono, Lennon pursued a successful solo career until his tragic assassination in 1980.

SERIES: The Beatles, one of four.

Royal Doulton
THE BEATLES
John Lennon
D 6725
Modelled by
Stanley James Taylor.
© ROYAL DOULTON TABLEWARE
LIMITED 198?

Designer: Stanley J. Taylor   **Handle:** Plain   **Backstamp:** See Backstamps

Colourway: See Variations

VARIATIONS

VARIATION NO. 1: Colourway: Turquoise jacket with maroon collar and epaulettes

BACKSTAMP: Doulton

Doulton Number	Size	Backstamp	Height	Intro.	Discon.	Current Market Value U.K. £	U.S. $	Can. $
D6725	Mid	Doulton	5 1/2"	1984	1991	45.00	65.00	95.00

VARIATION NO. 2: Colourway: Red jacket with yellow collar and epaulettes

BACKSTAMP: Doulton / John Sinclair "NEW COLOURWAY 1987 SPECIAL EDITION OF 1000 FOR JOHN SINCLAIR, SHEFFIELD"

Commissioned by John Sinclair, Sheffield. Issued in 1987 in a limited edition of 1,000 pieces.

Doulton Number	Size	Backstamp	Height	Intro.	Discon.	Current Market Value U.K. £	U.S. $	Can. $
D6797	Mid	Doulton/Sinclair	5 1/2"	1987	Ltd. Ed.	65.00	100.00	125.00

JOHN PEEL

(1776-1854). John Peel was a famous English huntsman, known for his enthusiam, skill and hospitality. Fond of drink, he hosted large, popular post-hunt celebrations. Peel has been immortalized in the song "D'ye ken John Peel," writeen by John Woodcock Graves.

"John Peel."
RᵈNº809559.

| **Designer:** Harry Fenton | **Handle:** Riding crop | **Backstamp:** Doulton |
| | **Colourway:** See Variations | |

VARIATIONS

VARIATION NO. 1: Colourway: Grey handle

| Doulton Number | Size | Variations | Height | Intro. | Discon. | Current Market Value | | |
						U.K. £	U.S. $	Can. $
D5612	Large	Var. 1	6 1/2"	1936	1960	75.00	150.00	195.00
D5731	Small	Var. 1	3 1/2"	1937	1960	45.00	75.00	110.00
D6130	Miniature	Var. 1	2 1/4"	1940	1960	35.00	55.00	85.00
D6259	Tiny	Var. 1	1 1/4"	1947	1960	90.00	200.00	225.00

VARIATION NO. 2: Colourway: Black and orange handle

| Doulton Number | Size | Variations | Height | Intro. | Discon. | Current Market Value | | |
						U.K. £	U.S. $	Can. $
D5612	Large	Var. 2	6 1/2"	Unknown		75.00	160.00	200.00

JOHN SHORTER

Commissioned by the Character and Toby Jug Collectors Society of Australia, this depiction of Australian retailer Shorter was released in 1991 in a limited edition of 1,500 pieces.

Royal Doulton®
JOHN SHORTER
D.6880
Modelled by
William K. Harper
© 1990 ROYAL DOULTON
Specially commissioned from Royal Doulton
by the Character and Toby Jug Collectors Society
of Australia to commemorate
the 10th anniversary of the Society 1980-1990.
ISSUED IN A WORLDWIDE
LIMITED EDITION OF 1,500.
THIS IS N° **372**

Designer: William K. Harper   **Handle:** A kangaroo and joey   **Backstamp:** Doulton / CJCSA

Colourway: Grey hair, black jacket, maroon and white polka-dot bow-tie

Doulton Number	Size	Backstamp	Height	Intro.	Discon.	Current Market Value		
						U.K. £	U.S. $	Can. $
D6880	Small	Doulton/CJCSA	4 1/4"	1991	Ltd. Ed.	60.00	100.00	110.00

JOHNNY APPLESEED

(1774-1845). John Chapman was an American pioneer who sold and gave saplings and apple seeds to colonizing families. He travelled the Eastern U.S., sowing apple orchards and tending his trees. After his death, Chapman became the hero of many legends.

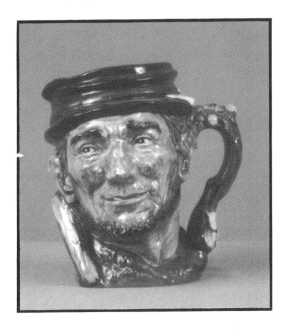

"Johnny Appleseed"
D 6372
COPR. 1952.
DOULTON & CO. LIMITED.
R^dN^o 868196
R^dN^o 98801
R^dN^o 30304
R^dN^o 6647.

Designer: Harry Fenton   **Handle:** An apple tree and knapsack   **Backstamp:** Doulton

Colourway: Maroon and grey cap, brown robes

Doulton Number	Size	Backstamp	Height	Intro.	Discon.	Current Market Value U.K. £	U.S. $	Can. $
D6372	Large	Doulton	6"	1953	1969	180.00	325.00	495.00

THE JUGGLER

A favourite performer at the circus, the juggler dazzles the audience as he tosses balls, hoops or flaming wands without missing a beat.

SERIES: The Circus, one of four.

Royal Doulton®

THE JUGGLER
D 6835
Modelled by

Stanley James Taylor

© 1988 ROYAL DOULTON

Designer: Stanley J. Taylor **Handle:** Skittles and balls **Backstamp:** Doulton

Colourway: Brown and black cap, yellow, red and black tunic

Doulton Number	Size	Backstamp	Height	Intro.	Discon.	Current Market Value		
						U.K. £	U.S. $	Can. $
D6835	Large	Doulton	6 1/2"	1989	Ltd. Ed.	57.00	175.00	225.00

KING ARTHUR AND GUINEVERE

Arthur is the legendary 5th century King of Britain, known for his courage and honesty. His twelve knights, with whom he ruled and planned his campaigns, sat at a round table so that none had precedence. His best friend, the knight Lancelot, betrayed him by falling in love with his beautiful wife Guinevere. Arthur died at Camelford in a battle against his usurping, nephew Mordred.

SERIES: The Star Crossed Lovers Collection (Two-faced Jug), one of four.

Designer: Stanley J. Taylor

Handle: A dagger backed by a chalice

Colourway: Blue-grey, yellow and white

Backstamp: Doulton

Doulton Number	Size	Backstamp	Height	Intro.	Discon.	Current Market Value U.K. £	U.S. $	Can. $
D6836	Large	Doulton	6 1/2"	1989	Ltd. Ed.	70.00	130.00	165.00

KING PHILIP OF SPAIN

(1527-1598). Reigning king of Spain during its most powerful and influential era, Philip was a strong defender of Catholicism and leader of an anti-reformation movement against Protestant leaders, such as Queen Elizabeth I. He lead a rebellion in the Netherlands, and waged wars against the Ottoman Empire and England in the name of his cause. His attempted invasion of England in 1588 was repressed in one of the most famous naval battles in history, and his **Armada** was defeated. Issued by Lawley's By Post in 1988, this jug is one of a pair, (with Queen Elizabeth I), produced to celebrate the 400th anniversary of the defeat of the Spanish Armada. Both jugs are limited editions of 9500 pieces.

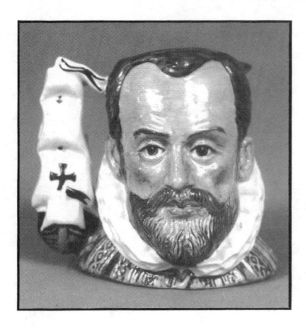

Designer: William K. Harper **Handle:** Galleon sailing on the left **Backstamp:** Doutlon / Lawley's

Colourway: Grey, white and brown

Doulton Number	Size	Backstamp	Height	Intro.	Discon.	Current Market Value U.K. £	U.S. $	Can. $
D6822	Small	Doulton/Lawley's	4"	1988	Ltd. Ed.	40.00	100.00	125.00

THE LAWYER

This solicitor is dressed in the old English tradition of lawyers that is still practiced today. The wig is horsehair and complements a stylized white collar and black robes.

Royal Doulton
THE LAWYER
D 6504
Modelled by

© ROYAL DOULTON TABLEWARE
LIMITED 1958

The Lawyer
D 6498
COPR 1958
DOULTON & CO LIMITED
Rd No 889569
Rd No 38225
Rd No 8035
Rd No 424/58

Designer: Max Henk   **Handle:** Feather quill   **Backstamp:** Doulton

Colourway: Grey wig, black robes, white shirt

Doulton Number	Size	Backstamp	Height	Intro.	Discon.	Current Market Value U.K. £	U.S. $	Can. $
D6498	Large	Doulton	7"	1959	Current	41.00	130.00	145.00
D6504	Small	Doulton	4"	1959	Current	22.50	65.00	80.00
D6524	Miniature	Doulton	2 1/2"	1960	Current	15.50	50.00	60.00

Miscellaneous "The Lawyer" Items

Doulton Number	Item	Height	Intro.	Discon.	Current Market Value U.K. £	U.S. $	Can. $
D6504	Table Lighter	3 1/2"	1962	1974	90.00	225.00	260.00

LEPRECHAUN

This wizened little elf is a legenday Irish sprite with a mischievous nature. The Irish believed that leprechauns guarded hoards of treasue hidden at the bottom of rainbows.

Designer: William K. Harper   **Handle:** Rainbow with a sack of gold at the base   **Backstamp:** See Backstamps

Colourway: Green cap, brown coat

BACKSTAMPS

A: Doulton

For General Release: 1991 (large) and 1992 (small)

B: Doulton / The Site of the Green (large)

Commissioned by The Site of The Green and issued in 1990 in a special edition of 500 pieces.

C: Doulton / The Site of The Green (small)

Commissioned by The Site of The Green and issued in 1991 in a special edition of 500 pieces.

Doulton Number	Size	Backstamp	Height	Intro.	Discon.	Current Market Value		
						U.K. £	U.S. $	Can. $
D6847	Large	Doulton	7 1/2"	1991	Current	57.00	175.00	195.00
D6847	Large	Doulton/Site	7 1/2"	1990	Sp. Ed.	100.00	195.00	225.00
D6899	Small	Doulton	4 1/2"	1992	Current	24.50	65.00	95.00
D6899	Small	Doulton/Site	4 1/2"	1991	Sp. Ed.	50.00	85.00	100.00

LITTLE MESTER MUSEUM PIECE

This jug was modelled on the likeness of Grinder Rowland Swindon, a grinder from Sheffield, England. One thousand jugs were bought by the World Student Games to help launch the games in Sheffield. Commissioned by John Sinclair, Sheffield, England. Issued in 1988 in a limited edition of 3,500 pieces.

Designer: Stanley J. Taylor   **Handle:** Bowie knife and grinder   **Backstamp:** Doulton / John Sinclair

Colourway: Black cap, blue jacket, white shirt and red scarf

Doulton Number	Size	Backstamp	Height	Intro.	Discon.	Current Market Value U.K. £	Current Market Value U.S. $	Current Market Value Can. $
D6819	Large	Doulton/Sinclair	6 3/4"	1988	Ltd. Ed.	65.00	150.00	175.00

LITTLE NELL

Little Nell is the ill-fated protagonist in Dickens' "The Old Curiosity Shop."

Issued to commemorate the 170th Anniversary of the birth of Charles Dickens. There are twelve jugs in this set, which were issued with a certificate of authenticity. A mahogany display shelf completes the set. The set was first sold by Lawley's By Post in the U.K. during 1982 to 1988, and in 1985 forward in North America and Austrialia.

SERIES: Charles Dickens Commemorative Set / Dickens Tinies, one of twelve.

> *Photograph*
> *Not Available*
> *At Press Time*

Designer: Michael Abberley   **Handle:** Plain   **Backstamp:** Doulton

Colourway: Yellow and black

Doulton Number	Size	Backstamp	Height	Intro.	Discon.	Current Market Value U.K. £	U.S. $	Can. $
D6681	Tiny	Doulton	1 1/2"	1982	1989	30.00	50.00	60.00

LOBSTER MAN

This hearty fisherman with the weathered face is out at sea in all weather, catching that hard-shelled creature that is such a delicacy to eat.

Royal Doulton®

LOBSTER MAN

D 6783

Modelled by

David B Biggs

© 1967 ROYAL DOULTON
NEW COLOURWAY 1987

LOBSTER MAN

D 6652

COPR 1967

DOULTON & CO LIMITED

Designer: David Biggs	**Handle:** Lobster	**Backstamp:** Doulton

Colourway: See Variations

VARIATIONS

VARIATION NO. 1: Colourway: Black cap, white fisherman's jersey

Doulton Number	Size	Backstamp	Height	Intro.	Discon.	Current Market Value U.K. £	U.S. $	Can. $
D6617	Large	Var. 1	7 1/2"	1968	Current	41.00	130.00	145.00
D6620	Small	Var. 1	3 3/4"	1968	Current	22.50	65.00	80.00
D6652	Miniature	Var. 1	2 3/4"	1980	Current	15.50	50.00	60.00

VARIATION NO. 2: Colourway: Dark blue cap, pale blue fisherman's jersey

Doulton Number	Size	Backstamp	Height	Intro.	Discon.	Current Market Value U.K. £	U.S. $	Can. $
D6783	Large	Var. 2	8"	1987	1989	45.00	130.00	150.00

THE LONDON 'BOBBY'

The constabulary of London have long been known by their affectionate nickname, "bobbies." Loyal and professional, they are never too busy to give directions to grateful visitors every year.

SERIES: The London Collection, one of ten.

Designer: Stanley J. Taylor   **Handle:** Tower of "Big Ben" and a whistle

Colourway: Black and white badge, see Variations

Backstamp: Doulton

Royal Doulton®
THE LONDON
'BOBBY'
D6744
Modelled by
Stanley James Taylor
© 1985 ROYAL DOULTON (UK)

VARIATIONS

VARIATION NO. 1: Hat badge embossed and hand painted

Doulton Number	Size	Variations	Height	Intro.	Discon.	Current Market Value U.K. £	U.S. $	Can. $
D6744	Large	Var. 1	7"	1986	1987	50.00	135.00	150.00

VARIATION NO. 2: Hat badge transfer decorated

Doulton Number	Size	Variations	Height	Intro.	Discon.	Current Market Value U.K. £	U.S. $	Can. $
D6744	Large	Var. 2	7 1/2"	1987	Current	47.00	130.00	145.00
D6762	Small	Var. 2	3 1/2"	1987	Current	24.50	65.00	80.00
D6763	Miniature	Var. 2	2 1/2"	1987	Current	16.50	50.00	60.00

LONG JOHN SILVER

This scoundrel pirate from Robert Louis Stevenson's famous adventure tale, "Treasure Island," had a wooden leg and a parrot companion. Together with the boy-hero Jim Hawkins, he set sail in a hair-raising search for buried treasure that has captured the imaginations of readers for over a century.

SERIES: Characters from Literature, one of eleven.

Designer: Max Henk   **Handle:** A Parrot

Colourway: See Variations

Backstamp: See Backstamps

`Long John Silver`
D.6335.
COPR 1951.
DOULTON & CO LIMITED
R⁴N° 864843.
R⁴N° 29156
R⁴N° 6404.
R⁴N° 112/51

VARIATIONS

VARIATION NO. 1: Colourway: Maroon shirt, green and grey parrot

BACKSTAMP: Doulton

Doulton Number	Size	Backstamp	Height	Intro.	Discon.	Current Market Value U.K. £	U.S. $	Can. $
D6335	Large	Doulton	7"	1952	Current	41.00	130.00	145.00
D6386	Small	Doulton	4"	1952	Current	22.50	65.00	80.00
D6512	Miniature	Doulton	2 1/2"	1960	Current	15.50	50.00	60.00

VARIATION NO. 2: Colourway: Yellow shirt, yellow-green parrot

BACKSTAMP: Doulton/D. H. Holmes "Specially Commissioned from Royal Doulton by D. H. Holmes Company Ltd. Celebrating the opening of The Royal Doulton Room D.H. Holmes, New Orleans, Louisiana, U.S.A."

Commissioned by D. H. Holmes Company Ltd. Issued in 1987 in a limited edition of 250 pieces

Doulton Number	Size	Backstamp	Height	Intro.	Discon.	Current Market Value U.K. £	U.S. $	Can. $
D6799	Large	Holmes	7"	1987	Ltd. Ed.	225.00	400.00	450.00

Miscellaneous "Long John Silver" Items

Doulton Number	Item	Height	Intro.	Discon.	Current Market Value U.K. £	U.S. $	Can. $
D6386	Lighter	3 1/2"	1958	1973	95.00	125.00	155.00
D6853	Teapot	7"	1990	Current	60.00	110.00	250.00

LORD MAYOR OF LONDON

The newly elected Mayor of the city of London first presents himself to the people on Mayor's Day. Annually, on the second Sunday in November, a procession takes the Mayor to Westminster to receive from the Lord Chancellor assent of the Crown to his election.

SERIES: The London Collection, one of ten.

Designer: Stanley J. Taylor   **Handle:** Sceptre of office   **Backstamp:** Doulton

Colourway: Black plume hat, red cloak and yellow chain of office.

Doulton Number	Size	Backstamp	Height	Intro.	Discon.	Current Market Value U.K. £	U.S. $	Can. $
D6864	Large	Doulton	7 1/4"	1990	Current	59.00	155.00	225.00

LORD NELSON

(1758-1805). Horatio Nelson, a member of the navy since the age of twelve, was made commander-in-chief of his own fleet in 1803. He saw action in the West Indies and Canada, but is most well-remembered for his courage at the battle of Trafalgar. In 1805 his fleet engaged and defeated the French and Spanish navies. Nelson died during the battle.

Designer: Geoff Blower   **Handle:** Plain   **Backstamp:** See Backstamps

Colourway: Blue tricorn and jacket with gold trim, white cravat

BACKSTAMPS

A: **Doulton**

B: **Doulton/Battle of Trafalgar "Commemorating the 150th Anniversary of the Battle of Trafalgar 21st October 1955"**

> Commissioned for the Admiralty to commemorate the 150th anniversary of Nelson's victory at Trafalgar, October 21st, 1955. Three of the jugs carry an added line to the backstamp, that of "First Lord", "First Sea Lord" and "Secretary," the intention being that these three jugs would be held in perpetuity at the respective offices.

Doulton Number	Size	Backstamp	Height	Intro.	Discon.	U.K. £	Current Market Value U.S. $	Can. $
D6336	Large	A	7"	1952	1969	250.00	425.00	500.00
D6336	Large	B	7"	1955	1955	750.00	1,250.00	1,500.00

LOUIS ARMSTRONG

(1900-1971). Daniel Louis Armstrong, ("Satchmo"), evolved from a self-taught cornet player at fourteen to the first internationally famous soloist in jazz music. He was well-known for both his brilliant technique on the trumpet and for his deep throaty singing voice. Appearing in many live shows, Broadway musicals and films, Armstrong's music made a lasting influence on jazz music.

SERIES: The Celebrity Collection, one of five.

THE CELEBRITY COLLECTION
by Royal Doulton
A hand-made, hand-decorated series
LOUIS ARMSTRONG ®
"Man, if you gotta ask, you'll never know"
(His reply when asked what Jazz was).

Designer: David Biggs   **Handle:** Trumpet and handkerchief   **Backstamp:** Doulton

Colourway: Brown and pink

Doulton Number	Size	Backstamp	Height	Intro.	Discon.	U.K. £	Current Market Value U.S. $	Can. $
D6707	Large	Doulton	7 1/2"	1984	1988	60.00	100.00	155.00

LUMBERJACK

From early colonial times, lumber has been one of Canada's main industries. The tasks of cutting down trees and hauling them to rivers for transportation was a dangerous and isolated one. These sturdy men would leave for "the bush" in the fall, to reappear with the logs in the spring thaw. Many legends have grown-up around this way of life. A small quantity of miniature prototypes are known to exist.

SERIES: Canadian Centennial Series 1867-1967, one of three.

Lumberjack
D 6610
COPR 1966
DOULTON & CO LIMITED
Rd No 924807
Rd No 49146
Rd No 10601
Rd No 53/66

CANADIAN CENTENNIAL SERIES
1867 - 1967

The Lumberjack
D 6610
COPR 1966
DOULTON & CO LIMITED
Rd No 924807
Rd No 49146
Rd No 10601
Rd No 53/66

Designer: Max Henk   **Handle:** Tree trunk and axe   **Backstamp:** See Backstamps

Colourway: Red cap, green jacket and white sweater

BACKSTAMPS

A: Doulton

B: Doulton / Canadian Centenary "Canadian Centennial Series 1867-1967"

Available in North America during 1967 only.

Doulton Number	Size	Backstamp	Height	Intro.	Discon.	Current Market Value U.K. £	Current Market Value U.S. $	Current Market Value Can. $
D6610	Large	Doulton	7 1/4"	1967	1982	55.00	90.00	155.00
D6610	Large	Centenary	7 1/4"	1967	1967	110.00	300.00	300.00
D6613	Small	Doulton	3 1/2"	1967	1982	35.00	60.00	95.00
D —	Miniature	Doulton	2 1/2"	Unknown		950.00	1,700.00	2,000.00

MACBETH

First perfomed in 1606, this Shakespearean tragedy is based upon Scottish history. With the help of his wife, Macbeth plots to usurp the throne. Three witches prophesy that he will succeed but that his enemy Banquo's heirs will one day rule the Kingdom. In a series of grisly events, their dark predicitons are fulfilled.

SERIES: The Shakespearean Collection, one of six.

Designer: Michael Abberley   **Handle:** The faces of the three witches are on the front of the handle facing forwards.   **Backstamp:** Doulton

Colourway: Brown, yellow and grey

Doulton Number	Size	Backstamp	Height	Intro.	Discon.	Current Market Value U.K. £	U.S. $	Can. $
D6667	Large	Doulton	7 1/4"	1982	1989	60.00	100.00	145.00

MACBETH

PROTOTYPE

This prototype jug has the faces of the three witches on the outer side of the handle. Only after the jug was in the final stages of completion did Doulton realize the hazards which might occur in shipping the jug. The possibility of the handle being damaged in packing was great.

Designer: Michael Abberley   **Handle:** Three witches facing to the right   **Backstamp:** Doulton

Colourway: Brown, yellow and grey

Doulton Number	Size	Backstamp	Height	Intro.	Discon.	Current Market Value		
						U.K. £	U.S. $	Can. $
D6667	Large	Doulton	7 1/4"	1981	1981		Extremely Rare	

MAD HATTER

A guest at a tea party which Alice attends uninvited, the Mad Hatter's watch keeps months rather than hours. The March Hare presides over tea and bread and butter, and the dormouse sleeps through the party.

SERIES: Alice in Wonderland, one of six.

Mad Hatter
D 6598
COPR 1970
DOULTON & CO LIMITED
Rd No 917231
Rd No 46577
Rd No 10000
Rd No 592/64

Designer: Max Henk   **Handle:** A dormouse above a pocket watch   **Backstamp:** See Backstamps

Colourway: See Variations

VARIATIONS

VARIATION NO. 1: Colourway: Black hat, dark red bow-tie

BACKSTAMP: Doulton

Doulton Number	Size	Variation	Height	Intro.	Discon.	Current Market Value U.K. £	U.S. $	Can. $
D6598	Large	Var. 1	7 1/4"	1965	1983	75.00	140.00	175.00
D6602	Small	Var. 1	3 3/4"	1965	1983	50.00	80.00	95.00
D6606	Miniature	Var. 1	2 1/2"	1965	1983	45.00	60.00	75.00

"MAD HATTER"
D. 6790
Specially Commissioned from
Royal Doulton®
by
THE HIGBEE COMPANY
To commemorate
the Second Anniversary of
the opening of
the First Royal Doulton Room
Higbee's, Cleveland, Ohio, U.S.A.
HAND MODELLED
AND HAND DECORATED
A LIMITED EDITION OF 500
THIS IS N° 2
© 1987 ROYAL DOULTON

VARIATION NO. 2: Colourway: Black hat, yellow bow-tie

BACKSTAMPS

A: Doulton/Higbee's (large)

> Commissioned by the Higbee Company to celebrate the opening of the Royal Doulton Room. Issued on October 28th, 1985 in a limited edition of 250 pieces.

B: Doulton/Higbee's (small)

> Commissioned by the Higbee Department Store to celebrate the second anniversary of the opening of the Royal Doulton Room.
> Issued in 1987 in a limited edition of 500 pieces.

Doulton Number	Size	Backstamp	Height	Intro.	Discon.	Current Market Value		
						U.K. £	U.S. $	Can. $
D6748	Large	A Higbee	7"	1985	Ltd. Ed.	375.00	650.00	750.00
D6790	Small	B Higbee	3 1/4"	1987	Ltd. Ed.	100.00	200.00	200.00

MAE WEST

(1892-1980). From her screen debut in 1932, Mae West became an instant hit. She is best known for the tough, sophisticated characters she played who loved luxury and men. The public adored her and her witty quips, the most famous of which appears on the base of the jug: "When I'm good, I'm very good. But when I'm bad, I'm better."

SERIES: The Celebrity Collection, one of five.

Designer: Colin M. Davidson

Handle: Umbrella with a bow tied around the handle

Backstamp: See Backstamps

Colourway: Yellow hair, white feather dress

BACKSTAMPS

A: Doulton

General Issue: 1983.

B: Doulton / American Express "Premier Edition for American Express"

This series was first introduced in the U.S.A. as a promotional jug for the American Express Company. Approximately five hundred jugs were given the special backstamp and were available only to the North American market.

Doulton Number	Size	Backstamp	Height	Intro.	Discon.	Current Market Value U.K. £	U.S. $	Can. $
D6688	Large	Doulton	7"	1983	1986	60.00	120.00	160.00
D6688	Large	Doulton/Amex	7"	1983	1983	250.00	500.00	600.00

MAORI

The Maori are a people of Polynesian descent who were the first inhabitants of present-day New Zealand. Beginning as hunters and fishers, the Maori later turned to agriculture. Master woodworkers, they are known for the complicated designs they carved on their houses and canoes. Today their population is about 300,000 or 9% of the whole of New Zealand.

STYLE ONE: *BLUE-GREY HAIR; FRIENDLY EXPRESSION*

Designer: Unknown   **Handle:** Plain with plaque of Maori   **Backstamp:** Doulton

Colourway: Brown and grey

Doulton Number	Size	Backstamp	Height	Intro.	Discon.	Current Market Value U.K. £	U.S. $	Can. $
D —	Large	Doulton	7"	1939	1939		Extremely Rare	

MAORI

STYLE TWO: *DARK HAIR, TWO WHITE TIPPED FEATHERS IN HAIR; SERIOUS FACIAL EXPRESSION*

Designer: Unknown   **Handle:** Plain with plaque of Maori   **Backstamp:** Doulton

Colourway: Brown and grey

Doulton Number	Size	Backstamp	Height	Intro.	Discon.	U.K. £	Current Market Value U.S. $	Can. $
D —	Large	Doulton	7"	1939	1939		Extremely Rare	

THE MARCH HARE

At the March Hare's home in Wonderland it is always 6 o'clock and time for tea. Not having a moment to tidy up in between, he and his friends the Mad Hatter and the dormouse sit at a table laid for a great number and change seats as they dirty the dishes. Alice makes herself unpopular by asking what they do when they arrive back at the beginning.

SERIES: Alice in Wonderland, one of six.

Royal Doulton®

THE MARCH HARE
D 6776
Modelled by

William K. Harper

© 1988 ROYAL DOULTON

Designer: William K. Harper   **Handle:** One of the hare's ears   **Backstamp:** Doulton

Colourway: Green hat, yellow bow-tie with blue spots

Doulton Number	Size	Backstamp	Height	Intro.	Discon.	Current Market Value		
						U.K. £	U.S. $	Can. $
D6776	Large	Doulton	6"	1989	Current	57.00	175.00	225.00

MARILYN MONROE

(1926-1962). Born Norma Jean Baker in Los Angeles, California, Monroe made her screen debut in 1948. Her beauty made her an international sex symbol and her career was a great success. Despite her fame, however, Monroe's private life was tragic -- she committed suicide by an overdose of sleeping pills at the age of thirty-six. Not issued due to copyright problems.

SERIES: The Celebrity Collection

PROTOTYPE

Designer: Eric Griffith **Handle:** A cine-camera encircled by a roll of film **Backstamp:** Doulton

Colourway: Yellow, white and grey

Doulton Number	Size	Variation	Height	Intro.	Discon.	U.K. £	Current Market Value U.S. $	Can. $
D —	Large	Prototype	7 1/4"	1983	1983		Extremely Rare	

MARK TWAIN

(1835-1910). Born Samuel Langhorne Clemens, Twain was an American writer and humourist, best loved for his classic adventure stories, "Tom Sawyer," (1876), and "The Adventures of Huckleberry Finn," (1884), which told of life in his native Mississippi.

The small jug was modelled for "The Queen's Table", Royal Doulton's Exhibit at the United Kingdom Showcase at Walt Disney's Epcot Centre in Orlando, Florida. The jug was sold exclusively to Epcot tourists visiting the exhibition during 1982.

Designer: Eric Griffiths   **Handle:** Quill and ink-pot

Colourway: Black coat and bow-tie, grey hair

Backstamp: Doulton

Royal Doulton
MARK TWAIN
D 6654
Modelled by

© ROYAL DOULTON TABLEWARE
LIMITED 1979

Doulton Number	Size	Backstamp	Height	Intro.	Discon.	Current Market Value U.K. £	U.S. $	Can. $
D6654	Large	Doulton	7 1/2"	1980	1990	45.00	75.00	145.00
D6694	Small	Doulton	4"	1983	1990	35.00	65.00	80.00
D6758	Miniature	Doulton	2 1/2"	1986	1990	30.00	55.00	60.00

THE MASTER (EQUESTRIAN)

Designer: Stanley J. Taylor   **Handle:** Horse head   **Backstamp:** Doulton

Colourway: Dark blue, red and white

Doulton Number	Size	Backstamp	Height	Intro.	Discon.	Current Market Value		
						U.K. £	U.S. $	Can. $
D6898	Small	Doulton	4"	1991	Current	27.50	70.00	100.00

McCALLUM

Produced as a promotional item for the D & J McCallum Distillery, Scotland, this jug exists in three different colour varieties, all in very limited quantities.

Designer: McCallum   **Handle:** Plain   **Backstamp:** Doulton

Colourway: See Variations

VARIATIONS

VARIATION NO. 1: Kingsware. Colourway: Light and dark browns.

Approximately 1,000 to 1,500 pieces were thought to have been made.

Doulton Number	Size	Variation	Height	Intro.	Discon.	U.K. £	Current Market Value U.S. $	Can. $
D269	Large	Kingsware glaze	7"	1930	Unknown	500.00	1,650.00	1,650.00

VARIATION NO. 2: Colourway: Ivory glaze.

Approximately 1,000 pieces

Doulton Number	Size	Variation	Height	Intro.	Discon.	Current Market Value U.K. £	U.S. $	Can. $
D270	Large	Ivory glaze	7"	1930	Unknown	600.00	950.00	950.00

VARIATION NO. 3: Colourway: Treacle body with green hat, collar and handle.

Doulton Number	Size	Variation	Height	Intro.	Discon.	Current Market Value U.K. £	U.S. $	Can. $
D270	Large	Treacle glaze	7"	1930	Unknown		Extremely Rare	

MEPHISTOPHELES
(Two-faced Jug)

First found in 16th century German legend, Mephistopheles became best-known in Johann von Geothe's drama, "Faust" (1808). He is portrayed as an evil spirit or devil to whom Faust sells his soul in return for services. Some of the jugs in this design are inscribed with the Rabelais verse:

> "When the devil was sick,
> The devil a saint would be.
> When the devil got well,
> the devil a saint was he."

Designer: Charles Noke
            Harry Fenton

Handle: Plain

Backstamp: See Backstamps

Colourway: Red and brown

BACKSTAMPS

A: Doulton/With verse

B: Doulton/Without verse

Doulton Number	Size	Backstamp	Height	Intro.	Discon.	Current Market Value U.K. £	U.S. $	Can. $
D5757	Large	With Verse	7"	1937	1948	900.00	950.00	2,200.00
D5757	Large	Without Verse	7"	1937	1948	850.00	1,850.00	2,200.00
D5758	Small		3 3/4"	1937	1948	450.00	950.00	1,100.00

MERLIN

In the legend of King Arthur of England, Merlin appears as wizard and aide to the King. He is credited with the manufacture of the famous Round Table as well as many prophesies.

SERIES: Characters from Literature, one of eleven.

Designer: Garry Sharpe

Handle: An owl

Colourway: Black, grey and brown

Backstamp: Doulton

Merlin
D 6543
COPR 1959
DOULTON & CO LIMITED
Rd No 893842
Rd No 39650
Rd No 8314
Rd No 41/959

Doulton Number	Size	Backstamp	Height	Intro.	Discon.	Current Market Value U.K. £	U.S. $	Can. $
D6529	Large	Doulton	7 1/4"	1960	Current	41.00	130.00	145.00
D6536	Small	Doulton	3 3/4"	1960	Current	22.50	65.00	80.00
D6543	Miniature	Doulton	2 3/4"	1960	Current	15.50	50.00	60.00

MICHAEL DOULTON

This jug was available only at stores where Michael Doulton made special appearances.

Designer: William K. Harper   **Handle:** Flag bearing the   **Backstamp:** Doulton
Royal Doulton logo

Colourway: Black, brown and blue

Doulton Number	Size	Backstamp	Height	Intro.	Discon.	Current Market Value		
						U.K. £	U.S. $	Can. $
D6808	Small	Doulton	4 1/4"	1988	1989	25.00	55.00	65.00

THE MIKADO

"Mikado," is the ancient title for the emperor of Japan. The Japanese ruling dynasty is considered to be one of the oldest in the world, with legend dating the reign of the Mikado Jimmu to 660 B.C. Believed by many to have descended from the all-powerful Sun Goddess, the same family line has been definitely traced through one hundred and twenty-four reigns. The "Mikado" is popularly known through the Gilbert and Sullivan operetta of the same name from 1885.

The Mikado
D 6 5 0 1
COPR 1958
DOULTON & CO LIMITED
Rd No 889572
Rd No 38228
Rd No 8038
Rd No 421,58

Designer: Max Henk   **Handle:** A Fan   **Backstamp:** Doulton

Colourway: Black and turquoise hat, green and white robes

Doulton Number	Size	Backstamp	Height	Intro.	Discon.	Current Market Value U.K. £	U.S. $	Can. $
D6501	Large	Doulton	6 1/2"	1959	1969	250.00	575.00	700.00
D6507	Small	Doulton	3 3/4"	1959	1969	150.00	325.00	425.00
D6525	Miniature	Doulton	2 1/2"	1960	1969	150.00	325.00	400.00

MINE HOST

The forerunner of today's English publican, this cheerful man would hang a pine bough on the door of his home to let travellers known that "refreshments" were available. As the handle shows, these often ran to a good pint of strong ale!

Mine Host
D.6513
COPR 1957
DOULTON & CO LIMITED
Rd No 888230
Rd No 37212
Rd No 7854
Rd No 389/57

Designer: Max Henk   **Handle:** Evergreen bough and barrel   **Backstamp:** Doulton

Colourway: Black tricorn, red coat, white bow-tie with gold spots

Doulton Number	Size	Backstamp	Height	Intro.	Discon.	Current Market Value U.K. £	U.S. $	Can. $
D6468	Large	Doulton	7"	1958	1982	50.00	100.00	155.00
D6470	Small	Doulton	3 1/2"	1958	1982	35.00	60.00	95.00
D6513	Miniature	Doulton	2 1/2"	1960	1982	25.00	50.00	75.00

MONTY

(1887-1976). Bernard Law, First Viscount Montgomery of Alamein was always referred familiarly as "Monty." The highlights of his long and distinguished military career included the first Allied victory of WWII in North Africa, in 1942, and the acceptance of the German surrender at Luneburg Heath in 1945. He was Deputy Supreme Commander of the Allied Powere in Europe from 1951 to 1958.

In 1954 a minor colourway change occurred when the yellow highlighting on the cap badge ceased.

Monty
D 6202

Designer: Harry Fenton   **Handle:** Plain   **Backstamp:** Doulton

Colourway: Brown beret, khaki uniform

Doulton Number	Size	Backstamp	Height	Intro.	Discon.	Current Market Value U.K. £	U.S. $	Can. $
D6202	Mid	Doulton	5 3/4"	1946	1991	41.00	130.00	145.00

MR BUMBLE

Mr. Bumble runs a local parish workhouse for orpans in Dickens' "Oliver Twist." The boy Oliver escapes from this dismal life and runs away to London.

Issued to commemorate the 170th Anniversary of the birth of Charles Dickens. There are twelve jugs in this set, which were issued with a certificate of authenticity. A mahogany display shelf completes the set. The set was first sold by Lawley's By Post in the U.K. during 1982 to 1988, and in 1985 forward in North America and Austrialia.

Series: Charles Dickens Commemorative Set / Dickens Tinies, one of twelve.

*Photograph
Not Available
At Press Time*

Designer: Robert Tabbenor   **Handle:** Plain   **Backstamp:** Doulton

Colourway: Yellow, dark blue and green

Doulton Number	Size	Backstamp	Height	Intro.	Discon.	Current Market Value U.K. £	U.S. $	Can. $
D6686	Tiny	Doulton	1 1/2"	1982	1989	30.00	50.00	60.00

MR MICAWBER

Wilkins Micawber, in Charles Dickins' classic, is David Copperfield's landlord and friend. A sauguine idler, Micawber unmasks Uriah Heap as a villian and is rewarded with passage to Australia where he settles happily in a prominent neighbourhood.

Designer: Leslie Harradine　　　　**Handle:** Plain　　　　**Backstamp:** Doulton
Harry Fenton

Colourway: Black hat, green coat and blue polka-dot bow-tie

Doulton Number	Size	Backstamp	Height	Intro.	Discon.	Current Market Value U.K. £	U.S. $	Can. $
D5843	Mid	Doulton	5 1/2"	1938	1948	90.00	175.00	200.00
D5843	Small	Doulton	3 1/4"	1948	1960	50.00	100.00	125.00
D6138	Miniature	Doulton	2 1/4"	1940	1960	35.00	50.00	75.00
D6143	Tiny	Doulton	1 1/4"	1940	1960	45.00	100.00	135.00

Miscellaneous "Mr Micawber" Items

Doulton Number	Item	Height	Intro.	Discon.	Current Market Value U.K. £	U.S. $	Can. $
D5843	Table Lighter	3 1/2"	1958	1959	90.00	200.00	250.00
D6050	Bust	2 1/4"	1939	1960	60.00	100.00	130.00
HN1615	Bookend	4"	1934	c. 1939	1,000.00	2,000.00	2,500.00
M58	Napkin Ring	3 1/2"	c. 1935	1939	350.00	600.00	700.00

MR PICKWICK

Founder and chairman of the Pickwick Club, this gentleman is the elegant and genial hero of Charles Dickens' "The Posthumous Papers of the Pickwick Club," first published in 1837.

Designer: Leslie Harradine   **Handle:** Plain   **Backstamp:** Doulton
Harry Fenton

Colourway: Green hat, brown coat, red bow-tie

Doulton Number	Size	Backstamp	Height	Intro.	Discon.	Current Market Value U.K. £	U.S. $	Can. $
D6060	Large	Doulton	7"	1940	1960	75.00	140.00	195.00
D5839	Mid	Doulton	4 1/4"	1938	1948	90.00	170.00	240.00
D5839	Small	Doulton	3 1/2"	1948	1960	45.00	65.00	110.00
D6254?	Miniature	Doulton	2 1/4"	1947	1960	40.00	65.00	90.00
D6260	Tiny	Doulton	1 1/4"	1947	1960	90.00	225.00	275.00

Miscellaneous "Mr Pickwick" Items

Doulton Number	Item	Height	Intro.	Discon.	Current Market Value U.K. £	U.S. $	Can. $
D5839	Table Lighter	3 1/2"	1958	1961	125.00	250.00	250.00
D6049	Bust	3 1/2"	1939	1960	65.00	95.00	125.00
HN1623	Bookend	4"	1934	c. 1939	450.00	800.00	900.00
M57	Napkin Ring	3 1/2"	c. 1935	c. 1939	325.00	550.00	650.00

MR QUAKER

These jugs were made as an advertising piece for the internal use of Quaker Oats Limited and the Royal Doulton International Collectors Club. They were issued with a certificate signed by Sir Richard Bailey, CBE and Michael Doulton.

Commissioned by Quaker Oats Limited. Issued in 1985 in a limited edition of 3,500 pieces.

D.6738
MR QUAKER ®
Specially Commissioned from
Royal Doulton ®
by
© QUAKER OATS LIMITED 1984
in celebration of the
Company's 85th year
Hand modelled & Hand Painted
Designed by *Harry Sales*
Modelled by *John G Tongue*
A LIMITED EDITION OF 3,500
of which this is no 1811

Designer: Harry Sales   **Handle:** A sheaf of wheat   **Backstamp:** Doulton/ Quaker Oats Ltd

Colourway: Black, white and yellow

Doulton Number	Size	Backstamp	Height	Intro.	Discon.	Current Market Value		
						U.K. £	U.S. $	Can. $
D6738	Large	Doulton/Quaker	7 1/2"	1985	Ltd. Ed.	195.00	425.00	500.00

MRS BARDELL

In Dickens' "The Pickwick Papers," Mrs. Bardell sues Mr. Pickwick for breach of promise.
Issued to commemorate the 170th Anniversary of the birth of Charles Dickens. There are twelve jugs in this set, which were issued with a certificate of authenticity. A mahogany display shelf completes the set. The set was first sold by Lawley's By Post in the U.K. during 1982 to 1988, and in 1985 forward in North America and Austrialia.

SERIES: Charles Dickens Commemorative Set / Dickens Tinies, one of twelve.

*Photograph
Not Available
At Press Time*

Designer: Robert Tabbenor   **Handle:** Plain   **Backstamp:** Doulton

Colourway: Yellow and green

Doulton Number	Size	Backstamp	Height	Intro.	Discon.	Current Market Value		
						U.K. £	U.S. $	Can. $
D6687	Tiny	Doulton	1 1/2"	1982	1989	30.00	50.00	60.00

NAPOLEON AND JOSEPHINE

Napoleon (1769-1821). "Le petit Caporal," standing only 5'2", was a military genius who amassed an empire that covered most of western and central Europe.

Josephine (1763-1814). The daughter of a French planter from Martinique, West Indies, Josephine first married Vicomte de Beauharnais at the age of seventeen. The Vicomte was killed during the Reign of Terror in the French Revolution and Josephine was imprisoned and nearly guillotined. As a member of fashionable society in Paris, she met Napoleon and married him in 1796. Unable to produce a child to satisfy the need for an heir, Napoleon divorced Josephine in 1809 to marry a younger woman.

Issued in 1986 in a limited edition of 9,500 pieces.

SERIES: Star Crossed Lovers (Two Faced Jug), one of four.

Designer: Michael Abberley

Handle: The French flag backed by a fan and mirror

Colourway: Black, white, yellow and brown

Backstamp: Doulton

Royal Doulton®

THE
S*TAR-CROSSED* **L***OVERS*
COLLECTION

Napoleon & Josephine
D 6750

Modelled by Michael Abberley.

Worldwide Limited Edition of 9,500
This is Number 1976
© 1985 Royal Doulton (UK)

Doulton Number	Size	Backstamp	Height	Intro.	Discon.	Current Market Value U.K. £	U.S. $	Can. $
D6750	Large	Doulton	7"	1986	Ltd. Ed.	63.00	120.00	195.00

NEPTUNE

In Roman mythology, Neptune is the god of the sea, horses and earthquakes. According to legend Neptune married the sea nymph Amphitrite and together they had a son named Triton who was half man and half fish.

Neptune
D 6552
COPR 1960
DOULTON & CO LIMITED
Rd No 897937
Rd No 40887
Rd No 8596
Rd No 547/60

Designer: Max Henk   **Handle:** A fish   **Backstamp:** Doulton

Colourway: White and green

Doulton Number	Size	Backstamp	Height	Intro.	Discon.	Current Market Value U.K. £	U.S. $	Can. $
D6548	Large	Doulton	6 1/2"	1961	1991	41.00	130.00	145.00
D6552	Small	Doulton	3 3/4"	1961	1991	22.50	65.00	80.00
D6555	Miniature	Doulton	2 1/2"	1961	1991	15.50	50.00	60.00

NIGHT WATCHMAN

When the sun sets and his colleague the guardsman's duty is over, the night watchman takes charge. Throughout the long "graveyard shift" he admits late travellers and looks out for any threat to the Williamsburg, Virginia, fortress.

SERIES: Character Jugs from Williamsburg, one of seven.

*Character Jugs from Williamsburg
Night Watchman*
D 6569
COPR 1962
DOULTON & CO LIMITED
Rd No 906339
Rd No 43446
Rd No 9225
Rd No 205/62

Designer: Max Henk   **Handle:** Lantern   **Backstamp:** Doulton

Colourway: Black-purple tricorn and cloak

Doulton Number	Size	Backstamp	Height	Intro.	Discon.	Current Market Value U.K. £	U.S. $	Can. $
D6569	Large	Doulton	7"	1963	1983	50.00	100.00	145.00
D6576	Small	Doulton	3 1/2"	1963	1983	40.00	65.00	95.00
D6583	Miniature	Doulton	2 1/2"	1963	1983	35.00	50.00	80.00

NORTH AMERICAN INDIAN

The misnomer "Indian" can be attributed to Christopher Columbus' landing in what he thought was the West Indies. The original inhabitants of North America, these people occupied most of the continent in different and unique cultures. Early white settlers, in the selfish pursuit of land and riches, massacred and subdued so many of these First Peoples that today much of their way of life has been forever destroyed.

SERIES: Canadian Centennial Series 1867-1967, one of three.

North American Indian
D 6614
COPR 1966
DOULTON & CO LIMITED
Rd No 924806
Rd No 49145
Rd No 10602
Rd No 54/66

CANADIAN CENTENNIAL SERIES
1867 — 1967

North American Indian
D 6611
COPR 1966
DOULTON & CO LIMITED
Rd No 924806
Rd No 49145
Rd No 10602
Rd No 54/66

OKOBOJI
75 ANNIVERSARY
1973

Designer: Max Henk	**Handle:** A totem pole
	Colourway: See Variations
	Backstamp: See Backstamps

North American Indian
D 6611
COPR 1966
DOULTON & CO LIMITED
Rd No 924806
Rd No 49145
Rd No 10602
Rd No 54/66

VARIATIONS

VARIATION NO. 1: Colourway: Red, white and black feathers, yellow and white band, green robes.
Handle: Dark brown.

BACKSTAMPS

A: Doulton

B: Doulton/Canadian Centenary "Canadian Centennial Series 1867-1967"

Available only in North America during 1967

C: Doulton/"Okoboji 75 Anniversary 1973"

Issued for the 75th Anniversary of the Okoboji trap shooting club. 180 jugs were presented to the club members at the 1973 annual "Pow-Wow".

Doulton Number	Size	Backstamp	Height	Intro.	Discon.	Current Market Value U.K. £	Current Market Value U.S. $	Current Market Value Can. $
D6611	Large	A	7 3/4"	1967	1991	41.00	130.00	145.00
D6611	Large	B	7 3/4"	1967	1967	110.00	350.00	300.00
D6611	Large	C	7 3/4"	1973	1973	425.00	750.00	850.00
D6614	Small	A	4 1/4"	1967	1991	22.50	65.00	80.00
D6665	Miniature	A	2 3/4"	1981	1991	15.50	50.00	60.00

Royal Doulton®

NORTH AMERICAN INDIAN

D 6786

Modelled by

© 1966 ROYAL DOULTON
NEW COLOURWAY 1987
SPECIAL EDITION OF 1,000
FOR JOHN SINCLAIR SHEFFIELD

VARIATION NO. 2: Colourway: Yellow, blue, white and black feathers, green and white band, orange robes. Handle: Light brown.

BACKSTAMP: Doulton / John Sinclair

Commissioned by John Sinclair, Sheffield, England. Issued in 1987 in a special edition of 1,000 pieces

Doulton Number	Size	Backstamp	Height	Intro.	Discon.	Current Market Value U.K. £	Current Market Value U.S. $	Current Market Value Can. $
D6786	Large	Doulton/Sinclair	7 1/2"	1987	Sp. Ed.	35.00	100.00	195.00

OLD CHARLEY

"10 o'clock and all's well" was the familiar call of the "Charlies," watchmen who originated in the reign of Charles II and were named after him. They enjoyed a career of almost two hundred years duration before finally being replaced by an early version of the present-day policeman, in the early 1800's.

Old Charley
D5420
DOULTON & CO LIMITED

1936

Designer: Charles Noke

Handle: Plain

Colourway: See Variations

Backstamp: See Backstamps

VARIATIONS

VARIATION NO. 1: Colourway: Brown hat, dark green coat, blue polka-dot bow-tie.

BACKSTAMPS

A: **Doulton**

B: **Doulton/Bentalls "Souvenir from Bentalls Jubilee Year 1935"**

Bentalls Ltd, a London Department Store.

C: **Doulton/Bentalls "Souvenir from Bentalls 1936"**

Doulton Number	Size	Backstamp	Height	Intro.	Discon.	Current Market Value U.K. £	U.S. $	Can. $
D5420	Large	Doulton	5 1/2"	1934	1983	50.00	85.00	125.00
D5527	Small	Doulton	3 1/4"	1935	1983	30.00	50.00	95.00
D5527	Small	Bentalls B	3 1/4"	1935	1935	350.00	600.00	850.00
D5527	Small	Bentalls C	3 1/4"	1936	1936	350.00	600.00	850.00
D6046	Miniature	Doulton	2 1/4"	1939	1983	25.00	40.00	70.00
D6144	Tiny	Doulton	1 1/4"	1940	1960	45.00	100.00	135.00

VARIATION NO. 2: Colourway: Black hat, maroon coat, black polka-dot bow-tie.

BACKSTAMPS

A: Doulton/Higbee "Specially Commissioned from Royal Doulton by The Higbee
Company To Commemorate the First Anniversary of the Opening
of the First Royal Doulton Room Higbee's, Cleveland, Ohio, U.S.A."

Commissioned by the Higbee Department Store to celebrate the first anniversary of the opening of the Higbee Doulton Shop in 1985. Issued in 1986 in a limited edition of 250 pieces.

B: Doulton/Higbee "Specially Commissioned from Royal Doulton by The Higbee
Company To Commemorate the Second Anniversary of the Opening
of the First Royal Doulton Room Higbee's, Cleveland, Ohio, U.S.A."

Commissioned by the Higbee Department Store to celebrate the second anniversary of the opening of the Royal Doulton Room.

Doulton Number	Size	Backstamp	Height	Intro.	Discon.	Current Market Value U.K. £	U.S. $	Can. $
D6761	Large	A Higbee	5 1/2"	1986	1986	350.00	400.00	525.00
D6791	Small	B Higbee	3 1/4"	1987	1987	145.00	200.00	230.00

Miscellaneous "Old Charley" Items

Doulton Number	Item	Height	Intro.	Discon.	Current Market Value U.K. £	U.S. $	Can. $
D5227	Table Lighter	3 1/2"	1959	1973	90.00	160.00	180.00
D5844	Tobacco Jar	5 1/2"	1937	1960	750.00	1,500.00	1,850.00
D5858	Musical Jug	5 1/2"	1938	1939	350.00	725.00	850.00
D5599	Ashtray	2 3/4	1936	1960	60.00	100.00	120.00
D5925	Ash Bowl	3"	1939	1960	60.00	100.00	120.00
D6012	Sugar Bowl	2 1/2"	1939	1960	350.00	1,000.00	1,200.00
D6017	Teapot	7"	1939	1960	750.00	1,500.00	1,850.00
D6110	Wall Pocket	7 1/4"	1940	1960	750.00	1,600.00	1,950.00
D6152	Toothpick Holder	2 1/4"	1940	1960	350.00	600.00	700.00

Note: Tune played on musical jug is "Here's a Health Unto His Majesty."

OLD KING COLE

"Old King Cole was a merry old soul," the ever-popular nursery rhyme, inspired the design of this cheerful and benevolent ruler.

The collar frill was remodelled circa 1939, variation number two can be found with both deep and shallow white ruff modellings.

Designer: Harry Fenton   **Handle:** Plain   **Backstamp:** See Backstamps

Colourway: See Variations

VARIATIONS

VARIATION NO. 1: Colourway: Yellow crown, frills in the white ruff are deep and pronounced.

BACKSTAMP: Doulton

Doulton Number	Size	Variations	Height	Intro.	Discon.	Current Market Value U.K. £	U.S. $	Can. $
D6036	Large	Var. 1	5 3/4"	1938	1939	1,200.00	5,000.00	5,000.00
D6037	Small	Var. 1	3 1/2"	1938	1939	900.00	2,500.00	2,750.00

VARIATION NO. 2: Colourway: Brown crown.

BACKSTAMPS

A: Doulton

B: Doulton/Royal Doulton International Collectors Club

Doulton Number	Size	Backstamp	Height	Intro.	Discon.	Current Market Value U.K. £	U.S. $	Can. $
D6036	Large	A	5 3/4"	1939	1960	120.00	275.00	295.00
D6037	Small	A	3 1/2"	1939	1960	90.00	150.00	195.00
D6871	Tiny	B	1 1/2"	1990	1990	45.00	50.00	95.00

Miscellaneous "Old King Cole" Items

Musical Jug

Doulton Number	Variation	Height	Intro.	Discon.	Current Market Value U.K. £	U.S. $	Can. $
D —	Yellow Crown	7 1/2"	1939	1939	1,500.00	3,000.00	3,500.00
D6014	Brown Crown	7 1/2"	1939	1939	750.00	1,700.00	2,000.00

Note: Tune played on musical jug "Old King Cole was a Merry Old Soul."

OLD SALT

With their weather-hardened faces and bottomless repetoire of stories, these retired seamen never tire of explaining just where they saw that mermaid.

When the minature jug was launched in 1984 it originally had a hollow crook in the mermaid's arm. Late that year, because of production problems, the arm was moulded as one with the body. The first versions of this miniature have attained almost "pilot" status and command a large premium over the general issue.

Old Salt
D 6551
COPR 1960
DOULTON & CO LIMITED
Rd No 898030
Rd No 40938
Rd No 8616
Rd No 572/60

Designer: Gary Sharpe , Large
and Small
Peter Gee, Miniature

Handle: A mermaid

Backstamp: Doulton

Colourway: See Variations

VARIATIONS

VARIATION NO. 1: Colourway: Dark blue fisherman's jersey.
Handle: Mermaid has blue tail.

Doulton Number	Size	Variation	Height	Intro.	Discon.	Current Market Value U.K. £	U.S. $	Can. $
D6551	Large	Var. 1	7 1/2"	1961	Current	41.00	130.00	145.00
D6554	Small	Var. 1	4"	1961	Current	22.50	65.00	80.00
D6557	Miniature	Var. 1	2 1/2"	1984	Current	15.50	50.00	60.00
D6557	Miniature	Pilot	2 1/2"	1984	1984	600.00	1,200.00	1,200.00

Royal Doulton®
OLD SALT
D 6782
Modelled by

Gary Sharpe

© 1960 ROYAL DOULTON
NEW COLOURWAY 1987

VARIATION NO. 2: Colourway: Light and dark blue fisherman's jersey.
Handle: Mermaid has yellow and black tail.

Doulton Number	Size	Variation	Height	Intro.	Discon.	Current Market Value U.K. £	U.S. $	Can. $
D6782	Large	Var. 2	8"	1987	1990	41.00	100.00	145.00

OLD SALT
EXCLUSIVELY FOR
COLLECTORS CLUB
© 1986 ROYAL DOULTON
MODELLED BY

Miscellaneous "Old Salt" Items

Doulton Number	Item	Height	Intro.	Discon.	Current Market Value U.K. £	U.S. $	Can. $
D6818	Teapot*	6 1/4"	1989	1989	95.00	150.00	295.00

* Issued for RDICC

OLIVER TWIST

The hero of Dickens' novel of Victoria, London, Oliver is and orphan who runs away from a workhouse to the city, only to be forced into thieving for the wicked Fagin.

Issued to commemorate the 170th Anniversary of the birth of Charles Dickens. There are twelve jugs in this set, which were issued with a certificate of authenticity. A mahogany display shelf completes the set. The set was first sold by Lawley's By Post in the U.K. during 1982 to 1988, and in 1985 forward in North America and Austrialia.

SERIES: Charles Dickens Commemorative Set / Dickens Tinies, one of twelve.

*Photograph
Not Available
At Press Time*

Designer: Robert Tabbenor   **Handle:** Plain   **Backstamp:** Doulton

Colourway: Dark and light blue

Doulton Number	Size	Backstamp	Height	Intro.	Discon.	U.K. £	Current Market Value U.S. $	Can. $
D6677	Tiny	Doulton	1 1/2"	1982	1989	30.00	50.00	60.00

OTHELLO

In Shakespeare's tragic play, (1604), Othello is a successful soldier to the Venetian state who marries the attractive Desdemona. His subordinate Iago, out of spite and jealousy, convinces Othello that Desdemona has been unfaithful. Outraged, Othello kills her then commits suicide from grief.

SERIES: The Shakespearean Collection, one of six.

© ROYAL DOULTON TABLEWARE LIMITED 1982
D 6673
The
Shakespearean
Collection
OTHELLO
A series of hand-made, hand-decorated Character Jugs by
Royal Doulton

Designer: Michael Abberley   **Handle:** A figure of Iago   **Backstamp:** Doulton

Colourway: Yellow turban, green, yellow and white robes

Doulton Number	Size	Backstamp	Height	Intro.	Current Market Value Discon.	U.K. £	U.S. $	Can. $
D6673	Large	Doulton	7 1/4"	1982	1989	60.00	100.00	145.00

PADDY

Paddy, a colloquial term for an Irishman, is derived from St. Patrick, the country's patron saint. Annually, on the 17th of March, a holiday is celebrated in his honour. This gent is dressed for the occasion in the green that is traditionally worn.

"Paddy."

Designer: Harry Fenton   **Handle:** Plain   **Backstamp:** Doulton

Colourway: Brown hat, green coat, yellow and red scarf

Doulton Number	Size	Backstamp	Height	Intro.	Discon.	Current Market Value U.K. £	U.S. $	Can. $
D5753	Large	Doulton	6"	1937	1960	65.00	150.00	200.00
D5768	Small	Doulton	3 1/4"	1937	1960	45.00	70.00	110.00
D6042	Miniature	Doulton	2 1/4"	1939	1960	35.00	50.00	85.00
D6145	Tiny	Doulton	1 1/4"	1940	1960	45.00	100.00	135.00

Miscellaneous "Paddy" Items

Doulton Number	Item	Backstamp	Height	Intro.	Discon.	Current Market Value U.K. £	U.S. $	Can. $
D5845	Tobacco Jar	Doulton	5 1/2"	1939	1942	750.00	1,500.00	1,850.00
D5845	Tobacco Jar	Salt River	5 1/2"	1939	1942	1,000.00	1,700.00	2,000.00
D5845	Tobacco Jar	Coleman's	5 1/2"	1939	1942	1,000.00	1,700.00	2,000.00
D5887	Musical Jug	Doulton	7"	1938	c. 1939	350.00	725.00	850.00
D5926	Ash bowl	Doulton	3"	1938	1960	60.00	120.00	140.00
D6151	Toothpick Holder	Doulton	2 1/4"	1940	1941	350.00	600.00	675.00

Note: Tune played on musical jug is "An Irish Jig."

PARSON BROWN

Typical of the country clergy found in England, Parson Brown would live in a home supplied by his church. In rural areas, the parsonage was often the cultural as well as spiritual centre of a village.

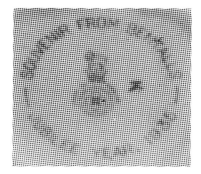

Designer: Charles Noke **Handle:** Plain **Backstamp:** See Backstamps

Colourway: Dark green

BACKSTAMPS

A: Doulton

B: Doulton/Bentalls "Souvenir from Bentalls Jubilee Year 1935"

Commissioned by Bentalls to celebrate the silver jubilee of King George VI.

Doulton Number	Size	Backstamp	Height	Intro.	Discon.	Current Market Value U.K. £	U.S. $	Can. $
D5486	Large	Doulton	6 1/2"	1935	1960	65.00	150.00	175.00
D5529	Small	Doulton	3 1/4"	1935	1960	45.00	70.00	110.00
D5529	Small	Doulton/Bentalls	3 1/4"	1935	1935	350.00	600.00	650.00

Miscellaneous "Parson Brown" Items

Doulton Number	Size	Backstamp	Height	Intro.	Discon.	Current Market Value U.K. £	U.S. $	Can. $
D5600	Ash Tray	Doulton	3 1/2"	1936	1960	85.00	120.00	170.00
D6008	Ash Bowl	Doulton	3"	1939	1960	85.00	120.00	170.00

PAUL McCARTNEY

(b. 1942). Singer/songwriter for the Beatles until 1970, McCartney went on to form his own successful band "Wings," who played together from 1971-1981. He remains active in the music field, writing and playing with various artists and on his own.

Issued only in Great Britain for copyright reasons.

SERIES: The Beatles, one of four.

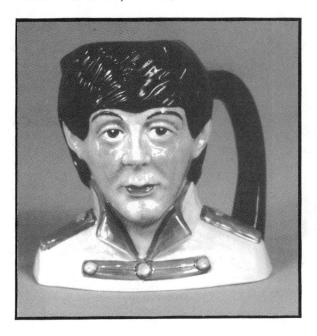

Royal Doulton
THE BEATLES
Paul McCartney
D 6724
Modelled by
Stanley James Taylor.
© ROYAL DOULTON TABLEWARE
LIMITED 1984

Designer: Stanley J. Taylor   **Handle:** Plain   **Backstamp:** Doulton

Colourway: Yellow tunic trimmed with blue collar and epaulettes

Doulton Number	Size	Backstamp	Height	Intro.	Discon.	Current Market Value		
						U.K. £	U.S. $	Can. $
D6724	Mid	Doulton	5 1/2"	1984	1991	45.00	60.00	95.00

PEARLY BOY

Pearly Boy is a coster or costermonger, who sold fruits and vegetables from a barrow in the streets of London. When he is dressed in his finest, pearl buttons or "pearlies" sewn to his clothes, he is known as Pearly Boy. 'Arry is Pearly Boy without his buttons. Please see 'Arry on page 18.

Designer: Harry Fenton   **Handle:** Plain   **Backstamp:** Doulton

Colourway: See Variations

VARIATIONS

VARIATION NO. 1: Colourway: Brown hat, blue coat, white buttons.

Doulton Number	Size	Variation	Height	Intro.	Discon.	Current Market Value U.K. £	Current Market Value U.S. $	Current Market Value Can. $
D —	Large	Var. 1	6 1/2"	1947	Unknown	3,500.00	5,500.00	6,500.00
D —	Small	Var. 1	3 1/2"	1947	Unknown	1,700.00	3,000.00	3,500.00
D —	Miniature	Var. 1	2 1/2"	1947	Unknown		Extremely Rare	

VARIATION NO. 2: Colourway: Brown hat, brown coat, white buttons.

Doulton Number	Size	Variation	Height	Intro.	Discon.	Current Market Value U.K. £	Current Market Value U.S. $	Current Market Value Can. $
D —	Large	Var. 2	6 1/2"	1947	Unknown	975.00	2,100.00	2,500.00
D —	Small	Var. 2	3 1/2"	1947	Unknown	750.00	1,275.00	1,500.00
D —	Miniature	Var. 2	2 1/2"	1947	Unknown	475.00	800.00	950.00

VARIATION NO. 3: Colourway: Brown hat, coat and buttons.

Doulton Number	Size	Variation	Height	Intro.	Discon.	Current Market Value U.K. £	U.S. $	Can. $
D —	Large	Var. 3	6 1/2"		Unknown	975.00	2,100.00	2,500.00
D —	Small	Var. 3	3 1/2"		Unknown	700.00	1,275.00	1,500.00
D —	Miniature	Var. 3	2 1/2"		Unknown	475.00	800.00	950.00

VARIATION NO. 4: Colourway: Beige hat, brown coat, white buttons.

Doulton Number	Size	Variation	Height	Intro.	Discon.	Current Market Value U.K. £	U.S. $	Can. $
D —	Large	Var. 4	6 1/2"		Unknown	975.00	2,100.00	2,500.00
D —	Small	Var. 4	3 1/2"		Unknown	700.00	1,275.00	1,500.00
D —	Miniature	Var. 4	2 1/2"		Unknown	475.00	800.00	950.00

PEARLY GIRL

Pearly Girl is Pearly Boy's female counterpart. She was a costermonger who sold her produce in the streets of London. Pearly Girl is 'Arriet dressed in her finest. Please see 'Arriet on page 17.

Designer: Harry Fenton	**Handle:** Hat feather	**Backstamp:** Doulton

Colourway: See Variations

VARIATIONS

VARIATION NO. 1: Colourway: Blue jacket, lime green feather, maroon hat and button, red scarf

Doulton Number	Size	Variation	Height	Intro.	Discon.	Current Market Value U.K. £	Current Market Value U.S. $	Current Market Value Can. $
D —	Large	Var. 1	6 1/2"	1946	Unknown		Extremely Rare	
D —	Small	Var. 1	3 1/4"	1946	Unknown	2,400.00	4,000.00	4,750.00

VARIATION NO. 2: Colourway: Dark brown jacket, lime green feather, pink hat and button

Doulton Number	Size	Variation	Height	Intro.	Discon.	Current Market Value U.K. £	Current Market Value U.S. $	Current Market Value Can. $
D —	Large	Var. 2	6 1/2"	1946	Unknown		Extremely Rare	
D —	Small	Var. 2	3 1/4"	1946	Unknown		Extremely Rare	

PEARLY KING

The Pearly King is the head spokesman of the street market costers of London. Over a hundred years ago his chief mandate was go between for the costers with the London police, but now with this need diminishing, the "Pearlies" have turned their energy to raising money for charity. With the elaborate pearl button designs sewn on their clothes they can bee seen at all the main function held throughout the year.

SERIES: The London Collection, one of ten.

Designer: Stanley J. Taylor   **Handle:** The "Bow Bells" and pearl buttons

Colourway: Black cap and jacket with silver buttons, yellow scarf

Backstamp: Doulton

Royal Doulton®

PEARLY KING

D 6760

Modelled by

Stanley James Taylor.

© 1986 ROYAL DOULTON

Doulton Number	Size	Backstamp	Height	Intro.	Discon.	Current Market Value U.K. £	U.S. $	Can. $
D6760	Large	Doulton	6 3/4"	1987	Current	47.00	130.00	145.00
D6844	Small	Doulton	3 1/2"	1990	Current	24.50	65.00	90.00

PEARLY QUEEN

The Pearly Queen, like the Pearly King, is the chief spokesperson for the street market costers of London. The office is both herediatry and elected.

SERIES: The London Collection, one of ten.

Designer: Stanley J. Taylor

Handle: The "Bow Bells" with pink and blue feathers

Colourway: Black coat with silver buttons, black hat with white, pink and blue feathers

Backstamp: Doulton

Royal Doulton®

PEARLY QUEEN

D 6759

Modelled by

Stanley James Taylor.

© 1986 ROYAL DOULTON

Doulton Number	Size	Backstamp	Height	Intro.	Discon.	Current Market Value		
						U.K. £	U.S. $	Can. $
D6759	Large	Doulton	7"	1987	Current	47.00	130.00	145.00
D6843	Small	Doulton	3 1/2"	1990	Current	24.50	65.00	90.00

THE PENDLE WITCH

This jug was the first and only jug issued in the proposed series Myths, Fantasies and Legends. Commissioned and distributed by Kevin Francis Ceramics (KFC). Issued in 1989 in a special edition of 5,000 pieces.

Designer: Stanley J. Taylor   **Handle:** A Hound   **Backstamp:** Doulton / Kevin Francis

Colourway: Grey hair, black dress

Doulton Number	Size	Backstamp	Height	Intro.	Discon.	Current Market Value		
						U.K. £	U.S. $	Can. $
D6826	Large	Doulton/KFC	7 1/4"	1989	Sp. Ed.	60.00	140.00	195.00

PIED PIPER

In the German legend, the town of Hamelin was infested with rats. A stranger came to town and told the mayor he would solved the problem for a sum of money. He walked through town playing a flute and the rats followed him to the Weser river where they drowned.

When the mayor refused to pay him, the Pied Piper again played his flute, and this time the village children followed him into a cave, never to be seen again.

STYLE ONE: *HANDLE: THREE BROWN RATS / FLUTE*

Pied Piper
D 6403
COPR 1953
DOULTON & CO LIMITED

Designer: Geoff Blower   **Handle:** Three brown rats atop a flute   **Backstamp:** Doulton

Colourway: Green cap, maroon and yellow tunic

Doulton Number	Size	Backstamp	Height	Intro.	Discon.	Current Market Value U.K. £	U.S. $	Can. $
D6403	Large	Doulton	7"	1954	1981	50.00	100.00	155.00
D6462	Small	Doulton	3 3/4"	1957	1981	30.00	60.00	90.00
D6514	Miniature	Doulton	2 5/8"	1960	1981	30.00	45.00	80.00

PIED PIPER

PROTOTYPE

STYLE TWO: *HANDLE: ONE WHITE RAT / FLUTE*

Designer: Geoff Blower   **Handle:** White rat at the top of a dark brown flute.   **Backstamp:** Doulton

Colourway: Light brown hat, blond hair

Doulton Number	Size	Variation	Height	Intro.	Discon.	Current Market Value U.K. £	U.S. $	Can. $
D6403	Large	Prototype	7"		Unknown		Unique	

PIERRE ELLIOT TRUDEAU

(b. 1919) Joseph Philippe Pierre Yves Elliott Trudeau, is a French Canadian, from the province of Quebec. A lawyer, he entered national politics in 1965 and became Minister of Justice and Attorney General in 1967. After the retirement of Prime Minister Lester Pearson, Trudeau was elected leader of the Liberal Party in 1968 and then Prime Minister. He served as Prime Minister from 1968 to 1979 and from 1980 to 1984.

Doulton was unable to obtain permission to issue this jug.

PROTOTYPE

Designer: Unknown   **Handle:** The Canadian Maple Leaf flag   **Backstamp:** Doulton

Colourway: Black and Grey

Doulton Number	Size	Variation	Height	Intro.	Discon.	U.K. £	U.S. $	Can. $
							Current Market Value	
D —	Large	Prototype	7"		Unknown		Unique	

THE POACHER

Poaching, or illegal hunting and fishing, was at one time punishable by death in England. Although no longer a capital offence, anyone caught committing this crime can still expect a heavy fine.

"The Poacher"
D 6429
COPR 1954
DOULTON & CO LIMITED
Rd No 875201
Rd No 33325
Rd No 7095
Rd No 321/54

Designer: Max Henk   **Handle:** A Salmon   **Backstamp:** Doulton

Colourway: See Variations

VARIATIONS

VARIATION NO. 1: Colourway: Green coat, red scarf, light brown hat.

Doulton Number	Size	Variation	Height	Intro.	Discon.	Current Market Value U.K. £	U.S. $	Can. $
D6429	Large	Var. 1	7"	1955	Current	41.00	130.00	145.00
D6464	Small	Var. 1	4"	1957	Current	22.50	65.00	80.00
D6515	Miniature	Var. 1	2 1/2"	1960	Current	15.50	50.00	60.00

Royal Doulton®
THE POACHER
D 6781
Modelled by

© 1954 ROYAL DOULTON
NEW COLOURWAY 1987

VARIATION NO 2: Colourway: Maroon coat, yellow striped scarf, black hat.

Doulton Number	Size	Variation	Height	Intro.	Discon.	Current Market Value		
						U.K. £	U.S. $	Can. $
D6781	Large	Var. 2	7"	1987	1989	45.00	100.00	145.00

Miscellaneous "The Poacher" Items

Doulton Number	Item	Backstamps	Height	Intro.	Discon.	Current Market Value		
						U.K. £	U.S. $	Can. $
D6464	Table Lighter	Doulton	4 3/4"	c. 1960	1973	95.00	125.00	190.00

THE POLICEMAN

The task of ensuring a govenment's law is carried out has been performed with varying degrees of violence throughout history and around the world. Happily, one can say that the English policeman is loyal and impartial, the exemplar of his field.

Commissioned by Lawley's By Post and issued in 1989 in a limited edition of 5,000 pieces. The Doulton backstamp is set within the design of a policeman's badge.

SERIES: Journey Through Britain, one of four.

Designer: Stanley J. Taylor   **Handle:** Handcuffs and truncheon   **Backstamp:** Doulton / Lawley's

Colourway: Black and white

Doulton Number	Size	Backstamp	Height	Intro.	Discon.	Current Market Value U.K. £	U.S. $	Can. $
D6852	Small	Douton	4"	1989	Ltd. Ed.	40.00	95.00	110.00

PORTHOS

One of the much-loved three musketeers, Porthos roamed Europe with his merry band in search of adventure in the 1844 novel by Alexandre Dumas.

SERIES: One of the "Three Musketeers", one of four.
Now part of the Characters from Literature, one of eleven.

Porthos
D 6440
COPR 1955
DOULTON & CO LIMITED

Porthos
(One of the "Three Musketeers")
D 6453
COPR 1955
DOULTON & CO LIMITED
Rd No 877526
Rd No 34107
Rd No 7246
Rd No 291/55

Designer: Max Henk   **Handle:** Handle of a sword   **Backstamp:** See Backstamps

Colourway: See Variations

VARIATIONS

VARIATION NO. 1: Colourway: Black hat, red cloak, black hair and moustache.

BACKSTAMPS

A: **Doulton**

B: **Doulton/(One of the "Three Musketeers")**

The wording "One of the Three Musketeers" was included in the early backstamp to enlighten the unknowledgeable that "Porthos" was one of the famous Musketeers.

Doulton Number	Size	Backstamp	Height	Intro.	Discon.	Current Market Value U.K. £	Current Market Value U.S. $	Current Market Value Can. $
D6440	Large	Doulton	7 1/4"	1956	Current	41.00	130.00	145.00
D6440	Large	Doulton/One	7 1/4"	1956	1970	45.00	135.00	150.00
D6453	Small	Doulton	4"	1956	Current	22.50	65.00	80.00
D6453	Small	Doulton/One	4"	1956	1970	30.00	70.00	85.00
D6516	Miniature	Doulton	2 3/4"	1960	Current	15.50	50.00	60.00

Royal Doulton®
PORTHOS
D 6828
Modelled by

© 1955 ROYAL DOULTON
NEW COLOURWAY 1988
SPECIAL COMMISSION 1000
PETER JONES CHINA
LEEDS AND WAKEFIELD

VARIATION NO. 2: Colourway: Maroon hat, blue cloak, ginger hair and moustache.

BACKSTAMP: Doulton/Peter Jones China Ltd.

Commissioned by Peter Jones China Ltd., Sheffield, England. Issued in 1988 in a limited edition of 1,000 pieces.

Doulton Number	Size	Backstamp	Height	Intro.	Discon.	Current Market Value U.K. £	Current Market Value U.S. $	Current Market Value Can. $
D6828	Large	Doulton/Jones	7 1/4"	1988	1988	35.00	150.00	195.00

Miscellaneous "Porthos" Items

Doulton Number	Item	Height	Intro.	Discon.	Current Market Value U.K. £	Current Market Value U.S. $	Current Market Value Can. $
D6453	Table Lighter	3 1/2"	1958	Unknown	95.00	125.00	175.00

THE POSTMAN

Even in this age of instant communication through telephone and facsimile machines, the postman continues to play an integral role in society, keeping even the most isolated places in touch with the world.

Commissioned by Lawley's By Postand issued in 1988 in a limited edition of 5,000 pieces. The Doulton backstamp is set within the design of a postage stamp.

SERIES: Journey Through Britain, one of four.

Designer: Stanley J. Taylor	**Handle:** A pillar box	**Backstamp:** Doulton / Lawley's

Colourway: Black, white and red

Doulton Number	Size	Backstamp	Height	Intro.	Discon.	Current Market Value U.K. £	Current Market Value U.S. $	Current Market Value Can. $
D6801	Small	Doulton/Lawley's	4"	1988	Ltd. Ed.	120.00	125.00	145.00

PUNCH AND JUDY MAN

Coming to England in the 17th century by way of Italy and France "commedia del 'arte," the Punch and Judy puppet show retains its original popularity today. Often performed by street musicians, the show features Punch, the hunchbacked boastful husband who beats his shrew-like wife Judy.

The colours on Punch's bat are occasionally reversed with no effect on the market value.

Designer: David Biggs   **Handle:** Punch   **Backstamp:** Doulton

Colourway: Brown hat, green coat, yellow scarf

Doulton Number	Size	Backstamp	Height	Intro.	Discon.	Current Market Value U.K. £	U.S. $	Can. $
D6590	Large	Doulton	7"	1964	1969	350.00	625.00	675.00
D6593	Small	Doulton	3 1/2"	1964	1969	180.00	400.00	425.00
D6596	Miniature	Doulton	2 1/2"	1964	1969	180.00	375.00	395.00

QUEEN ELIZABETH I

(1533-1603). Daughter of Anne Boleyn, second wife of Henry VIII, Elizabeth enjoyed a 45 year reign. The "Virgin Queen" never married and, without heirs, was in constant danger of usurption. Her biggest threat, after Mary Queen of Scots, was King Philip of Spain. With the leadership of Sir Francis Drake, her Royal Navy defeated the Spanish Armada and Philip's attempted invasion of England. Issued by Lawley's in 1988, this jug is one of a pair (with King Phillip of Spain) that was produced to celebrate the 400th anniversary of the defeat of the Spanish Armada in 1588. Both jugs were limited editions of 9,500 pieces.

Designer: William K. Harper **Handle:** Warship sailing on the right **Backstamp:** Doulton/Lawley's

Colourway: Grey, dark red and white

Doulton Number	Size	Backstamp	Height	Intro.	Discon.	Current Market Value U.K. £	U.S. $	Can. $
D6821	Small	Doulton	4"	1988	Ltd. Ed.	40.00	100.00	125.00

QUEEN VICTORIA

(1819-1901). Alexandrina Victoria succeeded her uncle, William IV, to the throne on her eighteenth birthday in 1837. Reigning until her death in 1901, she had a longer rule than any other British monarch. The marriages of their nine children allied the English royal house with those of Russia, Germany, Greece, Denmark and Romania and helped her reign become known as one of the most peaceful in English history.

Royal Doulton®

QUEEN VICTORIA

D 6816

Modelled by

Stanley James Taylor

© 1987 ROYAL DOULTON
NEW COLOURWAY 1988

Designer: Stanley J. Taylor **Handle:** Yellow sceptre **Backstamp:** See Backstamps

Colourway: See Variations

VARIATIONS

VARIATION NO. 1: Colourway: Black and yellow crown, purple veil with white frills.

BACKSTAMP: Doulton

Doulton Number	Size	Backstamp	Height	Intro.	Discon.	Current Market Value		
						U.K. £	U.S. $	Can. $
D6816	Large	Doulton	7 1/4"	1989	Current	49.00	130.00	180.00

VARIATION NO. 2: Colourway: Purple and yellow crown, grey veil with white frills.

BACKSTAMP: Guild of Specialist China & Glass Retailers, Peter Jones "The Guild of Specialist China & Glass Retailers"

Commissioned by the Guild of Specialist China and Glass Retailers in 1988 and issued in a limited edition of 3,000 pieces.

Doulton Number	Size	Backstamp	Height	Intro.	Discon.	Current Market Value U.K. £	U.S. $	Can. $
D6788	Large	Guild	7 1/4"	1988	Ltd. Ed.	45.00	90.00	195.00

THE RED QUEEN

"Off with his head" maybe the Red Queen should straighten a few more people out today, for we have confusion with names. "The Adventures in Wonderland" story is built around a pack of cards of which the Queen of hearts, showing her suit on the axe blade is one. While "Through the Looking Glass" the theme is tied into a chess game and of course the Red Queen is a chess piece. We have the Queen of Hearts being called the Red Queen, "Off with their heads."
Issued in 1987 as the first in the series.

SERIES: Alice in Wonderland, one of six.

Designer: William K. Harper

Handle: An axe

Colourway: Yellow, red and blue

Backstamp: Doulton

Royal Doulton®

THE RED QUEEN
D 6777
Modelled by

William K. Harper

© 1987 ROYAL DOULTON

Doulton Number	Size	Backstamp	Height	Intro.	Discon.	Current Market Value		
						U.K. £	U.S. $	Can. $
D6777	Large	Doulton	7 1/4"	1987	Current	49.00	130.00	180.00
D6859	Small	Doulton	3"	1990	Current	24.50	65.00	80.00
D6860	Miniature	Doulton	2"	1990	Current	16.50	60.00	60.00

REGENCY BEAU

The Regency of the Prince of Wales lasted from 1811 to 1820 witht he Prince becoming George IV in the latter year. The Regency Period, however, is a term loosely applied to the years from 1805 to 1830 when classical mythology, Greek and Roman authors were better known than their English counterparts.

The period was a time of excess in clothes and appearance.

Regency Beau
D 6559
COPR 1961
DOULTON & CO LIMITED
Rd No 902090
Rd No 42142
Rd No 3925
Rd No R84/6'

Designer: David Biggs   **Handle:** Cane and handkerchief   **Backstamp:** Doulton

Colourway: Green coat, green and yellow hat

Doulton Number	Size	Backstamp	Height	Intro.	Discon.	Current Market Value U.K. £	U.S. $	Can. $
D6559	Large	Doutlon	7 1/4"	1962	1967	500.00	925.00	950.00
D6562	Small	Doutlon	4 1/4"	1962	1967	300.00	625.00	675.00
D6565	Miniature	Doutlon	2 3/4"	1962	1967	350.00	700.00	850.00

THE RINGMASTER

The master-of-ceremonies of the circus is responsible, much as a theatre director, for the quality of his show. Usually operating from the centre of the ring, he must ensure that all of the acts proceed safely and smoothly, and be ready to respond to any last minute problems.

SERIES: The Circus, one of four.

Royal Doulton®
THE RING MASTER
D 6863
Modelled by

© 1990 ROYAL DOULTON

Designer: Stanley J. Taylor   **Handle:** Horse's head and plume   **Backstamp:** See Backstamps

Colourway: Black top hat with a light blue ribbon, red jacket, black lapel, green plume atop horses head.

The Maple Leaf Edition

BACKSTAMP

A: **Doulton**

For General Release: 1991.

B: **Doulton / The Maple Leaf Edition "The International Royal Doulton Collectors Weekend 1990 Toronto, Ontario, Canada. The Maple Leaf Edition."**

Commissioned to Commemorate The International Royal Doulton Collectors Weekend, September 14, 15 & 16th, 1990. The design incorporates a red maple leaf in honour of the 25th anniversary of Canada's Maple Leaf Flag. Issued with a certificate of authenticity. Pre-released in 1990 in a special edition of 750 pieces.

Doulton Number	Size	Backstamp	Height	Intro.	Discon.	U.K. £	U.S. $	Can. $
							Current Market Value	
D6863	Large	Doulton	7 1/2"	1991	Current	57.00	130.00	225.00
D6863	Large	Doulton/Maple	7 1/2"	1990	Sp. Ed.	145.00	250.00	300.00

RINGO STARR

(b. 1940). Richard Starkey was the drummer for the Beatles until they disbanded in 1970. Shyer than his three cohorts, Ringo neither wrote nor sang, beyond one or two notable exceptions.

SERIES: The Beatles, one of four.

Royal Doulton
THE BEATLES
Ringo Starr
D 6726
Modelled by
Stanley James Taylor.
© ROYAL DOULTON TABLEWARE
LIMITED 1984

Designer: Stanley J. Taylor   **Handle:** Plain   **Backstamp:** Doulton

Colourway: Black tunic trimmed with yellow collar and epaulettes

Doulton Number	Size	Backstamp	Height	Intro.	Discon.	Current Market Value U.K. £	U.S. $	Can. $
D6726	Mid	Doulton	5 1/2"	1984	1991	45.00	60.00	95.00

RIP VAN WINKLE

In 1820, the American writer, Washington Irving, wrote the story of Rip Van Winkle, based on legends he'd heard from Dutch settlers. Rip, while walking in the Catskill mountains of New England, drinks a fairy potion and falls asleep for twenty years. He wakes to find the world unrecognizable.

SERIES: Characters from Literature, one of eleven.

"Rip Van Winkle."
D.6438.
COPR.1954.
DOULTON & CO.LIMITED.
R⁴N° 874255.
R⁴N° 32854.
R⁴N° 7022.
R⁴N° 193/54.

Designer: Geoff Blower

Handle: A man resting against the trunk of a tree; a blackbird sits atop the tree

Colourway: See Variations

Backstamp: See Backstamps

VARIATIONS

VARIATION NO. 1: Colourway: Grey-blue cap, brown robes, figure resting against tree dressed in blue

BACKSTAMP: Doulton

Doulton Number	Size	Backstamp	Height	Intro.	Discon.	Current Market Value U.K. £	U.S. $	Can. $
D6438	Large	Doulton	6 1/2"	1955	Current	41.00	130.00	145.00
D6463	Small	Doulton	4"	1957	Current	22.50	65.00	80.00
D6517	Miniature	Doulton	2 1/2"	1960	Current	15.50	50.00	60.00

Royal Doulton®
RIP VAN WINKLE
D 6785
Modelled by

© 1954 ROYAL DOULTON
NEW COLOURWAY 1987
SPECIAL EDITION OF 1000
FOR JOHN SINCLAIR SHEFFIELD

VARIATION NO. 2: Colourway: Black cap, green robes, figure resting against tree dressed in black.

BACKSTAMP: Doulton/John Sinclair

Commissioned by John Sinclair, Sheffield, England. Issued in 1987 in a special edition of 1,000 pieces.

Doulton Number	Size	Backstamp	Height	Intro.	Discon.	Current Market Value U.K. £	U.S. $	Can. $
D6785	Large	Doulton/Sinclair	7"	1987	Sp. Ed.	35.00	125.00	195.00

Miscellaneous "Rip Van Winkle" Items

Doulton Number	Item	Height	Intro.	Discon.	Current Market Value U.K. £	U.S. $	Can. $
D6463	Table Lighter	3 1/2"	1958	Unknown	350.00	600.00	700.0

ROBIN HOOD

A legendary figure from the reign of Richard I in the 12th century, Robin Hood and his group of benevolent bandits are credited with many adventures while robbing the rich to help the poor of England.

STYLE ONE: *HAT WITH NO FEATHER, PLAIN HANDLE*

Robin Hood

COPR.1946.
DOULTON & CO LIMITED.
Rd No 847681.
Rd No 23906.
Rd No 134/46
Rd No 5192.

Designer: Harry Fenton **Handle:** Plain **Backstamp:** Doulton

Colourway: Brown hat, green robes

Doulton Number	Size	Backstamp	Height	Intro.	Discon.	Current Market Value U.K. £	Current Market Value U.S. $	Current Market Value Can. $
D6205	Large	Doulton	6 1/4"	1947	1960	75.00	150.00	195.00
D6234	Small	Doulton	3 1/4"	1947	1960	45.00	75.00	110.00
D6252	Miniature	Doulton	2 1/4"	1947	1960	40.00	55.00	85.00

ROBIN HOOD

STYLE TWO: *HAT WITH FEATHER, HANDLE: BOW, QUIVER AND ARROWS*

SERIES: Characters from Literature, one of eleven.

Robin Hood
D 6527
COPR 1959
DOULTON & CO LIMITED
Rd No 893840
Rd No 39648
Rd No 8312
Rd No 421/59

Royal Doulton
ROBIN HOOD
D 6541
© ROYAL DOULTON
TABLEWARE LTD 1959

Designer: Max Henk **Handle:** Bow and quiver of arrows **Backstamp:** Doulton

Colourway: Brown hat with white feather on one side and oak leaves
and acorns on the other, green robes

Doulton Number	Size	Backstamp	Height	Intro.	Discon.	Current Market Value		
						U.K. £	U.S. $	Can. $
D6527	Large	Doulton	7 1/2"	1960	Current	41.00	130.00	145.00
D6534	Small	Doulton	4"	1960	Current	22.50	65.00	80.00
D6541	Miniature	Doulton	2 3/4"	1960	Current	15.50	50.00	60.00

ROBINSON CRUSOE

In 1719, Daniel Defoe wrote a novel based on the experiences of Alexander Selkirk who was marooned on a deserted Pacific island for five years. The book became a huge success and has been read ever since.

Robinson Crusoe
D 6532
COPR 1959
DOULTON & CO LIMITED
Rd No 893845
Rd No 39653
Rd No 8317
Rd No 416/59

Designer: Max Henk   **Handle:** The man Friday peers from behind a palm tree   **Backstamp:** Doulton

Colourway: Brown and green

Doulton Number	Size	Backstamp	Height	Intro.	Discon.	Current Market Value U.K. £	U.S. $	Can. $
D6532	Large	Doulton	7 1/2"	1960	1982	50.00	90.00	155.00
D6539	Small	Doulton	4"	1960	1982	30.00	55.00	80.00
D6546	Miniature	Doulton	2 3/4"	1960	1982	25.00	45.00	70.00

ROMEO

The hero of Shakespeare's 1596 romantic play, Romeo falls in love with Juliet, the daughter of a Verona family feuding with his own. The lives of these two clandestine lovers end tragically and, as the bitter irony, cause the reconciliation of the two families.

SERIES: The Shakespearean Collection, one of six.

STYLE ONE: *HANDLE: A DAGGER SUPERIMPOSED ON THE COLUMN SUPPORTING A BALCONY*

© ROYAL DOULTON TABLEWARE LIMITED 1982
D 6670

The
Shakespearean
Collection
ROMEO
A series of hand-made, hand-decorated Character Jugs by
Royal Doulton

Designer: David Biggs   **Handle:** See above   **Backstamp:** Doulton

Colourway: Brown and white

Doulton Number	Size	Backstamp	Height	Intro.	Discon.	U.K. £	U.S. $	Can. $
						Current Market Value		
D6670	Large	Doulton	7 1/2"	1983	1989	60.00	90.00	145.00

ROMEO

PROTOTYPE

STYLE TWO: HANDLE: A PHIALL OF POISON SPILLS OVER A DAGGER BELOW

Designer: David Biggs   **Handle:** See above   **Backstamp:** Doulton

Colourway: Brown and white

Doulton Number	Size	Variation	Height	Intro.	Discon.	Current Market Value U.K. £	Current Market Value U.S. $	Current Market Value Can. $
D6670	Large	Prototype	7"	1981	1981		Extremely Rare	

RONALD REAGAN

(b. 1911). Ronald Wilson Reagan began as an Iowa sports announcer for a radio station. In 1937 he began acting, a profession that was to last thirty years and span fifty films, including the "Bonzo" series. In 1966, Reagan was elected governor of California, and his political career began. After losing the Republican Presidential nomination twice, he was elected President of the United States, he served two terms in office from 1980-1988.

This jug was commissioned for the Republican National Committee. Originally to be issued in a limited edition of 5,000 pieces, the jug did not sell well and only 2,000 pieces were said to have been produced.

Issued with a certificate and photograph of President Reagan in a decorative folio.

Designer: Eric Griffiths   **Handle:** The "Stars and Stripes"   **Backstamp:** Doulton / Reagan

Colourway: Blue and white

Doulton Number	Size	Backstamp	Height	Intro.	Discon.	Current Market Value U.K. £	U.S. $	Can. $
D6718	Large	Doulton/Reagan	7 3/4"	1984	Ltd. Ed.	195.00	400.00	500.00

THE SAILOR

One of the Armed Forces series, the sailor would be a member of the navy, operating the various carriers, fighters and submarines in the military arsenal.

SERIES: The Armed Forces, one of three.

STYLE ONE: *WITHOUT "R.C.N." ON BINOCULARS*

Designer: William K. Harper   **Handle:** Binoculars   **Backstamp:** Doulton

Colourway: White Royal Navy cap, brown coat and white sweater

Doulton Number	Size	Backstamp	Height	Intro.	Discon.	Current Market Value U.K. £	U.S. $	Can. $
D6875	Small	Doulton	4 1/2"	1991	Current	26.50	65.00	90.00

THE SAILOR

Commissioned by The British Toby in a limited edition of 250 pieces. Sold originally as a set for $465.00 Canadian Dollars.

SERIES: The Canadians, one of three.

STYLE TWO: WITH "R.C.N." ON BINOCULARS

| **Designer:** William K. Harper | **Handle:** R.C.N. Binoculars | **Backstamp:** Doulton /
The British Toby |

Colourway: White Royal Canadian Navy cap, brown coat and white sweater

Doulton Number	Size	Backstamp	Height	Intro.	Discon.	Current Market Value		
						U.K. £	U.S. $	Can. $
D6904	Small	Doulton/British	4 1/2"	1991	Ltd. Ed.	100.00	170.00	200.00

SAIREY GAMP

In Charles Dickins' 1843 novel "Martin Chizzelwit" Sairey Gamp is a gossiping, gin-drinking midwife and sick-nurse. Her ubiquitous old cotton umbrella has given rise to the colloquialism "gamp," for particulary untidy specimens.

Sairey Gamp
D 6045
DOULTON & CO LIMITED

Designer: Leslie Harradine
Harry Fenton

Handle: An Umbrella

Backstamp: See Backstamps

Colourway: See Variations

VARIATIONS

VARIATION NO. 1: Colourway: **Light green head scarf, pink bow**
Handle: **Black umbrella**

BACKSTAMPS

A: Doulton

B: Doulton/Bentalls "Souvenir From Bentalls Jubilee Year 1935"

Commissioned by Bentalls to commemorate the silver jubilee in 1935 of King George V.

Doulton Number	Size	Backstamp	Height	Intro.	Discon.	Current Market Value U.K. £	Current Market Value U.S. $	Current Market Value Can. $
D5451	Large	Doulton	6 1/4"	1935	1986	45.00	85.00	125.00
D5528	Small	Doulton	3 1/8"	1935	1986	30.00	50.00	75.00
D5528	Small	Doulton/Bentalls	3 1/8"	1935	1935	350.00	600.00	700.00
D6045	Miniature	Doulton	2 1/8"	1939	1986	20.00	35.00	60.00
D6146	Tiny	Doulton	1 1/4"	1940	1960	45.00	100.00	135.00

VARIATION NO. 2: Colourway: Yellow head scarf and bow.
Handle: Maroon umbrella

BACKSTAMPS

A: Strawbridge and Clothier "Celebrating the opening of The Royal Doulton Room at
Strawbridge and Clothier, Philadelphia, U.S.A."

Commissioned by Strawbridge and Clothier, Philadelphia. Issued in 1986 in a
limited edition of 250 pieces.

B: Strawbridge and Clothier "Made for the First Anniversary of the Royal Doulton
Room at Strawbridge and Clothier"

Commissioned by Strawbridge and Clothier in 1987 and issued in a limited
edition of 500 pieces.

Doulton Number	Size	Variations	Height	Intro.	Discon.	Current Market Value		
						U.K. £	U.S. $	Can. $
D6770	Large	Var. 2A	6 1/4"	1986	Ltd. Ed.	200.00	400.00	495.00
D6789	Small	Var. 2B	3"	1987	Ltd. Ed.	125.00	225.00	250.00

Miscellaneous "Sairey Gamp" Items

Doulton Number	Item	Height	Intro.	Discon.	Current Market Value		
					U.K. £	U.S. $	Can. $
D6009	Ash Bowl	3"	1939	1960	65.00	110.00	130.00
D6011	Sugar Bowl	2 1/2"	1939	1942	400.00	725.00	850.00
D6015	Teapot	7"	1939	1942	750.00	1,500.00	1,750.00
D6047	Bust	2 1/4"	1939	1960	65.00	110.00	130.00
D6150	Toothpick Holder	2 3/4"	1940	1942	250.00	425.00	500.00
HN1625	Bookend	3 1/2"	1934	1939	1,000.00	2,000.00	2,500.00
M62	Napkin Ring	3 1/2"	c. 1935	1939	350.00	550.00	650.00

SAM JOHNSON

(1709-1784). A celebrated poet, essayist and lexicographer, Dr. Johnson's "Dictionary" (1755) was the first systematic study of the English language. His "Literary Club" met regulary at a London pub and included such famous figures as David Garrick, Oliver Goldsmith and Edmund Burke.

"Sam Johnson."

COPR. 1949.
DOULTON & CO. LIMITED.
R.No 857579
R.No 5906.
R.No 77/49

Designer: H. Fenton   **Handle:** Plain   **Backstamp:** Doulton

Colourway: Dark brown hat, light brown, maroon and white robes

Doulton Number	Size	Backstamp	Height	Intro.	Discon.	Current Market Value U.K. £	U.S. $	Can. $
D6289	Large	Doulton	6 1/4"	1950	1960	180.00	325.00	395.00
D6296	Small	Doulton	3 1/4"	1950	1960	120.00	225.00	265.00

SAM WELLER

In the 1837 Charles Dickens' novel "The Pickwick Papers," Sam was a "Boots" employed at the White Hart Inn. He becomes the faithful aide and valet of Mr. Pickwick and eventually marries Napkins' housemaid.

This character jug is unusual in that it's modelling changes dramatically between the large and smaller versions.

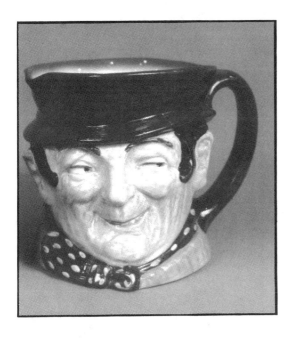

"Sam Weller"
R^d N° 822824
REG^d IN AUSTRALIA

Designer: Leslie Harradine   **Handle:** Plain   **Backstamp:** Doulton
Harry Fenton

Colourway: Dark brown hat, light brown coat, red kerchief with white spots

Doulton Number	Size	Backstamp	Height	Intro.	Discon.	U.K. £	U.S. $	Can. $
							Current Market Value	
D6064	Large	Doulton	6 1/2"	1940	1960	75.00	140.00	195.00
D5841	Mid	Doulton	4 1/2"	1938	1948	90.00	175.00	200.00
D5841	Small	Doulton	3 1/4"	1948	1960	50.00	75.00	110.00
D6140	Miniature	Doulton	2 1/4"	1940	1960	35.00	55.00	95.00
D6147	Tiny	Doulton	1 1/4"	1940	1960	50.00	100.00	135.00

Miscellaneous "Sam Weller" Items

Doulton Number	Item	Height	Intro.	Discon.	U.K. £	U.S. $	Can. $
						Current Market Value	
D6052	Bust	2 1/2"	1939	1960	60.00	90.00	130.00
M61	Napkin Ring	3 1/2"	c. 1939	1939	350.00	550.00	650.00

SAMSON AND DELILAH

Samson was an Israelite judge from Biblical times, famous for his strength.

Delilah, a Philistine woman, was paid to find the secret of Samson's strength so that her people could overthrow their Isrealite enemies. Samson fell in love with Delilah and told her that his strength lay in his hair. She shaved his head while he slept and the Philistines captured and blinded him. Samson avenged himself when his hair grew back by pulling down a Philistine temple, killing himself and many of his enemies.

Issued in 1988 in a limited edition of 9,500 pieces but not yet sold out.

SERIES: The Star-Crossed Lovers Collection (Two-faced Jug), one of four.

Designer: Stanley J. Taylor

Handle: A column backed by the jawbone of an ass

Colourway: Brown, black and cream

Backstamp: Doulton

Doulton Number	Size	Backstamp	Height	Intro.	Discon.	Current Market Value		
						U.K. £	U.S. $	Can. $
D6787	Large	Doulton	7"	1988	Ltd. Ed.	63.00	130.00	165.00

SANCHO PANÇA

This amiable peasant is employed as the squire to Don Quixote in Cervantes' 17th century novel. Accompanying Quixote on many adventures, his down-to-earth common sense acts as a foil to his master's romantic musing.

Sancho Panca
(A Servant to Don Quixote)
D 6461
COPR 1956
DOULTON & CO LIMITED
Rd No 881510
Rd No 35706
Rd No 7561
Rd No 332/56

Designer: Geoff Blower   **Handle:** Head of a mule   **Backstamp:** See Backstamps

Colourway: Black hat with a white feather, black coat with a white collar

BACKSTAMPS

A: Doulton

B: Doulton / Sancho Panca ("A Servant to Don Quixote")

Produced from 1957 to the early 1970's, with no cedilla.

C: Doulton / Sancho Pança

The spelling of the name Pança with the cedilla makes the "c" sibilant, giving a soft "s" sound in pronunciation. Early versions of the backstamp included the cedilla, but it was dropped in the late fifties. The incised name shows that the cedilla was included in the modelling.

Doulton Number	Size	Backstamp	Height	Intro.	Discon.	Current Market Value U.K. £	U.S. $	Can. $
D6456	Large	Doulton	6 1/2"	1957	1983	60.00	110.00	150.00
D6456	Large	"A Servant"	6 1/2"	1957	1970	60.00	110.00	150.00
D6456	Large	Cedilla	6 1/2	1957	1959	60.00	110.00	150.00
D6461	Small	Doulton	3 1/4"	1957	1983	40.00	60.00	80.00
D6461	Small	"A Servant"	3 1/4"	1957	1970	40.00	60.00	80.00
D6461	Small	Cedilla	3 1/4"	1957	1959	40.00	60.00	80.00
D6518	Miniature	Doulton	2 1/2"	1960	1983	40.00	50.00	60.00
D6518	Miniature	"A Servant"	2 1/2"	1960	1970	40.00	50.00	60.00

Note: The dates for the discontinuance of the backstamp varieties are only approximate.

SANTA CLAUS

A figure who needs no introduction, the Santa Claus jug was introduced in 1981 and was the first to undergo annual design changes. From 1981, the jug handle has changed, featuring different well-known Christmas themes.

STYLE ONE: HANDLE: A DOLL AND DRUM

Designer: Michael Abberley   **Handle:** A doll stands on a drum   **Backstamp:** Doulton

Colourway: Red, white and light brown

Doulton Number	Size	Backstamp	Height	Intro.	Discon.	Current Market Value U.K. £	U.S. $	Can. $
D6668	Large	Doulton	7 1/2"	1981	1981	65.00	100.00	155.00

SANTA CLAUS

STYLE TWO: *HANDLE: THE HEAD OF A REINDEER*

© **ROYAL DOULTON**
TABLEWARE LTD 1982

Santa Claus

D.6675

Designer: Michael Abberley   **Handle:** The head of a reindeer   **Backstamp:** Doulton

Colourway: Red, white and brown

Doulton Number	Size	Backstamp	Height	Intro.	Discon.	Current Market Value		
						U.K. £	U.S. $	Can. $
D6675	Large	Doulton	7 1/4"	1982	1982	55.00	125.00	155.00

SANTA CLAUS

STYLE THREE: *HANDLE: A SACK OF TOYS*

ROYAL DOULTON
TABLEWARE LTD. 1983

Santa Claus
D 6690

Designer: Michael Abberley   **Handle:** A sack of toys   **Backstamp:** Doulton

Colourway: Red, white and light brown

Doulton Number	Size	Backstamp	Height	Intro.	Discon.	Current Market Value		
						U.K. £	U.S. $	Can. $
D6690	Large	Doulton	7 1/2"	1983	1983	80.00	160.00	155.00

SANTA CLAUS

STYLE FOUR: HANDLE: PLAIN RED

Designer: Michael Abberley

Handle: Plain

Colourway: Red and white

Backstamp: Doulton

Royal Doulton
SANTA CLAUS
D6704
Modelled by

© ROYAL DOULTON TABLEWARE
LIMITED 1983

Doulton Number	Size	Backstamp	Height	Intro.	Discon.	Current Market Value U.K. £	U.S. $	Can. $
D6704	Large	Doulton	7 1/2"	1984	Current	41.00	130.00	145.00
D6705	Small	Doulton	3 1/4"	1984	Current	22.50	65.00	80.00
D6706	Miniature	Doulton	2 1/2"	1984	Current	15.50	50.00	60.00

SANTA CLAUS

STYLE FIVE: *HANDLE: A HOLLY WREATH*

Designer: Michael Abberley   **Handle:** A holly wreath   **Backstamp:** See Backstamps

Colourway: Red, white and green

BACKSTAMPS

A: Doulton

Miniature - Issued in a limited edition of 5,000 Christmas 1991

B: Doulton / Home Shopping

Large - Commissioned by "Home Shopping Network", Florida
Issued in a special edition of 5,000

Doulton Number	Size	Backstamp	Height	Intro.	Discon.	Current Market Value U.K. £	U.S. $	Can. $
D6794	Large	Doulton/Home	7"	1988	Sp. Ed.	125.00	285.00	350.00
D6900	Miniature	Doulton	2 1/2"	1991	Ltd. Ed.	25.00	50.00	60.00

SANTA CLAUS

STYLE SIX: *HANDLE: A CANDY CANE*

Designer: Michael Abberley   **Handle:** See Variations   **Backstamp:** See Backstamps

Colourway: Red and white

VARIATIONS

VARIATION NO. 1: Handle: Candy cane with red and white stripes.

BACKSTAMP: Doulton/Cable Value

Commissioned by the "Cable Value Network". Issued in a special edition of 1,000

Doulton Number	Size	Backstamp	Height	Intro.	Discon.	U.K. £	Current Market Value U.S. $	Can. $
D6793	Large	Cable Value	7 1/2"	1988	Sp. Ed.	250.00	800.00	850.00

VARIATION NO. 2: Handle: Candy cane with red, white and green stripes

BACKSTAMP: Doulton/American Collectors Society

Commissioned by the "American Collectors Society". Issued in 1989 in a special edition of 1,000 pieces.

Doulton Number	Size	Backstamp	Height	Intro.	Discon.	Current Market Value U.K. £	Current Market Value U.S. $	Current Market Value Can. $
D6840	Large	Doulton/ American	7 1/2"	1989	Sp. Ed.	125.00	225.00	300.00

SCARAMOUCHE

In the 17th century "commedia dell'arte," Scaramouche appears as a boastful, foolish character, dressed in the old Spanish style. He was first featured on his own in the Edward Ravenscroft comedy produced in 1677.

STYLE ONE *HANDLE: A GUITAR WITH THE TWO MASKS OF COMEDY AND TRAGEDY*

```
Scaramouche
    D6558
  COPR 1961
DOULTON & CO LIMITED
  Rd No 902089
  Rd No 42141
  Rd No 8924
  Rd No R83/61
```

Designer: Max Henk   **Handle:** A guitar   **Backstamp:** Doulton

Colourway: Blue-black, brown and green

Doulton Number	Size	Backstamp	Height	Intro.	Discon.	Current Market Value U.K. £	U.S. $	Can. $
D6558	Large	Doulton	7"	1962	1967	400.00	700.00	700.00
D6561	Small	Doulton	3 1/4"	1962	1967	250.00	450.00	550.00
D6564	Miniature	Doulton	2 1/2"	1962	1967	250.00	425.00	450.00

SCARAMOUCHE

STYLE TWO: *HANDLE: A CURTAIN WITH THE TWO MASKS OF COMEDY AND TRAGEDY*

SERIES: Characters from Literature, one of eleven.

Designer: Stanley J. Taylor   **Handle:** The masks of tragedy and comedy rest against a curtain   **Backstamp:** See Backstamps

Colourway: See Variations

VARIATIONS

VARIATION NO. 1: Colourway: Black hat, green tunic and white ruff, dark brown hair; yellow handle

BACKSTAMP: Doulton

Doulton Number	Size	Variations	Height	Intro.	Discon.	Current Market Value U.K. £	U.S. $	Can. $
D6814	Large	Var. 1	6 3/4"	1988	Current	49.00	130.00	180.00

VARIATION NO. 2: Colourway: Yellow hat, turquoise tunic and white ruff, light brown hair. Handle: Lavender

BACKSTAMP: Doulton/Guild

Commmissioned by the Guild of Specialist China & Glass Retailers in 1987 and issued in a limited edition of 1,500 pieces.

Doulton Number	Size	Variations	Height	Intro.	Discon.	Current Market Value		
						U.K. £	U.S. $	Can. $
D6774	Large	Var. 2	6 3/4"	1987	Ltd. Ed.	45.00	225.00	300.00

SCARLET PIMPERNEL

In a 1905 novel by the Hungarian Baroness Orczy, the league of the Scarlet Pimpernel were a group of Englishmen who dedicated themselves to the rescue of victims of the Reign of Terror in Paris. Sir Percy Blakeney, the group's leader, bests his opponents by clever wit and courage while disguising his identity from his friends back home in England.

PROTOTYPE

Designer: Geoff Blower   **Handle:** Characters in assorted disguises   **Backstamp:** Doulton

Colourway: Black, white and blue

Doulton Number	Size	Backstamp	Height	Intro.	Discon.	Current Market Value U.K. £	U.S. $	Can. $
D —	Large	Doulton	7"		Unknown		Unique	

SCROOGE

In Dickens' famous novel, "A Christmas Carol," Scrooge is a loveless, miserly businessman who changes his ways after being visited by the three ghosts of Christmas on Christmas Eve.

Issued to commemorate the 170th Anniversary of the birth of Charles Dickens. There are twelve jugs in this set, which were issued with a certificate of authenticity. A mahogany display shelf completes the set. The set was first sold by Lawley's By Post in the U.K. during 1982 to 1988, and in 1985 forward in North America and Austrialia.

SERIES: Charles Dickens Commemorative Set / Dickens Tinies, one of eleven.

*Photograph
Not Available
At Press Time*

Designer: Michael Abberley   **Handle:** Plain   **Backstamp:** Doulton

Colourway: Yellow and brown

Doulton Number	Size	Backstamp	Height	Intro.	Discon.	U.K. £	Current Market Value U.S. $	Can. $
D6683	Tiny	Doulton	1 1/2"	1982	1989	30.00	50.00	60.00

SIMON THE CELLARER

Simon was the subject of a 19th century English folksong. The keys on the handle are those to his cellar of great wines and ales, and he was always good for standing a drink for his friends.

Designer: Charles Noke   **Handle:** A bunch of keys   **Backstamp:** Doulton
Harry Fenton

Colourway: Maroon hat, white ruff

Doulton Number	Size	Backstamp	Height	Intro.	Discon.	Current Market Value U.K. £	U.S. $	Can. $
D5504	Large	Doutlon	6 1/2"	1935	1960	65.00	135.00	175.00
D5616	Small	Doulton	3 1/2"	1936	1960	45.00	75.00	110.00

SIMPLE SIMON

Dating back to a 17th century nursery rhyme of Simon and a "pieman" he meets, the real identity of this character has been lost.

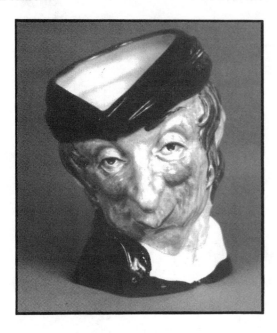

Designer: Geoff Blower   **Handle:** Plain   **Backstamp:** Doulton

Colourway: Green, brown and white

Doulton Number	Size	Backstamp	Height	Intro.	Discon.	Current Market Value		
						U.K. £	U.S. $	Can. $
D6374	Large	Doulton	7"	1953	1960	250.00	525.00	650.00

SIR FRANCIS DRAKE

This version of the Drake jug was produced to celebrate the 400th anniversary of the defeat of the Spanish Armada in 1588. Commissioned by the Guild of Specialist China and Glass Retailers, this jug was issued in 1988 in a limited edition of 6,000 pieces.

Designer: Peter Gee   **Handle:** The Golden Hind's bow and sails   **Backstamp:** Doulton / Guild

Colourway: Black and white

Doulton Number	Size	Backstamp	Height	Intro.	Discon.	Current Market Value U.K. £	U.S. $	Can. $
D6805	Large	Doulton/Guild	7"	1988	Ltd. Ed.	65.00	85.00	175.00

SIR HENRY DOULTON

(1820-1897) In the mid 1830's Henry joined his father's firm just in time to capitalize on the large expanding market that was developing in London for modern sanitation products. The manufacture of stoneware sewer and water pipes led Doulton and Company, as they were known after 1854, to become a large and flourishing concern. John Doulton retired around this time leaving Doulton and Company in the hands of his son Henry. In the 1860's with decorative wares expanding Henry Doulton was persuaded to hire students from the Lambeth School of Art as designers and decorators of the new ornamental wares his company was introducing. Their outstanding artist-signed creations heralded the beginning of the studio art pottery movement.

SERIES: Royal Doulton International Collectors Club

Designer: Eric Griffiths   **Handle:** A Doulton art pottery vase   **Backstamp:** Doulton / RDICC

Colourway: Brown, yellow and greys.

Doulton Number	Size	Backstamp	Height	Intro.	Discon.	Current Market Value		
						U.K. £	U.S. $	Can. $
D6703	Small	RDICC	4 1/2"	1984	1984	75.00	130.00	155.00

SIR THOMAS MORE

(1478-1535) More entered the service of King Henry VIII in 1518 as royal counciller. He was knighted and became Lord Chanceller after the dismissal of Cardinal Wolsey in 1529. Henry at this time was embroiled in a battle with Rome over his decision to divorce Catherine of Aragon. Unable to support his King, More resigned.

In 1534 More was arrested for high treason when he refused to swear an Oath of Supremacy, stating that Henry VIII ranked above all foreign leaders, including the Pope. He was beheaded in 1535 and canonized by the Catholic Church 400 years later in 1935.

SERIES: Henry and his Six Wives, one of eight.

Royal Doulton®
SIR THOMAS MORE
D 6792
Modelled by
Stanley James Taylor
© 1987 ROYAL DOULTON

Designer: Stanley J. Taylor   **Handle:** A window arch and a bible   **Backstamp:** Doulton

Colourway: Black hat, brown fur trim, gold chain of office.

Doulton Number	Size	Backstamp	Height	Intro.	Discon.	Current Market Value		
						U.K. £	U.S. $	Can. $
D6792	Large	Doulton	6 3/4"	1988	Current	41.00	130.00	145.00

SIR WINSTON CHURCHILL

This Churchill jug is a new design, commissioned by Lawley's By Post. Issued in 1989 as a set of three, and limited to 9,500 pieces.

SERIES: Heroic Leaders, one of three.

Royal Doulton®
SIR WINSTON CHURCHILL
1874-1965
D 6849
Modelled by
Stanley James Taylor
© 1989 ROYAL DOULTON
A LIMITED EDITION OF 9500
THIS IS NO. 1609

Designer: Stanley J. Taylor   **Handle:** The Union Jack flag   **Backstamp:** Doulton / Lawley's

Colourway: Black, grey and white

Doulton Number	Size	Backstamp	Height	Intro.	Discon.	Current Market Value U.K. £	Current Market Value U.S. $	Current Market Value Can. $
D6849	Small	Doulton/Lawley's	3 1/4"	1989	Ltd. Ed.	60.00	125.00	150.00

THE SLEUTH

The unsuccessful doctor, Arthur Conan Doyle, (1859-1930), published the first of his widely popular detective stories in 1887. The amateur sleuth Sherlock Holmes shared rooms on Baker Street and many adventures with his friend and foil Dr. Watson.

The Sleuth
D 6631
© DOULTON & CO LIMITED 1972
REGISTRATION APPLIED FOR

Designer: Alan Moore   **Handle:** A pipe and magnifying glass   **Backstamp:** See Backstamps

Colourway: See Variations

VARIATIONS

VARIATION NO. 1: Colourway: Black deerstalker hat, brown cloak

BACKSTAMP: Doutlon

Doulton Number	Size	Backstamp	Height	Intro.	Discon.	Current Market Value U.K. £	U.S. $	Can. $
D6631	Large	Doulton	7"	1973	Current	41.00	130.00	145.00
D6635	Small	Doulton	3 1/4"	1973	Current	22.50	65.00	80.00
D6639	Miniature	Doulton	2 3/4"	1973	Current	15.50	50.00	60.00

VARIATION NO 2: Colourway: Brown deerstalker, red cloak

BACKSTAMP: DOULTON/LAWLEY'S "THIS LIMITED EDITION OF 5,000 COMMEMORATES THE CENTENARY OF THE PUBLICATION OF THE FIRST SHERLOCK HOLMES STORY "A STUDY IN SCARLET"

Commissioned by Lawley's By Post to celebrate 100 years since the publication of the first Sherlock Holmes story "A Study in Scarlet".
Issued in 1987 in a limited edition of 5,000 pieces.

Doulton Number	Size	Backstamp	Height	Intro.	Discon.	Current Market Value U.K. £	U.S. $	Can. $
D6773	Small	Lawley's	3 1/4"	1987	Ltd. Ed.	45.00	85.00	125.00

SMUGGLER

Smuggling most certainly has been practiced ever since the first trade embargo was introduced. The illegal importation of goods remains today a very lucrative, dangerous business.

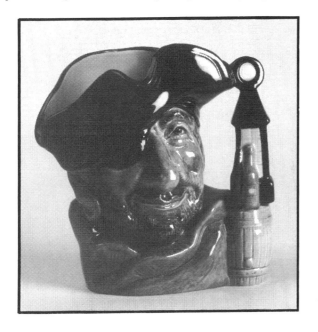

Smuggler
D6616
COPR. 1967
DOULTON & CO. LIMITED
Rd No 932050
Rd No 51328
Rd No 11138
Rd No 630/67

Designer: David Biggs   **Handle:** Lantern above a barrel   **Backstamp:** Doulton

Colourway: Green hat, red scarf

Doulton Number	Size	Backstamp	Height	Intro.	Discon.	Current Market Value U.K. £	U.S. $	Can. $
D6616	Large	Doulton	7 1/4"	1968	1981	60.00	100.00	145.00
D6619	Small	Doulton	3 1/4"	1968	1981	40.00	60.00	80.00

SMUTS

(1870-1950). A South African attorney, militaryman and politician, Jan Christiaan Smuts enjoyed a long and distinguished career. Serving as a member of the British War Cabinet in WWI, Smuts was one of the authors of the Covenent of the League of Nations. In 1945, after again serving the Allies in WWII, Smuts is credited with writing the preamble to the Charter of the United Nations.

In South Africa, he served as Attorney General and Minister of Defence, becoming Prime Minister in 1919 and again in 1939.

Designer: Harry Fenton   **Handle:** Springbok   **Backstamp:** Doulton

Colourway: Light brown

Doulton Number	Size	Backstamp	Height	Intro.	Discon.	Current Market Value U.K. £	U.S. $	Can. $
D6198	Large	Doulton	6 1/2"	1946	1948	750.00	1,250.00	1,500.00

THE SNOOKER PLAYER

Snooker is a billiard game, and like billiards requires great accuracy. The speed and angle at which one hits a ball with the cue must be carefully caluclated before each move.

SERIES: Characters from Life, one of seven.

Royal Doulton®

THE SNOOKER PLAYER
D 6879
Modelled by

Stanley James Taylor

© 1990 ROYAL DOULTON

Designer: Stanley J. Taylor   **Handle:** Cue with chalk, red and black cue balls   **Backstamp:** Doulton

Colourway: Black hair, white shirt, black bow-tie and vest

Doulton Number	Size	Backstamp	Height	Intro.	Discon.	Current Market Value U.K. £	U.S. $	Can. $
D6879	Small	Doulton	4"	1991	Current	26.50	65.00	90.00

THE SOLDIER

In the Armed Forces, the soldier is a member of the Army, that wing which lights the ground battles during a war. The term has come to mean, in general, anyone involved in a military career.

SERIES: The Armed Forces, one of three

STYLE ONE: *WITHOUT "RED PATCH ON CANTEEN"*

Royal Doulton®
THE SOLDIER
D 6876
Modelled by

William K. Harper

© 1990 ROYAL DOULTON

Designer: William K. Harper   **Handle:** Bayonet and water canteen   **Backstamp:** Doulton

Colourway: Army steel helmet with netting, khaki tunic

Doulton Number	Size	Backstamp	Height	Intro.	Discon.	Current Market Value U.K. £	U.S. $	Can. $
D6876	Small	Doulton	4 1/2"	1991	Current	26.50	65.00	90.00

THE SOLDIER

Commissioned by The British Toby in a limited edition of 250 pieces. Originally sold in a set for $465.00 Canadian Dollars.

SERIES: The Canadians, one of three.

STYLE TWO: WITH "RED PATCH ON CANTEEN"

Designer: William K. Harper **Handle:** Bayonet and water canteen with red patch **Backstamp:** Doulton / The British Toby

Colourway: Army steel helmet with netting, khaki tunic

Doulton Number	Size	Backstamp	Height	Intro.	Discon.	Current Market Value U.K. £	U.S. $	Can. $
D6905	Small	Doulton/British	4 1/2"	1991	Ltd. Ed.	100.00	170.00	200.00

ST GEORGE

The patron saint of England since the 13th century, George is the hero of a legend which describes him as a chivalrous knight who single-handedly slays a huge dragon, thus saving the princess Melisande.

Designer: Max Henk

Handle: A dragon

Colourway: Grey helmet, turquoise armour

Backstamp: Doulton

St George
D 6618
COPR 1967
DOULTON & CO LIMITED
Rd No 932048
Rd No 51330
Rd No 11140
Rd No 628/67

Doulton Number	Size	Backstamp	Height	Intro.	Discon.	Current Market Value U.K. £	U.S. $	Can. $
D6618	Large	Doulton	7 1/2"	1968	1975	120.00	225.00	275.00
D6621	Small	Doulton	3 3/4"	1968	1975	75.00	175.00	140.00

TAM O'SHANTER

In a poem by Robert Burns, written in 1791, Tam O'Shanter is a drunken farmer who happens upon witches who pursue him and his horse. He escapes, but his horse doesn't quite make it - one witch pulls its tail off.

The Scottish woollen cap called a tam is reputedly name after this poem's hero.

Tam o'Shanter
D 6632
©DOULTON & CO. LIMITED 1972
REGISTRATION APPLIED FOR

Designer: Max Henk   **Handle:** Witch holding horse's tail above a mug of ale   **Backstamp:** Doulton

Colourway: Dark blue tam, green cloak

Doulton Number	Size	Backstamp	Height	Intro.	Discon.	Current Market Value U.K. £	U.S. $	Can. $
D6632	Large	Doulton	7"	1973	1980	65.00	110.00	155.00
D6636	Small	Doulton	3 1/4"	1973	1980	45.00	60.00	95.00
D6640	Miniature	Doulton	2 1/2"	1973	1980	40.00	50.00	85.00

TERRY FOX

(1958-1981). Canadian Terrance Stanley Fox was a student and athlete until diagnosed with osteogenic sarcoma, a rare form of bone cancer. While recovering from the amputation of most of one leg, Fox conceived of the idea of a "Marathon of Hope", a run across Canada to raise money for cancer research. He began on April 12, 1980 but had to abort his run on September 1st, after being diagnosed with lung cancer. He raised over $24 million and became a source of inspiration for millions of people. Only three jugs were produced; one was given to his family, one was put up for auction at the International Royal Doulton Collectors Weekend, September 14-16, 1990, and the third resides in the Sir Henry Doulton Gallery.

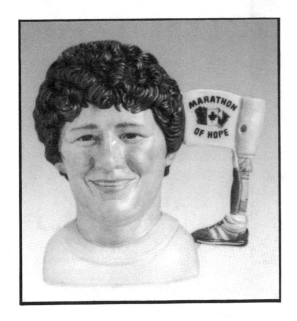

Designer: William K. Harper	**Handle:** Fox's artificial leg	**Backstamp:** Doulton

Colourway: Brown and white

Doulton Number	Size	Backstamp	Height	Intro.	Discon.	Current Market Value U.K. £	U.S. $	Can. $
D6881	Large	Doulton	7"	1990	Ltd. Ed.		Extremely Rare	

TOBY GILLETTE

Jimmy Saville's British television show, "Jim'll Fix It," invites public requests and received one from Toby Gillette to have a character jug created in his likeness.

In 1984, three were produced; one was given to Toby Gillette, one remains in the Sir Henry Doulton Gallery, and the third was auctioned by Sotheby's with the proceeds going to one of the charities Jimmy Saville supported.

In 1986, Toby Gillette sold his own jug at a Sotheby's auction.

Designer: Eric Griffiths   **Handle:** Plain   **Backstamp:** Doulton

Colourway: Brown

Doulton Number	Size	Backstamp	Height	Intro.	Discon.	U.K. £	Current Market Value U.S. $	Can. $
D6717	Large	Doulton	7"	1984	Ltd. Ed.		Extremely Rare	

TOBY PHILPOTS

A "thirsty old soul" in an 18th century drinking song, Toby is thought by some to be the source of the traditional British Toby jug, in which a character sits astride a barrel of ale. Popular opinion suggests his name is a derivation of the French topé, to toast.

Designer: Charles Noke   **Handle:** Plain   **Backstamp:** See Backstamps

Colourway: Dark green hat, maroon coat, blue scarf with white spots

BACKSTAMPS

A: **Doulton**

B: **Doulton / Toby Philpotts**

Incised name on jug "Toby Philpots", but on the backstamp "Toby Philpotts"

C: **Doulton / Toby Philpots"**

Incised name on jug "Toby Philpots", but on the backstamp the corrected spelling of "Toby Philpots"

Doulton Number	Size	Backstamp	Height	Intro.	Discon.	Current Market Value U.K. £	U.S. $	Can. $
D5736	Large	A Doulton	6 1/4"	1937	1951	65.00	145.00	195.00
D5736	Large	B Philpotts	6 1/4"	1937	1951	65.00	145.00	195.00
D5736	Large	C Philpots	6 1/4"	1952	1969	65.00	145.00	195.00
D5737	Small	A Doulton	3 1/4"	1937	1951	40.00	70.00	110.00
D5737	Small	B Philpotts	3 1/4"	1937	1951	40.00	70.00	110.00
D5737	Small	C Philpots	3 1/4"	1952	1969	40.00	70.00	110.00
D6043	Miniature	A Doulton	2 1/4"	1939	1951	35.00	50.00	85.00
D6043	Miniature	B Philpotts	2 1/4"	1939	1951	35.00	50.00	85.00
D6043	Miniature	C Philpots	2 1/4"	1952	1969	35.00	50.00	85.00

TONY WELLER

In Charles Dickens' "The Pickwick Papers," (1837), Tony is a stage-coachman who inherits a pub from his wife. He is the father of Sam Weller, who works for him at the inn.

Designer: Leslie Harradine   **Handle:** Plain   **Backstamp:** See Backstamps
Harry Fenton

Colourway: Grey hat, maroon coat, white bow with yellow spots

BACKSTAMPS

A: Doulton

B: Doulton / Darley & Son "Souvenir From Darley & Son Sheffield & Rotheram"

> Commissioned by Darley & Son, Sheffield and Rotheram

C: Doulton / Bentalls "Souvenir From Bentalls Jubilee Year 1935"

> Commissioned by Bentalls to commemorate the silver jubilee in 1935 of King George V.

D: Doulton / Bentalls "Souvenir from Bentalls - 1936"

Doulton Number	Size	Backstamp	Height	Intro.	Discon.	Current Market Value U.K. £	U.S. $	Can. $
D5531	Ext. Large	Doulton	8 1/2"	1936	1942	120.00	200.00	250.00
D5531	Large	Doulton	6 1/2"	1936	1960	75.00	145.00	195.00
D5530	Small	Doulton	3 1/4"	1936	1960	45.00	70.00	90.00
D5530	Small	Doulton/Darley	3 1/4"	1936	1936	350.00	550.00	650.00
D5530	Small	Doulton/Bentalls	3 1/4"	1935	1935	350.00	550.00	650.00
D5530	Small	Doulton/Bentalls	3 1/4"	1936	1936	350.00	550.00	650.00
D6044	Miniature	Doulton	2 1/4"	1939	1960	35.00	45.00	85.00

Miscellaneous "Tony Weller" Items

Doulton Number	Item	Height	Intro.	Discon.	Current Market Value U.K. £	U.S. $	Can. $
D5888	Musical Jug	6 1/2"	1937	1939	250.00	400.00	500.00
D6013	Sugar bowl	2 1/2"	1939	1960	250.00	400.00	500.00
D6016	Teapot	7"	1939	1960	750.00	1,650.00	1,950.00
D6051	Bust	4"	1939	1960	65.00	90.00	130.00
HN1616	Bookend	4"	1934	1939	1,000.00	2,000.00	2,500.00
M60	Napkin Ring	3 1/2"	1935	1939	350.00	550.00	550.00

TOUCHSTONE

In Shakespeare's comedy, "As You Like It," Touchstone is the jester to the exiled Duke of Frederick's court who accompanies Rosalind and Celia into the Forest of Arden.

Designer: Charles Noke   **Handle:** Head of a clown   **Backstamp:** Doulton

Colourway: Purple, green and brown

Doulton Number	Size	Backstamp	Height	Intro.	Discon.	Current Market Value U.K. £	U.S. $	Can. $
D5613	Large	Doulton	7"	1936	1960	120.00	200.00	275.00

TOWN CRIER

With his familiar "Hear Ye! Hear Ye!" the crier would gain the attention of passersby to read his proclamation of news, serving as the only vehicle for passing official information in his time.

STYLE ONE: HANDLE: BELL ON SCROLL

Designer: David Biggs   **Handle:** Bell on scroll   **Backstamp:** Doulton

Colourway: Black hat trimmed with gold, scarlet coat trimmed with gold

Doulton Number	Size	Backstamp	Height	Intro.	Discon.	Current Market Value U.K. £	U.S. $	Can. $
D6530	Large	Doulton	7"	1960	1973	125.00	240.00	275.00
D6537	Small	Doulton	3 1/4"	1960	1973	90.00	125.00	185.00
D6544	Miniature	Doulton	2 1/2"	1960	1973	110.00	130.00	175.00

TOWN CRIER

STYLE TWO: HANDLE: SCROLL WRAPPED AROUND BELL

Designer: Stanley J. Taylor   **Handle:** Scroll wrapped around bell   **Backstamp:** Doulton

Colourway: Black, maroon and white

Doulton Number	Size	Backstamp	Height	Intro.	Discon.	Current Market Value		
						U.K. £	U.S. $	Can. $
D6895	Large	Doulton	7"	1991	Current	59.00	150.00	200.00

THE TRAPPER

An integral part of Canadian history, the early trappers, or voyageurs, were largely responsible for the early exploration of the country. In search of animal pelts for export to the European market, these rugged men spent the winter travelling by canoe, snowshoe, and foot through the wild Canadian north. Trapping is still practised to a smaller extent today, mostly by Canada's native people.

The miniature version of The Trapper character jug was put into production briefly in 1983, however before any quantity was produced, it was decided to withdraw the character. Several dozen have appeared on the market. The Royal Doulton International Collectors Club was not involved as reported.

SERIES: Canadian Centennial Series 1867-1967, one of three.

The Trapper
D 6612
COPR 1966
DOULTON & CO LIMITED
Rd No 924808
Rd No 49144
Rd No 10600
Rd No 52/66

CANADIAN CENTENNIAL SERIES
1867 — 1967

The Trapper
D 6612
COPR 1966
DOULTON & CO LIMITED
Rd No 924808
Rd No 10600
Rd No 52/66

Designer: Max Henk
David Biggs

Handle: A horn and a pair of snowshoes

Backstamp: See Backstamps

Colourway: Dark green and white hat, brown and green clothing

BACKSTAMPS

A: Doulton

B: Doulton / Canadian Centennial Series 1867-1967

Doulton Number	Size	Backstamp	Height	Intro.	Discon.	U.K. £	U.S. $	Can. $
						Current Market Value		
D6609	Large	Doulton	7 1/4"	1967	1983	65.00	100.00	155.00
D6609	Large	Doul/Cent	7 1/4	1967	1967	150.00	350.00	300.00
D6612	Small	Doulton	3 3/4"	1967	1983	45.00	55.00	95.00
D —	Miniature	Doulton	2 1/2"	1983	1983	950.00	3,500.00	2,000.00

UGLY DUCHESS

The very ugly Duchess lives in Wonderland and plays croquet with the Queen. Alice found the game a curious one, with live hedgehogs for balls, flamingos for mallets, and playing cards soldiers who doubled over to serve as the arches.

SERIES: Alice in Wonderland, one of six.

Ugly Duchess
D 6599
COPR 1964
DOULTON & CO LIMITED
Rd No 917232
Rd No 46578
Rd No 10001
Rd No 593/64

Designer: Max Henk   **Handle:** A flamingo   **Backstamp:** Doulton

Colourway: Green, purple and pink

Doulton Number	Size	Backstamp	Height	Intro.	Discon.	Current Market Value		
						U.K. £	U.S. $	Can. $
D6599	Large	Doulton	6 3/4"	1965	1973	250.00	500.00	700.00
D6603	Small	Doulton	3 1/2"	1965	1973	180.00	300.00	425.00
D6607	Miniature	Doulton	2 1/2"	1965	1973	180.00	300.00	375.00

ULYSSES S. GRANT AND ROBERT E. LEE

Ulysses Samuel Grant (1822-1885). An Ohio native, Grant was made Lieutenant General by President Lincoln and put in command of the Union army in the American Civil War. His successes led to his election as president in 1868.

Robert E. Lee (1807-1870). The general in command of the Confederate army during the American Civil War. He was ruthlessly pursued by General Grant, who forced him to retreat from his defence of Richmond, Virginia in 1865. His troops were surrounded at the great battle of Appotomax, where he and the Confederate army surrendered and lost the war.

Issued in 1983 in a limited edition of 9,500 pieces.

SERIES: The Antagonists Collection (Two Faced Jug), one of four.

Designer: Michael Abberley **Handle:** Flags of the Confederacy and the Union **Backstamp:** Doulton

Colourway: Black, grey, brown and red

Doulton Number	Size	Backstamp	Height	Intro.	Discon.	Current Market Value U.K. £	U.S. $	Can. $
D6698	Large	Doulton	7"	1983	Ltd. Ed.	125.00	225.00	350.00

UNCLE TOM COBBLEIGH

In the popular 18th century Devonshire song, Tom Cobbleigh and six friends borrow Tom Pearse's old mare to ride to the fair. Unable to support so many, the mare becomes sick and dies and can be found haunting the nightime moors to this day.

Designer: Max Henk   **Handle:** Plain   **Backstamp:** Doulton

Colourway: Dark brown hat, green coat

Doulton Number	Size	Backstamp	Height	Intro.	Discon.	Current Market Value U.K. £	U.S. $	Can. $
D6337	Large	Doulton	7"	1952	1960	180.00	435.00	625.00

URIAH HEEP

Issued to commemorate the 170th Anniversary of the birth of Charles Dickens. There are twelve jugs in this set, which were issued with a certificate of authenticity. A mahogany display shelf completes the set. The set was first sold by Lawley's By Post in the U.K. during 1982 to 1988, and in 1985 forward in North America and Austrialia.

SERIES: Charles Dickens Commemorative Set / Dickens Tinies, one of twelve.

*Photograph
Not Available
At Press Time*

Designer: Robert Tabbenor   **Handle:** Plain   **Backstamp:** Doulton

Colourway: Grey and green

Doulton Number	Size	Backstamp	Height	Intro.	Discon.	Current Market Value U.K. £	U.S. $	Can. $
D6682	Tiny	Doulton	1 1/2"	1982	1989	30.00	50.00	60.00

VETERAN MOTORIST

In a tradition celebrating the 1896 act of parliament no longer requiring automobiles to be led by a man waving a cautionary flag, a commemorative drive is held each year. Motorists, all in vintage cars, drove from London's Hyde Park south to the coastal town of Brighton to mark the day.

Veteran Motorist
D.6637
Ⓒ DOULTON & CO. LIMITED.1972
REGISTRATION APPLIED FOR.

Designer: David Biggs   **Handle:** A horn   **Backstamp:** Doulton

Colourway: Yellow hat, green coat, white scarf

Doulton Number	Size	Backstamp	Height	Intro.	Discon.	Current Market Value U.K. £	U.S. $	Can. $
D6633	Large	Doulton	7 1/2"	1973	1983	75.00	110.00	155.00
D6637	Small	Doulton	3 1/4"	1973	1983	50.00	65.00	90.00
D6641	Miniature	Doulton	2 1/2"	1973	1983	50.00	55.00	60.00

VICAR OF BRAY

In a popular song of the 18th century, this very adaptable parson boasted that he was able to accommodate himself to the religious views of Charles, James, William, Anne and George, and that "whosoever King may reign, he would always be the Vicar of Bray."

Prior to 1940 these jugs had a distinctive yellow rim.

"Vicar of Bray."
R.N.807475.

Designer: Charles Noke	**Handle:** Plain	**Backstamp:** Doulton
Harry Fenton		

Colourway: Brown hat, green coat

Doulton Number	Size	Backstamp	Height	Intro.	Discon.	Current Market Value		
						U.K. £	U.S. $	Can. $
D5615	Large	Doulton	6 3/4"	1936	1960	120.00	190.00	300.00

VIKING

Also known as Norsemen, the Viking were Scandinavians living between the 8th and 10th centuries who sailed in pirating raids throughout Europe, discovering and settling much of it. Some historians believe they made it as far as North America before any other Europeans.

The Viking large size character is reported to carry the Stoke on Trent backstamp.

Designer: Max Henk   **Handle:** The prow of a viking long ship   **Backstamp:** Doulton

Colourway: Black, green and brown

Doulton Number	Size	Backstamp	Height	Intro.	Discon.	Current Market Value		
						U.K. £	U.S. $	Can. $
D6496	Large	Doulton	7 1/4"	1959	1975	120.00	200.00	275.00
D6502	Small	Doulton	4"	1959	1975	75.00	95.00	185.00
D6526	Miniature	Doulton	2 1/2"	1960	1975	75.00	135.00	175.00

VISCOUNT MONTGOMERY OF ALAMEIN

This new design was specially commissioned by Lawley's By Post and produced in a limited edition of 9,500 pieces. It was sold in a set of three: Montgomery, Mountbatten and Churchill.

SERIES: Heroic Leaders, one of three.

Royal Doulton®
VISCOUNT MONTGOMERY OF ALAMEIN
1887-1976
D 6850
Modelled by
Stanley James Taylor
© 1989 ROYAL DOULTON
A LIMITED EDITION OF 9500
THIS IS NO. 1609

Designer: Stanley J. Taylor   **Handle:** Imperial Army flag   **Backstamp:** Doulton / Lawley's

Colourway: Black beret, khaki uniform, red flag

Doulton Number	Size	Backstamp	Height	Intro.	Discon.	Current Market Value		
						U.K. £	U.S. $	Can. $
D6850	Small	Doulton/Lawley's	3 1/4"	1989	Ltd. Ed.	60.00	125.00	150.00

W. C. FIELDS

(1880-1946). Born Claude William Dukenfield, W.C. Fields began his entertainment career at the age of eleven as a juggler. Much later he appeared in the "Ziegfeld Follies" and then in 1925 began his work in film. With his rasping voice and bulbous nose, he became a very successful satiric comedian.

The following quote appears on the base of the jug.

"I was in love with a beautiful blonde once. She drove me to drink - 'tis the one thing I'm indebted to her for."

SERIES: The Celebrity Collection, one of five.

Designer: David Biggs   **Handle:** A walking cane   **Backstamp:** See Backstamps

Colourway: Black, grey and yellow

BACKSTAMPS

A: Doulton

B: Doulton/American Express "Premier Edition for American Express"

Introduced in the U.S.A. as a promotional jug for American Express.
Approximately 1,500 jugs bore the special backstamp.

Doulton Number	Size	Backstamp	Height	Intro.	Discon.	Current Market Value U.K. £	U.S. $	Can. $
D6674	Large	Doulton	7"	1983	1986	65.00	110.00	145.00
D6674	Large	Amex	7 1/2"	1983	Sp. Ed.	75.00	125.00	175.00

W. G. GRACE

(1848-1915). Wiliam Gilbert Grace's exceptional skill as a cricket batsman provided the game with its greatest single development in modern sports history. Debuting in professional cricket at the age of sixteen, Grace rose quickly to the status of England's best batsman, earning the title "the Champion." Throughout his long career, he set many early land-mark records, retiring at the age of sixty after forty-four seasons.

Commissioned by Lawley's By Post. Issued in 1989 in a limited edition of 9,500 pieces.

Designer: Stanley J. Taylor   **Handle:** Cricket bat and ball   **Backstamp:** Doulton/ Lawley's

Colourway: Yellow and orange striped cap, black beard

Doulton Number	Size	Backstamp	Height	Intro.	Discon.	Current Market Value U.K. £	Current Market Value U.S. $	Current Market Value Can. $
D6845	Small	Doulton	3 1/4"	1989	Ltd. Ed.	45.00	120.00	135.00

THE WALRUS AND CARPENTER

On a beach in Wonderland, the walrus and carpenter invite a number of oysters for evening conversation, with the poem

> "The time has come the Walrus said
> To talk of many things
> Like ships and string and sealing wax
> And cabbages and kings."

And then promptly ate them.

SERIES: Alice in Wonderland, one of six.

Designer: Max Henk   **Handle:** A walrus

Colourway: Black, green and red

Backstamp: Doulton

The Walrus & Carpenter
D 6600
COPR 1964
DOULTON & CO LIMITED
Rd No 917233
Rd No 46579
Rd No 10002
Rd No 591/64

Doulton Number	Size	Backstamp	Height	Intro.	Discon.	Current Market Value U.K. £	U.S. $	Can. $
D6600	Large	Doulton	7 1/4"	1965	1980	65.00	120.00	160.00
D6604	Small	Doulton	3 1/4"	1965	1980	45.00	70.00	95.00
D6608	Miniature	Doulton	2 1/2"	1965	1980	45.00	55.00	70.00

WILD BILL HICKOCK

(1837-1876). James Butler Hickock, after serving as a Union scout in the American Civil War, became a marshall and then sheriff of western frontier towns. An excellent gunman, he earned his nickname from his trigger-happy method of carrying out the law at the many shoutouts which erupted from poker games.

He toured briefly with Buffalo Bill's Wild West Show, (1872-1873), and was later murdered at Deadwood.

SERIES: The Wild West Collection, one of six.

Royal Doulton

THE WILD WEST
Collection
WILD BILL HICKOCK
D6736
Modelled by

© ROYAL DOULTON (UK) 1984

Designer: Michael Abberley

Handle: An upturned whiskey bottle flowing into a glass

Colourway: Black, brown and white

Backstamp: Doulton

Doulton Number	Size	Backstamp	Height	Intro.	Discon.	Current Market Value U.K. £	U.S. $	Can. $
D6736	Mid	Doulton	5 1/2"	1985	1989	45.00	75.00	110.00

WILLIAM SHAKESPEARE

(1564-1616). Shakespeare was born in Stratford upon Avon. There exists very little infomation about his early life in Stratford beyond records of his marriage and the births of his children. He apparently moved to London in 1585 and by 1592 had emerged as a promising actor and playwright. He was a part of the theatre company, the "King's Men of James I" throughout his London career, and in 1599 the new owner of the Globe theatre. Immensely successful in his life as playwright, director, poet and actor, Shakespeare was said to be quite wealthy by the time he returned to Stratford in 1613.

SERIES: The Shakespearean Collection, one of six.

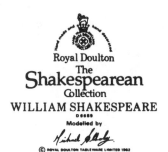

Designer: Michael Abberley   **Handle:** A feather quill stands in an ink pot   **Backstamp:** Doulton

Colourway: White, grey and yellow

Doulton Number	Size	Backstamp	Height	Intro.	Current Market Value Discon.	U.K. £	U.S. $	Can. $
D6689	Large	Doulton	7 3/4"	1983	Current	49.00	130.00	145.00

WITCH

Practitioners of magic and sorcery, these powerful women were the source of fear for many. Throughout history, women suspected of practicing witchcraft were persecuted as pagans and devils, often being killed by superstitious Christians in ritualistic ways.

SERIES: Mystical, one of three.

Designer: Stanley J. Taylor   **Handle:** Part of the witch's hat   **Backstamp:** Doulton

Colourway: Black and greys

Doulton Number	Size	Backstamp	Height	Intro.	Current Market Value Discon.	U.K. £	U.S. $	Can. $
D6893	Large	Doulton	7"	1991	Current	50.00	140.00	180.00

THE WIZARD

Although defined as a male witch, the term wizard is more often associated with strange and magical powers, instead of evil. Most legends of wizards portray them as heros and champions of evil.

SERIES: Mystical, one of three.

Royal Doulton®
THE WIZARD
D 6862
Modelled by

Stanley James Taylor

© 1990 ROYAL DOULTON

Designer: Stanley J. Taylor   **Handle:** Cat and a magic wand   **Backstamp:** Doulton

Colourway: Blue-grey, black and white

Doulton Number	Size	Backstamp	Height	Intro.	Discon.	Current Market Value U.K. £	U.S. $	Can. $
D6862	Large	Doulton	6 3/4"	1990	Current	57.00	155.00	225.00

WYATT EARP

(1848-1929). Wyatt Berry Stapp Earp, like his cohorts, was an expert gunfighter. He worked as a police officer and armed guard and, in 1881 was involved in the famous shootout at O.K. Corral while waging war on the "outlaw element." Later Earp travelled around the West, opening and operating a number of saloons.

SERIES: The Wild West Collection, one of six.

Designer: Stanley J. Taylor   **Handle:** A gun and sheriff's badge   **Backstamp:** Doulton

Colourway: Brown coat, light brown hat with red band

Doulton Number	Size	Backstamp	Height	Intro.	Discon.	Current Market Value U.K. £	U.S. $	Can. $
D6711	Mid	Doulton	5 1/2"	1985	1989	45.00	75.00	110.00

YACHTSMAN

Sailing has a history as old as that of man, and seems to remain constant in its popularity. Small and miniature jugs were piloted but never put into production.

STYLE ONE: *YACHTSMAN WITH LIFE JACKET*

Designer: David Biggs   **Handle:** A yacht sailing from the front to back   **Backstamp:** Doulton

Colourway: Blue cap and jersey, yellow lifejacket

Doulton Number	Size	Backstamp	Height	Intro.	Discon.	Current Market Value U.K. £	U.S. $	Can. $
D6622	Large	Doulton	8"	1971	1980	95.00	110.00	185.00

YACHTSMAN

STYLE TWO: *YATCHSMAN WITH PEEK CAP AND SCARF*

Royal Doulton®
YACHTSMAN
D 6820
Modelled by
Stanley James Taylor
© 1988 ROYAL DOULTON

Designer: Stanley J. Taylor   **Handle:** Sailboat with white sails and   **Backstamp:** See Backstamps
green trim sailing back to front

Colourway: Black hat, black and brown shirt, grey scarf

BACKSTAMPS

A: Doulton

For General Release: 1989.

B: Doulton / Canadian Doulton Show and Sale

Issued to commemorate the first Canadian Doulton Show and Sale at Durham, Ontario July 29th to 31st, 1988. Issued in a special edition of 750 pieces.

Doulton Number	Size	Backstamp	Height	Intro.	Discon.	Current Market Value U.K. £	U.S. $	Can. $
D6820	Large	Doulton	6 1/2"	1989	Current	49.00	155.00	180.00
D6820	Large	Doulton/Durham	6 1/2"	1988	Sp. Ed.	110.00	190.00	225.00

THE YEOMAN OF THE GUARD

In 1485, Henry VIII organized the Yeoman of the Guard, who formed a bodyguard to the monarch of England. Today the Yeoman, or Beefeaters as they are more commonly known, serve as bodyguards on formal occasions, however, their duties are purely ceremonial.

SERIES: The London Collection, one of ten.

Royal Doulton®

THE YEOMAN OF THE GUARD

D 6873

Modelled by

Stanley James Taylor

© 1990 ROYAL DOULTON

Designer: Stanley J. Taylor   **Handle:** Raven and tree trunk   **Backstamp:** See Backstamps

Colourway: Black hat, white frills and red jacket

BACKSTAMPS

A: Doulton

Pre-released in the U.S.A. to commemorate the anniversaries of the opening of four Royal Doulton Rooms at different retailers. Special edition of 450 pieces bearing a special backstamp.

B: Doulton / Dillards "To Commemorate the third anniversary of the opening of the Royal Doulton Room Dillards, New Orleans, Louisiana, U.S.A."

Dillards, Louisanna, Georgia, 50 pieces.

C: Doulton / Joseph Horne "To Commemorate the third anniversary of the opening of the Royal Doulton Room Joseph Horne, Pittsburgh, Pennsylvania, U.S.A."

Joseph Horne's, Pittsburgh, Pennsylvania, 75 pieces.

D: Doulton / Strawbridge and Clothier "To Commemorate the fourth anniversary of the opening of the Royal Doulton Room Strawbridge and Clothier, Philadelphia, Pennsylvania, U.S.A."

Strawbridge and Clothier, Philadelphia, Pennsylvania, 75 pieces.

E: Doulton / Higbee "To Commemorate the fifth anniversary of the opening of the Royal Doulton Room Higbee Cleveland, Ohio, U.S.A."

Higbee's, Cleveland, Ohio, 250 pieces.

Doulton Number	Size	Backstamp	Height	Intro.	Discon.	Current Market Value		
						U.K. £	U.S. $	Can. $
D6873	Large	Doulton	7"	1991	Current	57.00	130.00	180.00
D6883	Large	Dillards	7"	1990	Ltd. Ed.	175.00	250.00	275.00
D —	Large	Horne	7"	1990	Ltd. Ed.	135.00	250.00	275.00
D6885	Large	Strawbridge	7"	1990	Ltd. Ed.	135.00	250.00	275.00
D —	Large	Higbee	7"	1990	Ltd. Ed.	120.00	250.00	275.00

TOBY JUGS

ALBERT SAGGER
THE POTTER

Issued for the Royal Doulton International Collectors Club in 1986.

SERIES: The Doultonville Collection, one of twenty-five.

ALBERT SAGGER THE POTTER
FROM THE DOULTONVILLE COLLECTION
EXCLUSIVELY FOR
COLLECTORS CLUB
© 1986 ROYAL DOULTON (U.K)
MODELLED BY

Designer: William K. Harper **Handle:** Plain **Backstamp:** Doulton / RDICC

Colourway: Brown and white

Doulton Number	Size	Backstamp	Height	Intro.	Discon.	Current Market Value U.K. £	U.S. $	Can. $
D6745	Small	Doulton/RDICC	4"	1986	1986	55.00	85.00	100.00

ALDERMAN MACE
THE LORD MAYOR

SERIES: The Doultonville Collection, one of twenty-five.

Designer: William K. Harper   **Handle:** Plain   **Backstamp:** Doulton

Colourway: Red, white and black

Doulton Number	Size	Backstamp	Height	Intro.	Discon.	Current Market Value U.K. £	U.S. $	Can. $
D6766	Small	Doulton	4"	1987	Current	20.00	55.00	72.50

THE BEST IS NOT TOO GOOD

Designer: Harry Fenton   **Handle:** Plain   **Backstamp:** Doulton

Colourway: Reds and black

Doulton Number	Size	Backstamp	Height	Intro.	Discon.	Current Market Value U.K. £	U.S. $	Can. $
D6107	Small	Doulton	4 1/2"	1939	1960	180.00	300.00	400.00

BETTY BITTERS
THE BARMAID

SERIES: The Doultonville Collection, one of twenty-five.

Designer: William K. Harper   **Handle:** Plain   **Backstamp:** Doulton

Colourway: Turquoise, brown and yellow

Doulton Number	Size	Backstamp	Height	Intro.	Discon.	Current Market Value U.K. £	U.S. $	Can. $
D6716	Small	Doulton	4"	1984	1990	25.00	50.00	60.00

CAP'N CUTTLE

Designer: Harry Fenton   **Handle:** Plain   **Backstamp:** Doulton

Colourway: Browns

Doulton Number	Size	Backstamp	Height	Intro.	Discon.	Current Market Value U.K. £	U.S. $	Can. $
D6266	Small	Doulton	4 1/2"	1948	1960	95.00	200.00	230.00

CAPTAIN PROP
THE PILOT

SERIES: The Doultonville Collection, one of twenty-five.

Designer: William K. Harper   **Handle:** Plain   **Backstamp:** Doulton

Colourway: Grey, brown and white

Doulton Number	Size	Backstamp	Height	Intro.	Discon.	Current Market Value U.K. £	U.S. $	Can. $
D6812	Small	Doulton	4"	1989	Current	20.00	55.00	72.50

CAPTAIN SALT
THE SEA CAPTAIN

SERIES: The Doultonville Collection, one of twenty-five.

Designer: William K. Harper   **Handle:** Plain   **Backstamp:** Doulton

Colourway: Black

Doulton Number	Size	Backstamp	Height	Intro.	Discon.	U.K. £	U.S. $	Can. $
						Current Market Value		
D6721	Small	Doulton	4"	1985	Current	20.00	55.00	72.50

CHARLIE

The figure of Charlie Chaplain has a removeable bowler hat. He stands on a green base and the lettering incised in the base "Charlie."

Designer: Unknown		**Handle:** Plain	**Backstamp:** Doulton

Colourway: Black, plaid vest

Doulton Number	Size	Backstamp	Height	Intro.	Discon.	Current Market Value U.K. £	Current Market Value U.S. $	Current Market Value Can. $
Unknown	Large	Doulton	11"	1918	Unknown	1,500.00	2,500.00	3,000.00

CHARLIE CHEER
THE CLOWN

SERIES: The Doultonville Collection, one of twenty-five.

Designer: William K. Harper   **Handle:** Plain   **Backstamp:** Doulton

Colourway: Orange

Doulton Number	Size	Backstamp	Height	Intro.	Discon.	Current Market Value U.K. £	U.S. $	Can. $
D6768	Small	Doulton	4"	1987	Current	20.00	55.00	72.50

CHARRINGTON & CO. LTD.

These three jugs were made as advertising pieces for Charrington & Co. Ltd., Mile End, London. The three versions differ only in the wording on the base and were in production from the 1930's to the 1960's.

Designer: Hoare & Co. Ltd   **Handle:** Plain   **Backstamp:** Doulton

Colourway: Black, green and maroon

VARIATIONS

VARIATION NO. 1: Inscription on Base: Toby Ale

Doulton Number	Size	Backstamp	Height	Intro.	Discon.	Current Market Value U.K. £	U.S. $	Can. $
D —	Large	Toby Ale	9 1/4"	1934	1938	180.00	500.00	350.00

VARIATION NO. 2: Inscription on Base: One Toby Leads to Another

Doulton Number	Size	Backstamp	Height	Intro.	Discon.	Current Market Value U.K. £	U.S. $	Can. $
D —	Large	One Toby	9 1/4"	1934	1938	350.00	575.00	700.00

VARIATION NO. 3: Inscription on Base: Charrington's

Doulton Number	Size	Backstamp	Height	Intro.	Discon.	Current Market Value U.K. £	U.S. $	Can. $
D —	Large	Charrington's	9 1/4"	1934	1938	450.00	750.00	900.00

CLIFF CORNELL

In 1956 an American industrialist commissioned these toby jugs as gifts to friends and associates.
Inscription on base: Greetings Cliff Cornelll Famous Cornell Fluxes Cleveland Flux Company
Approximatley 500 pieces were issued for the large size blue and dark brown jugs and 375 pieces for the small size.
The numbers produced of the light brown jug are unknown.

GREETINGS
CLIFF CORNELL

"FAMOUS CORNELL FLUXES"
CLEVELAND FLUX COMPANY

Designer: Unknown   **Handle: Plain**   **Backstamp:** Doulton

Colourway: See Variations

VARIATIONS

VARIATION NO. 1: Colourway: Light brown suit

Doulton Number	Size	Variation	Height	Intro.	Discon.	Current Market Value U.K. £	U.S. $	Can. $
D —	Large	Var. 1	9"	1956	1956	300.00	525.00	600.00
D —	Small	Var. 1	5 1/2"	1956	1956	300.00	500.00	600.00

VARIATION NO. 2   VARIATION NO. 3

VARIATION NO. 2: Colourway: Blue suit.

Doulton Number	Size	Variation	Height	Intro.	Discon.	Current Market Value U.K. £	U.S. $	Can. $
D —	Large	Var. 2	9"	1956	1956	250.00	350.00	400.00
D —	Small	Var. 2	5 1/2"	1956	1956	250.00	475.00	550.00

VARIATION NO. 3: Colourway: Dark brown suit.

Doulton Number	Size	Variation	Height	Intro.	Discon.	Current Market Value U.K. £	U.S. $	Can. $
D —	Large	Var. 3	9"	1956	1956	250.00	350.00	400.00
D —	Small	Var. 3	5 1/2"	1956	1956	250.00	450.00	550.00

DR. PULSE
THE PHYSICIAN

SERIES: The Doultonville Collection, one of twenty-five.

Designer: William K. Harper

Handle: Plain

Backstamp: Doulton

Colourway: Light brown

Doulton Number	Size	Backstamp	Height	Intro.	Discon.	Current Market Value U.K. £	U.S. $	Can. $
D6723	Small	Doulton	4"	1985	Current	20.00	55.00	72.50

FALSTAFF

FALSTAFF

Designer: Charles Noke   **Handle:** Plain   **Backstamp:** Doulton

Colourway: Red

Doulton Number	Size	Backstamp	Height	Intro.	Discon.	Current Market Value U.S. £	U.S. $	Can. $
D6062	Large	Doulton	8 1/2"	1939	Current	53.00	145.00	175.00
D6063	Small	Doulton	5 1/4"	1939	Current	25.00	75.00	90.00

WORLD-WIDE LIMITED EDITION ONLY 1500 CHARACTER JUGS

Allocation of this world-wide limited quantity of jugs makes the number of collectors who may own a Queen Victoria small size jug even more select. Of the 1500 jugs commissioned by
PASCOE & COMPANY:

500 allocated to the US market
150 to the Canadian market
500 to the UK market
150 to the Australian market
200 are reserved for the RDICC

RESERVE YOUR JUG TODAY!

Delivery will begin February 1992

London, 27th Feb., 1900

Pascoe & Company

ROYAL DOULTON SPECIALISTS
545 Michigan Ave.
Miami Beach, Florida, 33139

FAT BOY

Designer: Harry Fenton   **Handle:** Plain   **Backstamp:** Doulton

Colourway: Brown

Doulton Number	Size	Backstamp	Height	Intro.	Discon.	Current Market Value U.S. £	Current Market Value U.S. $	Current Market Value Can. $
D6264	Small	Doulton	4 1/2"	1948	1960	90.00	200.00	230.00

FLORA FUCHSIA
THE FLORIST

SERIES: The Doultonville Collection, one of twenty-five.

Designer: William K. Harper   **Handle:** Plain   **Backstamp:** Doulton

Colourway: Light blue and brown

Doulton Number	Size	Backstamp	Height	Intro.	Discon.	Current Market Value U.K. £	U.S. $	Can. $
D6767	Small	Doulton	4"	1987	1990	35.00	50.00	60.00

FRED FEARLESS
THE FIREMAN

SERIES: The Doultonville Collection, one of twenty-five.

Designer: William K. Harper   **Handle:** Plain   **Backstamp:** Doulton

Colourway: Black and yellow

Doulton Number	Size	Backstamp	Height	Intro.	Discon.	Current Market Value U.K. £	Current Market Value U.S. $	Current Market Value Can. $
D6809	Small	Doulton	4"	1989	Current	20.00	55.00	72.50

FRED FLY
THE FISHERMAN

SERIES: The Doultonville Collection, one of twenty-five.

Designer: William K. Harper   **Handle:** Plain   **Backstamp:** Doulton

Colourway: Light brown

Doulton Number	Size	Backstamp	Height	Intro.	Discon.	Current Market Value U.K. £	U.S. $	Can. $
D6742	Small	Doulton	4"	1986	Current	20.00	55.00	72.50

GEORGE ROBEY

The hat is detachable. "George Robey" incised in base. George Robey, a star of the British Music Hall, entertained millions during his long career.

Designer: Unknown   **Handle:** Plain   **Backstamp:** Doulton

Colourway: Black and green

Doulton Number	Size	Backstamp	Height	Intro.	Discon.	U.K. £	U.S. $	Can. $
							Current Market Value	
Unknown	Large	Doulton	10 1/2"	1920's	Unknown	1,500.00	2,500.00	3,000.00

HAPPY JOHN

HAPPY JOHN

Designer: Harry Fenton

Handle: Plain

Colourway: Black hat, grey coat

Backstamp: Doulton

Doulton Number	Size	Backstamp	Height	Intro.	Discon.	Current Market Value		
						U.K. £	U.S. $	Can. $
D6031	Large	Doulton	9"	1939	Current	53.00	145.00	175.00
D6070	Small	Doulton	5 1/2"	1939	Current	25.00	75.00	90.00

HONEST MEASURE

Honest Measure

Designer: Harry Fenton   **Handle:** Plain   **Backstamp:** Doulton

Colourway: Dark red hat, green coat, orange vest

Inscription on Base: "Honest Measure: Drink as Leisure"

Doulton Number	Size	Backstamp	Height	Intro.	Discon.	Current Market Value U.K. £	U.S. $	Can. $
D6108	Small	Doulton	4 1/4"	1939	Current	25.00	75.00	90.00

THE HUNTSMAN

THE HUNTSMAN

Designer: Harry Fenton   **Handle:** Plain   **Backstamp:** See Backstamps

Colourway: See Variations

VARIATIONS

VARIATION NO. 1: Colourway: Black hat, maroon coat

BACKSTAMP: Doulton

Doulton Number	Size	Variation	Height	Intro.	Discon.	Current Market Value U.K. £	U.S. $	Can. $
D6320	Large	Var. 1	7 3/4"	1950	Current	53.00	145.00	175.00

VARIATION NO. 2   VARIATION NO. 3

VARIATION NO. 2: Kingsware
Colourway: Browns

BACKSTAMP: Doulton / Burslem

Doulton Number	Size	Variation	Height	Intro.	Discon.	Current Market Value		
						U.K. £	U.S. $	Can. $
D —	Large	Var. 2	7 1/2"	1910	1910	250.00	425.00	500.00

VARIATION NO. 3: Black hat, red coat, silver rim.

BACKSTAMP: Doulton

Doulton Number	Size	Variation	Height	Intro.	Discon.	Current Market Value		
						U.K. £	U.S. $	Can. $
D —	Large	Var. 3	7 1/2"	1930	1930	450.00	750.00	900.00

JOLLY TOBY

Designer: Harry Fenton   **Handle:** Plain   **Backstamp:** Doulton

Colourway: Black hat, dark red coat, yellow vest

Doulton Number	Size	Backstamp	Height	Intro.	Discon.	Current Market Value U.K. £	U.S. $	Can. $
D6109	Medium	Doulton	6 1/2"	1939	Current	35.00	92.00	115.00

LEN LIFEBELT
THE LIFEBOATMAN

SERIES: The Doultonville Collection, one of twenty-five.

Designer: William K. Harper   **Handle:** Plain   **Backstamp:** Doulton

Colourway: Yellow, black and white

Doulton Number	Size	Backstamp	Height	Intro.	Discon.	Current Market Value U.K. £	U.S. $	Can. $
D6811	Small	Doulton	4"	1989	Current	20.00	55.00	72.50

MADAME CRYSTAL
THE CLAIRVOYANT

SERIES: The Doultonville Collection, one of twenty-five.

Designer: William K. Harper   **Handle:** Plain   **Backstamp:** Doulton

Colourway: Green, grey and blue

Doulton Number	Size	Backstamp	Height	Intro.	Discon.	Current Market Value U.K. £	U.S. $	Can. $
D6714	Small	Doulton	4"	1984	1989	35.00	50.00	60.00

MAJOR GREEN
THE GOLFER

SERIES: The Doultonville Collection, one of twenty-five.

Designer: William K. Harper   **Handle:** Plain   **Backstamp:** Doulton

Colourway: Light brown, yellow and green

Doulton Number	Size	Backstamp	Height	Intro.	Discon.	Current Market Value U.K. £	U.S. $	Can. $
D6740	Small	Doulton	4"	1986	Current	20.00	55.00	72.50

MIKE MINERAL
THE MINER

SERIES: The Doultonville Collection, one of twenty-five.

Designer: William K. Harper   **Handle:** Plain   **Backstamp:** Doulton

Colourway: Light brown

Doulton Number	Size	Backstamp	Height	Intro.	Discon.	Current Market Value U.K. £	U.S. $	Can. $
D6741	Small	Doulton	4"	1986	1989	35.00	50.00	60.00

MRS. LOAN
THE LIBRARIAN

SERIES: The Doultonville Collection, one of twenty-five.

Designer: William K. Harper   **Handle:** Plain   **Backstamp:** Doulton

Colourway: Blue and white

Doulton Number	Size	Backstamp	Height	Intro.	Discon.	Current Market Value U.K. £	U.S. $	Can. $
D6715	Small	Doulton	4"	1984	1989	35.00	50.00	60.00

MISS NOSTRUM
THE NURSE

SERIES: The Doultonville Collection, one of twenty-five.

Designer: William K. Harper   **Handle:** Plain   **Backstamp:** Doulton

Colourway: Blue and white

Doulton Number	Size	Backstamp	Height	Intro.	Discon.	Current Market Value U.K. £	U.S. $	Can. $
D6700	Small	Doulton	4"	1983	Current	20.00	55.00	72.50

MISS STUDIOUS
THE SCHOOLMISTRESS

SERIES: The Doultonville Collection, one of twenty-five.

Designer: William K. Harper   **Handle:** Plain   **Backstamp:** Doulton

Colourway: Yellow and black

Doulton Number	Size	Backstamp	Height	Intro.	Discon.	U.K. £	Current Market Value U.S. $	Can. $
D6722	Small	Doulton	4"	1985	1989	35.00	50.00	60.00

MONSIEUR CHASSEUR
THE CHEF

SERIES: The Doultonville Collection, one of twenty-five.

Designer: William K. Harper   **Handle:** Plain   **Backstamp:** Doulton

Colourway: White and blue

Doulton Number	Size	Backstamp	Height	Intro.	Discon.	Current Market Value		
						U.K. £	U.S. $	Can. $
D6769	Small	Doulton	4"	1987	Current	20.00	55.00	72.50

MR. BRISKET
THE BUTCHER

SERIES: The Doultonville Collection, one of twenty-five.

Designer: William K. Harper   **Handle:** Plain   **Backstamp:** Doulton

Colourway: Pale blue, white and yellow

Doulton Number	Size	Backstamp	Height	Intro.	Discon.	Current Market Value U.K. £	U.S. $	Can. $
D6743	Small	Doulton	4"	1986	Current	20.00	55.00	72.50

MR. FURROW
THE FARMER

SERIES: The Doultonville Collection, one of twenty-five.

Designer: William K. Harper   **Handle:** Plain   **Backstamp:** Doulton

Colourway: Black and light brown

Doulton Number	Size	Backstamp	Height	Intro.	Discon.	Current Market Value		
						U.K. £	U.S. $	Can. $
D6701	Small	Doulton	4"	1983	1989	35.00	50.00	60.00

MR. LITIGATE
THE LAWYER

SERIES: The Doultonville Collection, one of twenty-five.

Designer: William K. Harper   **Handle:** Plain   **Backstamp:** Doulton

Colourway: Black

Doulton Number	Size	Backstamp	Height	Intro.	Discon.	Current Market Value		
						U.K. £	U.S. $	Can. $
D6699	Small	Doulton	4"	1983	Current	20.00	55.00	72.50

MR MICAWBER

Designer: Harry Fenton   **Handle:** Plain   **Backstamp:** Doulton

Colourway: Browns

Doulton Number	Size	Backstamp	Height	Intro.	Discon.	Current Market Value U.K. £	U.S. $	Can. $
D6262	Small	Doulton	4 1/2"	1948	1960	120.00	200.00	230.00

MR PICKWICK

Designer: Harry Fenton **Handle:** Plain **Backstamp:** Doulton

Colourway: Browns

Doulton Number	Size	Backstamp	Height	Intro.	Discon.	Current Market Value		
						U.K. £	U.S. $	Can. $
D6261	Small	Doulton	4 1/2"	1948	1960	120.00	200.00	230.00

MR. TONSIL
THE TOWNCRIER

SERIES: The Doultonville Collection, one of twenty-five.

Designer: William K. Harper   **Handle:** Plain   **Backstamp:** Doulton

Colourway: Red, white, black and yellow

Doulton Number	Size	Backstamp	Height	Intro.	Discon.	Current Market Value		
						U.K. £	U.S. $	Can. $
D6713	Small	Doulton	4"	1984	Current	20.00	55.00	72.50

OLD CHARLIE

Old Charlie

Designer: Harry Fenton   **Handle:** Plain   **Backstamp:** Doulton

Colourway: Brown, green and red

Doulton Number	Size	Backstamp	Height	Intro.	Discon.	Current Market Value U.K. £	Current Market Value U.S. $	Current Market Value Can. $
D6030	Large	Doulton	8 3/4"	1939	1960	150.00	300.00	400.00
D6069	Small	Doulton	5 1/2"	1939	1960	90.00	200.00	230.00

PAT PARCEL
THE POSTMAN

SERIES: The Doultonville Collection, one of twenty-five.

Designer: William K. Harper   **Handle:** Plain   **Backstamp:** Doulton

Colourway: Black

Doulton Number	Size	Backstamp	Height	Intro.	Discon.	Current Market Value		
						U.K. £	U.S. $	Can. $
D6813	Small	Doulton	4"	1989	Current	20.00	55.00	72.50

REV. CASSOCK
THE CLERGYMAN

SERIES: The Doultonville Collection, one of twenty-five.

Designer: William K. Harper   **Handle:** Plain   **Backstamp:** Doulton

Colourway: Black and white

Doulton Number	Size	Backstamp	Height	Intro.	Discon.	Current Market Value U.K. £	U.S. $	Can. $
D6702	Small	Doulton	4"	1983	1990	25.00	45.00	55.00

SAIREY GAMP

Designer: Harry Fenton   **Handle:** Plain   **Backstamp:** Doulton

Colourway: Browns

Doulton Number	Size	Backstamp	Height	Intro.	Discon.	Current Market Value		
						U.K. £	U.S. $	Can. $
D6263	Small	Doulton	4 1/2"	1948	1960	120.00	200.00	230.00

SAM WELLER

Designer: Harry Fenton   **Handle:** Plain   **Backstamp:** Doulton

Colourway: Browns

Doulton Number	Size	Backstamp	Height	Intro.	Discon.	Current Market Value U.K. £	U.S. $	Can. $
D6265	Small	Doulton	4 1/2"	1948	1960	120.00	200.00	230.00

SGT. PEELER
THE POLICEMAN

SERIES: The Doultonville Collection, one of twenty-five.

Designer: William K. Harper

Handle: Plain

Colourway: Black

Backstamp: Doulton

Doulton Number	Size	Backstamp	Height	Intro.	Discon.	Current Market Value		
						U.K. £	U.S. $	Can. $
D6720	Small	Doulton	4"	1985	Current	20.00	55.00	72.50

SHERLOCK HOLMES

Designer: Robert Tabbenor   **Handle:** Plain   **Backstamp:** Doulton

Colourway: Black hat and cloak, brown coat

Inscription on Base: "To Commemorate the 50th Anniversary of the Death of Sir Arthur Conan Doyle"

Doulton Number	Size	Backstamp	Height	Intro.	Discon.	Current Market Value U.K. £	U.S. $	Can. $
D6661	Large	Doulton	8 3/4"	1981	Current	53.00	145.00	175.00

SIR FRANCIS DRAKE

Issued to commemorate the 400th Anniversary of the circumnavigation of the world.

Designer: Michael Abberley   **Handle:** Plain   **Backstamp:** Doulton

Colourway: Black hat with white feather, tan tunic, brown boots

Doulton Number	Size	Backstamp	Height	Intro.	Discon.	Current Market Value		
						U.K. £	U.S. $	Can. $
D6660	Large	Doutlon	9"	1981	Current	53.00	145.00	175.00

THE SQUIRE

The Squire
B6319
COPR 1950
DOULTON & CO LIMITED

Designer: Harry Fenton   **Handle:** Plain   **Backstamp:** Doulton

Colourway: Brown hat, green coat, orange vest

VARIATIONS

VARIATION NO. 1: Bone China

Doulton Number	Size	Variation	Height	Intro.	Discon.	Current Market Value U.K. £	U.S. $	Can. $
D6319	Medium	Var. 1	5 3/4"	1950	1969	280.00	350.00	400.00

VARIATION NO. 2: Kingsware

Doulton Number	Size	Variation	Height	Intro.	Discon.	Current Market Value U.K. £	U.S. $	Can. $
D —	Large	Var. 2	8"		Unknown	375.00	600.00	700.00

TOBY XX

Also known as "Double XX" and "The Man on the Barrel."

Designer: Harry Fenton   **Handle:** Plain   **Backstamp:** Doulton

Colourway: Brown hat, maroon coat, orange vest

Doulton Number	Size	Backstamp	Height	Intro.	Discon.	Current Market Value		
						U.K. £	U.S. $	Can. $
D6088	Medium	Doulton	6 1/4"	1939	1969	150.00	375.00	375.00

WINSTON CHURCHILL

Designer: Harry Fenton   **Handle:** Plain

Colourway: Black hat, brown coat, black suit

Backstamp: Doulton   **WINSTON CHURCHILL**

Inscription on Base: "Winston Churchill Prime Minister
of Great Britain 1940"

Doulton Number	Size	Backstamp	Height	Intro.	Discon.	Current Market Value U.K. £	U.S. $	Can. $
D6171	Large	Doulton	9"	1941	Current	53.00	145.00	175.00
D6172	Medium	Doulton	5 1/2"	1941	Current	35.00	92.00	115.00
D6175	Small	Doulton	4"	1941	Current	25.00	75.00	90.00

LIQUOR CONTAINERS & JUGS

CAPTAIN COOK

Commissioned By: Pick-Kwik Wines And Spirits, in a limited edition of 2,000 pieces.

SERIES: The International Collection, one of four.

LIQUOR CONTAINER

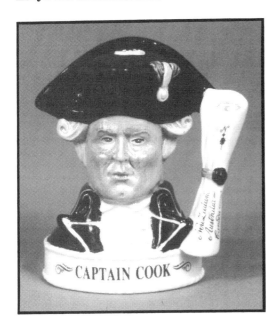

THIRD OF A SERIES
THE INTERNATIONAL COLLECTION
Specially Commissioned
from
Royal Doulton®
200ml. JIM BEAM BOURBON WHISKEY 40% Vol.
PICK-KWIK WINES & SPIRITS
MICKLEOVER, DERBY, ENGLAND
with special permission from
JAMES B. BEAM DISTILLING INTERNATIONAL CO.

Designer: Harry Sales
Modeller: Graham Tongue

Handle: Scroll

Backstamp: Doulton / Pick-Kwik

Colourway: Black hat, black and yellow uniform

Inscription on Base: "Captain Cook"

Doulton Number	Size	Backstamp	Height	Intro.	Discon.	Current Market Value U.K. £	U.S. $	Can. $
D —	Small	Doulton	4 3/4"	1985	1985	55.00	70.00	80.00

FALSTAFF

Falstaff, the Poacher and Rip Van Winkle character jugs were adapted to liqueur containers for "Bols" Liqueur by Doulton for the bottling firm of W. Walklate Ltd. The small size jugs were commissioned circa 1960.

Commissioned By: W. Walklate Ltd

LIQUEUR CONTAINER

Designer: Harry Fenton   **Handle:** Plain   **Backstamp:** Doulton

Colourway: Rose-pink tunic, black hat trimmed with rose-pink plumes, grey beard

Doulton Number	Size	Backstamp	Height	Intro.	Discon.	Current Market Value U.K. £	U.S. $	Can. $
D6385	Small	Falstaff	4"	c. 1960	c. 1960	45.00	110.00	130.00

IRISHMAN

Two whiskey flasks depicting a Scotsman and an Irishman set within a wooden tantalus. These were made in the 1930's for Asprey and Co., New Bond Street, London.

The heads of the flasks are detachable, and naturally the Scotsman contains Scottish whisky and the Irishman, Irish whisky. Normally traded as a set, see page 278 for the Scotsman.

Commissioned By: Asprey and Co.

WHISKEY DECANTER

Designer: Harry Fenton   **Backstamp:** Doulton

Colourway: Black hat and coat, green cravat, maroon vest

Doulton Number	Size	Backstamp	Height	Intro.	Discon.	Current Market Value U.K. £	U.S. $	Can. $
D6873	Large	Doulton	9 1/2"	1920	1930	750.00	1,250.00	1,500.00

JOHN BULL

Commissioned By: Pick-kwik Wines And Spirits in a limited edtion of 2,000 pieces.

SERIES: The International Collection, one of four

LIQUOR CONTAINER

SECOND OF A SERIES
THE INTERNATIONAL COLLECTION
Specially Commissioned from
Royal Doulton®

200ml.   JIM BEAM BOURBON WHISKEY   40% Vol.
PICK-KWIK WINES & SPIRITS
MICKLEOVER, DERBY, ENGLAND
with special permission from
JAMES B. BEAM DISTILLING INTERNATIONAL CO

Designer: Harry Sales   **Handle:** Cane with bull dog head   **Backstamp:** Doulton / Pick-Kwik
Modeller: Graham Tongue

Colourway: Black hat with yellow band, red coat

Inscription on Base: "John Bull"

Doulton Number	Size	Backstamp	Height	Intro.	Discon.	Current Market Value		
						U.K. £	U.S. $	Can. $
D —	Small	Doulton	5"	1985	1985	55.00	70.00	80.00

MR MICAWBER

Commissioned By: Pick-Kwik Wines and Spirits

STYLE ONE: LIQUOR CONTAINER

Designer: Harry Sales	**Handle:** See Variations	**Backstamp:** Doulton / Pick-Kwik
Modeller: Graham Tongue		

Colourway: See Variations

Inscription on Base: See Variations

VARIATIONS

VARIATION NO. 1: **Colourway: Brown hat, dark blue blazer, maroon cravat**
Handle: Dewar's
Inscription on Base: "Dewar's"
Issued: 2,000 pieces

Doulton Number	Size	Backstamp	Height	Intro.	Discon.	Current Market Value		
						U.K. £	U.S. $	Can. $
D —	Small	Var. 1	5"	1983	1983	55.00	70.00	80.00

VARIATION NO. 2: Colourway: Grey hat, green blazer, light blue cravat
Handle: Pickwick
Inscription on Base: "Pickwick Deluxe Whisky"
Issued: 2,000 pieces

Doulton Number	Size	Backstamp	Height	Intro.	Discon.	Current Market Value		
						U.K. £	U.S. $	Can. $
D —	Small	Var. 2	5"	1983	1983	55.00	70.00	80.00

VARIATION NO. 3: Colourway: White
Handle: Pickwick Deluxe
Inscription on Base: "Pickwick Deluxe Whisky"
Issued: 100 pieces

Doulton Number	Size	Backstamp	Height	Intro.	Discon.	Current Market Value		
						U.K. £	U.S. $	Can. $
D —	Small	Var. 3	5"	1985	1985	100.00	170.00	200.00

MR MICAWBER

Commissioned By: Pick-Kwik Wines And Spirits

STYLE TWO: CHARACTER JUG

Designer: Harry Sales   **Handle:** See Variations   **Backstamp:** Doulton / Pick-Kwik
Modeller: Graham Tongue

Colourway: See Variations

Inscription on Base: See Variations

VARIATIONS

VARIATION NO. 1: Colourway: Brown hat, blue blazer, maroon cravat
Handle: Dewar's
Inscription on Base: Dewar's
Issued: 100 pieces

Doulton Number	Size	Variation	Height	Intro.	Discon.	Current Market Value		
						U.K. £	U.S. $	Can. $
D —	Small	Var. 1	4"	1985	1985	125.00	210.00	250.00

VARIATION NO. 2   VARIATION NO. 3   VARIATION NO. 4

VARIATION NO. 2: Colourway: White
Handle: Dewar's
Inscription on Base: "Dewar's" in red
Issued: 100 pieces

Doulton Number	Size	Variation	Height	Intro.	Discon.	Current Market Value U.K. £	U.S. $	Can. $
D —	Small	Var. 2	4"	1985	1985	125.00	210.00	250.00

VARIATION NO. 3: Colourway: Grey hat, green blazer, light blue cravat
Handle: Pickwick Deluxe
Inscription on Base: "Pickwick Deluxe Whisky"
Issued: 100 pieces

Doulton Number	Size	Variation	Height	Intro.	Discon.	Current Market Value U.K. £	U.S. $	Can. $
D —	Small	Var. 3	4"	1985	1985	125.00	210.00	250.00

VARIATION NO. 4: Colourway: White
Handle: Pickwick Deluxe
Inscription on Base: "Pickwick Deluxe Whisky"
Issued: 100 pieces

Doulton Number	Size	Variation	Height	Intro.	Discon.	Current Market Value U.K. £	U.S. $	Can. $
D —	Small	Var. 4	4"	1985	1985	125.00	210.00	250.00

MR. PICWICK

Commissioned By: Pick-Kwik Wines and Spirits

CHARACTER JUG

MR PICKWICK
(FOUNDER & GENERAL CHAIRMAN
OF THE PICKWICK CLUB)
THE MOST FAMOUS OF
CHARLES DICKENS' CHARACTERS FROM
"PICKWICK PAPERS"
FIRST PUBLISHED IN 1846

Designer: Harry Sales   **Handle:** Pick-Kwik   **Backstamp:** Doulton / Pick-Kwik
Modeller: Graham Tongue

Colourway: See Variations

Inscription on Base: See Variations

VARIATIONS

VARIAITON NO. 1: Colourway: Green hat, black coat
Handle: No label / Whisky
Inscription on Base: "Pick-Kwik Derby Whiskies Wines Ales"
Issued: 2,000 pieces

Name	Size	Variation	Height	Intro.	Discon.	Current Market Value U.K. £	U.S. $	Can. $
D —	Small	Var. 1	4"	1982	1982	65.00	100.00	125.00

VARIATION NO. 4   VARIATION NO. 6   VARIATION NO. 2

VARIATION NO. 2: Colourway: Brown hat, dark brown coat
Handle: Jim Beam
Inscription on Base: "Pick-Kwik Derby Sells Jim Beam Whiskey"
Issued: 2,000 pieces

Name	Size	Variation	Height	Intro.	Discon.	Current Market Value		
						U.K. £	U.S. $	Can. $
D —	Small	Var. 2	4"	1984	1984	65.00	100.00	125.00

VARIATION NO. 3: Colourway: Beige hat, brown coat
Handle: Jim Beam
Inscription on Base: "Beam Whiskey"
Issued: 1,000 pieces

Name	Size	Variation	Height	Intro.	Discon.	Current Market Value		
						U.K. £	U.S. $	Can. $
D —	Small	Var. 3	5 1/4"	1984	1984	65.00	100.00	90.00

VARIATION NO. 4: Colourway: Beige hat, brown coat
Handle: Beam's Black Label
Inscription on Base: "Beam Whiskey"
Issued: 1,000 pieces

Name	Size	Variation	Height	Intro.	Discon.	Current Market Value		
						U.K. £	U.S. $	Can. $
D —	Small	Var. 4	5 1/4"	1984	1984	65.00	100.00	90.00

VARIATION NO. 5: Colourway: White
Handle: No label/"Whisky"
Inscription on Base: "Pick Kwik Derby"
Issued: 100 pieces

Name	Size	Variation	Height	Intro.	Discon.	Current Market Value U.K. £	Current Market Value U.S. $	Current Market Value Can. $
D —	Small	Var. 5	5 1/4"	1985	1985	100.00	170.00	200.00

VARIATION NO. 6: Colourway: White with red transfers
Handle: Jim Beam
Inscription on Base: "Pick Kwik Derby Sells Jim Beam Whisky"
Issued: 100 pieces

Name	Size	Variation	Height	Intro.	Discon.	Current Market Value U.K. £	Current Market Value U.S. $	Current Market Value Can. $
D —	Small	Var. 6	5 1/4"	1985	1985	100.00	170.00	200.00

THE PICKWICK COLLECTION

MR PICKWICK / SAM WELLER

Commissioned By: Pick-Kwik Wines and Spirits, in a limited edition of 2,000 pieces.
This is a two faced liquor container

LIQUOR CONTAINER

Photograph
Not Available
At Press Time

Designer: Harry Sales
Modeller: Graham Tongue

Handle: Jim Beam
Plain bottle

Backstamp: Doutlon / Pick-Kwik

Colourway: Black coat, pink bow-tie
Grey coat, yellow cravat

Inscription on Base: "Beam Whiskey"
"The World's Finest Bourbon"

Name	Size	Backstamp	Height	Intro.	Discon.	Current Market Value		
						U.K. £	U.S. $	Can. $
D —	Doulton	Small	5"	1985	1985	55.00	70.00	80.00

OLD MR. TURVERYDROP

Commissioned By: Pick-Kwik Wines and Spirits in a limited edition of 2,000 pieces.

LIQUOR CONTAINER

THE PICKWICK COLLECTION
Specially Commissioned from
Royal Doulton®

200ml.   JIM BEAM BOURBON WHISKEY   40% Vol.
PICK-KWIK WINES & SPIRITS
MICKLEOVER, DERBY, ENGLAND
with special permission from
JAMES B. BEAM DISTILLING INTERNATIONAL CO.

Designer: Harry Sales   Handle: Jim Beam   Backstamp: Doulton / Pick-Kwik
Modeller: Graham Tongue

Colourway: Yellow hat, black coat

Inscription on Base: "Beam Whiskey"

Name	Size	Backstamp	Height	Intro.	Discon.	U.K. £	Current Market Value U.S. $	Can. $
D —	Small	Doulton	5"	1985	1985	55.00	70.00	80.00

THE POACHER

Commissioned By: W. Walklate Ltd

Falstaff, the Poacher and Rip Van Winkle character jugs were adapted to liqueur containers for "Bols" Liqueurs by Doulton for the bottling firm W. Walklate Ltd. The small size jugs were commissioned circa 1960.

LIQUEUR CONTAINER

Designer: Max Henk   **Handle:** A Salmon   **Backstamp:** Doulton

Colourway: Green coat, red scarf, light brown hat

Doulton Number	Size	Backstamp	Height	Intro.	Discon.	Current Market Value U.K. £	U.S. $	Can. $
D6464	Small	Doulton	4"	c. 1960	c. 1960	65.00	110.00	130.00

RIP VAN WINKLE

Commissioned By: W. Walklate Ltd

Falstaff, the Poacher and Rip Van Winkle character jugs were adapted to liqueur containers for "Bols" Liqueurs by Doulton for the bottling firm W. Walklate Ltd. The small size jugs were commissioned circa 1960.

LIQUEUR CONTAINER

Designer: Geoff Blower   **Handle:** A man resting against a tree   **Backstamp:** see Backstamps

Colourway: Grey-blue cap, brown robes, figure rssting against tree dressed in blue

Doulton Number	Size	Backstamp	Height	Intro.	Discon.	Current Market Value		
						U.K. £	U.S. $	Can. $
D6463	Small	Doulton	4"	c. 1960	c. 1960	65.00	110.00	140.00

SAMURAI WARRIOR

Commissioned By: Pick-Kwik Wines And Spirits in a limited edtion of 2,000 pieces.

SERIES: The International Collection, one of four.

LIQUOR CONTAINER

FOURTH OF A SERIES
THE INTERNATIONAL COLLECTION
Specially Commissioned from
Royal Doulton®
200ml. JIM BEAM BOURBON WHISKEY 40% Vol.
PICK-KWIK WINES & SPIRITS
MICKLEOVER, DERBY, ENGLAND
with special permission from
JAMES B. BEAM DISTILLING INTERNATIONAL CO.

Designer: Harry Sales **Handle:** Sword **Backstamp:** Doulton / Pick-Kwik
Modeller: Graham Tongue

Colourway: Black hair, white face

Inscription on Base: "Samurai Warrior"

Name	Size	Backstamp	Height	Intro.	Discon.	Current Market Value U.K. £	U.S. $	Can. $
D —	Small	Doulton	5"	1986	1986	55.00	70.00	80.00

SCOTSMAN

Two whiskey flasks depicting a Scotsman and an Irishman set within a wooden tantalus. These were made in the 1930's for Asprey and Co., New Bond Street, London.

The heads of the flasks are detachable, and naturally the Scotsman contains Scottish whisky and the Irishman, Irish whisky. Normally traded as a set, see page 365 for the Irishman.

Commissioned By: Asprey and Co.

WHISKEY DECANTERS

Designer: Harry Fenton   **Backstamp:** Doulton

Colourway: Red tam, black coat

Doulton Number	Size	Backstamp	Height	Intro.	Discon.	Current Market Value U.K. £	U.S. $	Can. $
D6873	Large	Doulton	9 1/2"	1920	1930	750.00	1,250.00	1,500.00

SGT BUZ FUZ

Commissioned By: Pick-Kwik Wines And Spirits

CHARACTER JUG

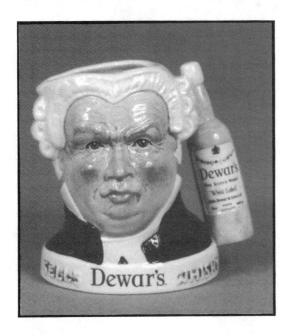

Designer: Harry Sales **Handle:** See Variations **Backstamp:** Doulton / Pick-Kwik
Modeller: Graham Tongue

Colourway: See Variations

Inscription on Base: See Variations

VARIATIONS

VARIAITON NO. 1: Colourway: White hair, black coat
Handle: Dewar's
Inscription on Base: Pick-Kwik Derby Sells Dewar's Whisky
Issued: 2,000 pieces

Doulton Number	Size	Variation	Height	Intro.	Discon.	Current Market Value		
						U.K. £	U.S. $	Can. $
D —	Small	Var. 1	4"	1982	1982	65.00	100.00	125.00

VARIATION NO. 2: Colourway: White with red transfers
Handle: Dewar's
Inscription on Base: Pick-Kwik Derby Sells Dewar's Whisky
Issued: 100 pieces

Doulton Number	Size	Variation	Height	Intro.	Discon.	Current Market Value U.K. £	U.S. $	Can. $
D —	Small	Var. 2	4"	1985	1985	75.00	150.00	185.00

VARIATION NO. 3: Colourway: White
Handle: Plain bottle
Inscription on Base: Pick-Kwik Derby Sells Whisky
Issued: 100 pieces

Doulton Number	Size	Backstamp	Height	Intro.	Discon.	Current Market Value U.K. £	U.S. $	Can. $
D —	Small	Doulton	4"	1985	1985	100.00	170.00	200.00

THE INTERNATIONAL COLLECTION

TOWN CRIER OF EATANSWILL

Commissioned By: Pick-Kwik Wines and Spirits, issued in a limited edition of 2,000 pieces.

LIQUOR CONTAINER

THE PICKWICK COLLECTION
Specially Commissioned
from
Royal Doulton®

200ml. JIM BEAM BOURBON WHISKEY 40% Vol.
PICK-KWIK WINES & SPIRITS
MICKLEOVER, DERBY, ENGLAND
with special permission from
JAMES B. BEAM DISTILLING INTERNATIONAL CO.

Designer: Harry Sales   Handle: Jim Beam   Backstamp: Doulton / Pick-Kwik
Modeller: Graham Tongue

Colourway: Black hat and maroon coat with yellow trim

Inscription on Base: "Beam Whiskey"

Doulton Number	Size	Backstamp	Height	Intro.	Discon.	Current Market Value		
						U.K. £	U.S. $	Can. $
D —	Small	Doulton	5"	1986	1986	55.00	70.00	80.00

UNCLE SAM

Commissioned By: Pick-Kwik Wines And Spirits, issued in a limited edition of 2,000 pieces.

SERIES: The International Collection, one of four.

STYLE ONE: *LIQUOR CONTAINER*

Specially Commissioned from

Royal Doulton

200ml. JIM BEAM BOURBON WHISKEY 40%Vol.
PICK-KWIK WINES & SPIRITS
MICKLEOVER, DERBY, ENGLAND
with special permission from
JAMES B. BEAM DISTILLING INTERNATIONAL CO.

Designer: Harry Sales   **Handle:** See Variations   **Backstamp:** Doulton / Pick-Kwik
Modeller: Graham Tongue

Colourway: Red, white and blue

Inscription on Base: See Variations

VARIATIONS

VARIATION NO. 1: Handle: Eagle
Inscription on Base: "Beam Whiskey"

Doulton Number	Size	Backstamp	Height	Intro.	Discon.	Current Market Value U.K. £	U.S. $	Can. $
D —	Small	Var. 1	5"	1984	1984	55.00	70.00	80.00

VARIATION NO. 2: Handle: Jim Beam
Inscription on Base: "Uncle Sam"

Doulton Number	Size	Backstamp	Height	Intro.	Discon.	Current Market Value U.K. £	U.S. $	Can. $
D —	Small	Var. 2	5"	1984	1984	55.00	70.00	80.00

UNCLE SAM

Commissioned By: Pick-Kwik Wines And Spirits, issued as promotional items in a limited edtion of 500 pieces.

STYLE TWO: *CHARACTER JUG*

Designer: Harry Sales   **Handle:** Eagle   **Backstamp:** Doulton / Pick-Kwik
Modeller: Graham Tongue

Colourway: Red, white and blue

Inscription on Base: "In God We Trust"

Doulton Number	Size	Backstamp	Height	Intro.	Discon.	Current Market Value U.K. £	U.S. $	Can. $
D —	Small	Doulton	5"	1986	1986	110.00	200.00	225.00

WILLIAM GRANT

Issued to commemorate the centenary of the founding of the Glenfiddich distillery. The jug containss 750 ml of 25 year old Grants whisky.

The uniform if that of a Major of the 6th Volunteer Battalion of the Gordon Highlanders. The Glengarry cap features the symbol of a stamgs head. This symbol also appears on all of the companies bottles of whisky.

STYLE ONE: HANDLE: FOUR OAK CASKS

LIQUOR CONTAINER

Designer: Graham Tongue

Handle: Four oak casks

Colourway: Scarlet

Backstamp: see Backstamps

BACKSTAMPS

A: Doulton / William Grant **100th Anniversary**

> Issued in 1986 in a limited edition of 500 pieces to commemorate the 100th Anniversary of the Founding.

B: Doulton / William Grant **100 Years**

> Issued in 1987 in a limited edition of 2,500 pieces to celebrate the 100 years since whisky first flowed from the stills.

Doulton Number	Size	Backstamp	Height	Intro.	Discon.	Current Market Value U.K. £	U.S. $	Can. $
D —	Large	Doul/100th Ann.	7"	1986	1986	145.00	250.00	300.00
D —	Large	Doulton/100 yrs.	7"	1987	1987	125.00	200.00	250.00

WILLIAM GRANT

Commissioned By: Grants Glenfiddich Distillery. Issued in 1988 in a limited edition of 5,000 pieces.

STYLE TWO: *HANDLE: FIELD OFFICER'S SWORD*

LIQUOR CONTAINER

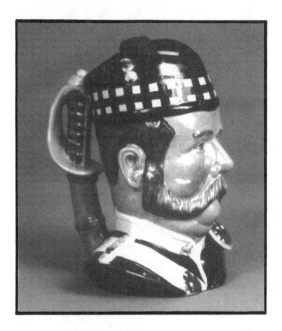

William Grant
Founder of William Grant & Sons Ltd
An independent family company for five generations
Specially Commissioned from
Royal Doulton®
Hand Modelled and Hand Painted
Designed and Modelled by *Graham Tongues*
William Grant's 25 Year Old
Very Rare Blended Scotch Whisky
One of a limited edition of 5000
William Grant Character Jugs specially styled
with a Field Officer's sword handle
Blended and Bottled by
William Grant & Sons Ltd
The Glenfiddich Distillery. Banffshire, Scotland
Product of Scotland
750ml 43% vol.

Designer: Graham Tongues   **Handle:** Field Officer's Sword   **Backstamp:** Doulton/ William Grant

Colourway: Scarlet

Doulton Number	Size	Backstamp	Height	Intro.	Discon.	Current Market Value U.K. £	U.S. $	Can. $
D —	Large	Doulton/Grant	7"	1988	1988	125.00	200.00	250.00

INDEX

CHARACTER JUGS

TOBY JUGS

LIQUOR CONTAINERS AND JUGS

ADVERTISERS

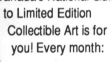